PRAISE FOR **UPLIFTED**

All aglow in the work.

~ VIRGIL

Where is human nature so weak as in the bookstore?

~ HENRY WARD BEECHER

D1118028

"I have had the great pleasure of knowing Susan for decades—since she was a young child, barely walking—and I can tell you for certain that she is one of the most positive, humorous, and kind people you could ever meet. I've read many of her books, and I have to say that this one, *Uplifted*, is now my favorite. In her typical reader-friendly, motivating, and inspiring writing style, Susan tells us how to be more hopeful, positive, and vibrantly healthy, even when uncertainty and stress may be our constant daily companions.

"As a medical doctor, I appreciate her holistic approach to living more healthfully, which fosters vitality, no matter one's age, not just physically but also mentally, emotionally, and spiritually. If you would like some practical, effective ways to feel more uplifted each day; if you desire to be healthier, kinder, or more peaceful; if you want some insightful guidance on how to live a more balanced, successful life; or if you simply want to enrich your experience of living, making your life a great adventure and celebration, then Susan's empowering *Uplifted* book is just for you!"

—PETER W. BROWN, MD, LOS ALTOS, CA

"Books that I love become more than ink on paper; they become good friends. This powerful and life-transforming book, *Uplifted*, is sure to become one of my very best friends forever. Long after I read such books, even as they sit on the shelf, their vibrations continue to bless, heal, enrich, and nurture me.

"For decades I have been producing and hosting radio programs, and for fifteen years, Susan has been a monthly guest on my radio show, *This Week in America*. She is the only person I've ever invited on my program monthly because she's that good, and my listeners around the world can't seem to get enough of her joyful, upbeat, and bright personality. Her enthusiasm, experience, and vast knowledge in the fields of holistic health, nutrition, fitness, human potential, and mental well-being are great gifts to my listeners. Her wit, wisdom, and humor blend to create a truly contagious field of joyous energy.

"These same characteristics about Susan's personality shine through on every page of this wonderful book. She makes you wish you were her next-door neighbor so you could visit with her in person and go for walks or visit with her in her home over some tea or fresh juice. Susan has a way of living the principles she speaks and writes about in this book that causes others to follow her way of healthy living. In *Uplifted*, it feels as if an angel of light has been dropped into our midst to bless us, just when the world needs it the most, in ways that will last for a long time. If we all lived as Susan suggests, America and the world could close most of its hospitals and jails and become nations at peace with each other. *Uplifted* is a beautiful and outstanding guide to living a life that is rooted in physical, mental, emotional, and spiritual vitality, no matter one's age. *Uplifted* is definitely essential reading."

—RIC BRATTON, FOUNDER AND HOST OF
THIS WEEK IN AMERICA

"Every chapter is this book is uplifting to read; the writing style is engaging; and the message of the book is insightful and profound, yet easy to assimilate and understand. It is inspiring to think of all the possible ways to apply the myriad suggestions Susan offers to your life right away. She reminds us that it is often the little things, the small revelations, the simple random acts of kindness, that make a great deal of difference in handling life's struggles, whether disappointment or frustration, sadness or loss, or any other struggle. I appreciate the beautiful way Susan phrases her thoughts, as well as the uplifting quotations, the illuminating stories, the powerful insights and Bible passages, and the many life-enriching recommendations that will stir you into action and help you regain a sense of balance and perspective in your life.

"'Everything good and positive that broadens our appreciation and appetite for life,' says Susan, 'should be one of our lifetime goals.' The reality of her faith-based lifestyle is truly inspiring and, in the Workbook, she encourages us to examine our life very carefully so that we can know ourselves better and aspire to a more rewarding and fulfilling life. There are over 100 easy-to-apply Action Steps in which we can all participate in only 12 or fewer minutes. Like favorite hymns, her many quotations will become familiar and comfortable, useful, timely, and uplifting. As you find yourself thinking, *Susan has written this just for me,* you will feel an extraordinary surge of energy, joy, and peace. *Uplifted* is sure to bring you inspiration, ideas, energy, unlimited possibilities, and motivation that will enrich the quality of your life."

—Olin Idol, ND, CNC, Vice President of Health at the Hallelujah Diet

"The human body is an amazing machine and requires attention, regular maintenance, and loving care to run as efficiently as possible. This wonderful book teaches us how to both honor our body and keep our mind uplifted and positive. But it's so much more than what to eat (and not eat), how to exercise for best results, when to reinvigorate the body, and why to live by the Golden Rule. Susan enlightens us on how to believe in possibilities, be courageous in our daily lives, live in the now, move more toward love, remain calm in the midst of uncertainty, reduce daily stress and anxiety, create joy in the middle of chaos, dream big and achieve goals, become a magnet for blessings and miracles, use affirmations to uplift sadness, foster fulfilling relationships, brighten our day first thing in the morning, and much more.

"I have had the pleasure of knowing Susan for many years and I can say for certain that she is one of the most joyful, kind, faith-filled, loving, peaceful, and upbeat people I've ever met. She definitely walks her talk. Whenever we visit, I always feel uplifted afterward—the theme of this book. Her message is about the art of living fully and using beauty, grace, and inspiration to illuminate our lives. *Uplifted* shows us how we can nurture ourselves by what we feed our mind, and how we can all live with divine connection and timing as we endure, persevere, prevail, and thrive. Susan's 12-Minute Action Steps are genius because we can all find this small chunk of time daily to uplift ourselves and others.

"Because of the healing and health wisdom permeating every page of this glorious book, my life has been greatly enriched. If you want to find warmth, affirmation, encouragement, and optimism, this is the book for you. If you need guidance on joy, love, courage, wholeness, grief, risk, loss, growth, and success, this book will be your godsend. If you simply want to read some of the most inspiring quotations ever written to guide you on your physical and spiritual journey, *Uplifted* will be your gift. With courage and confidence, Susan will take you on a delightful physical, mental, and spiritual journey, helping to restore you to serenity, grace, and positivity."

—MYRAN THOMAS, LA ESTHETIQUE WELLNESS

UPLIFTED

12 Minutes to More Joy, Faith, Peace, Kindness & Vitality

SUSAN SMITH JONES, PhD

Books to UPLIFT
Rejuvenating Your Health & Enriching Your Life

Disclaimer: The health suggestions and recommendations in this book are based on the training, research, and personal experiences of the author. Because each person and each situation are unique, the author and publisher encourage the reader to check with his or her physician or other health professional before using any procedure outlined in this book. Neither the author nor the publisher is responsible for any adverse consequences resulting from any of the suggestions in this book.

Published by
Books to UPLIFT
LOS ANGELES, CA

Copyright by Susan Smith Jones, PhD

ISBN-13: 978-0-9991492-8-7

Cover and book design: Gary A. Rosenberg
Editing: Carol Killman Rosenberg

For further information and permission approval, contact:
Health Unlimited, PO Box 49215, Los Angeles, CA 90049, Attn: Manager

Hitch your wagon to a star.

~ Ralph Waldo Emerson

If you can keep your head when all about you
Are losing theirs and blaming it on you . . .
Yours is the Earth and everything that's in it.

~ Rudyard Kipling

Memories are everyone's second chance
at happiness.

~ Queen Elizabeth

Each day comes bearing precious gifts for you
from God. Untie the ribbon.

~ Fritzie (Susan's grandmother)

Other Books by Susan Smith Jones, PhD

Nature always wears the color of spirit.
~ RALPH WALDO EMERSON

*Anything that's human is mentionable, and anything
that is mentionable can be more manageable.
When we can talk about our feelings, they become less
overwhelming, less upsetting, and less scary.*
~ FRED ROGERS

Wired for High-Level Wellness
Invest in Yourself with Exercise
A Hug in a Mug
Choose to Thrive
Be the Change
Kitchen Gardening
Living on the Lighter Side
The Curative Kitchen & Lifestyle
Body Temple Vitality
Healthy, Happy & Radiant . . . at Any Age

Please refer to **SusanSmithJones.com** to learn more about
these books or to get autographed copies by the author, which
include a notecard and bookmark.

Genius is 1% inspiration, 99% perspiration.
~ THOMAS EDISON

If you want to live a happy life,
tie it to a goal, not to people or objects.
~ ALBERT EINSTEIN

Faith is an invisible and invincible
magnet and attracts to itself whatever it
fervently desires and persistently expects.
~ RALPH WALDO TRINE

Promise me you'll always remember—
you're braver than you believe, and stronger
than you seem, and smarter than you think.
~ CHRISTOPHER ROBIN TO WINNIE THE POOH

Fear is a reaction. Courage is a decision.

~ Winston Churchill

The most beautiful people we have known are those who have known defeat, known suffering, known struggle, known loss, and have found their way out of the depths . . . Beautiful people do not just happen.

~ Elisabeth Kübler-Ross

Contents

Dedication & Gratitudes

Peace I leave with you; my peace I give to you.
~ Jesus Christ, John 14:27

Not until we are lost do we begin to understand ourselves.
~ Henry David Thoreau

This book is lovingly dedicated to:

My wonderful mom, June, whose presence and kindliness I still feel watching over me daily. She nourished me in immeasurable ways, always enthusiastic and kindhearted, and supported me in being happy and healthy. Throughout my glorious decades with her, she taught me what it meant to love someone as well as what it's like to be loved unconditionally. How blessed and privileged I was, and still am, to call her Mom.

My cherished and supportive friends and family for enriching my life in myriad ways and blessing me with kindness, joy, and upliftment, including David Craddock, MA; Ginny Swabek; Lucy Boyadzhian; Myran Thomas; Jay Solton; Janis Faye; Steven Crithfield; Mamiko Matsuda; Flechelle Morin; Agnes Nagy; Edwin Basye; Olin Idol, ND, CNC; Ric Bratton: Peter W. Brown, MD; Alexandra Stoddard; Peter Brough, PhD; Sophia Craddock; Barbara de Noronha; Sati Dent; Louise Deaville; Joanne Zimbler; Wanda Huberman; Tiana Brandon; Lara Kajajian; Julia Wouk-Brown; my loving grandparents Fritzie and Benny Benoit; and my wonderful sisters, June Smith Brugger, and Jamie Carr.

My invaluable team, Carol and Gary Rosenberg, known as The Book Couple, who brought this book to life and also lent a helping hand with my entire series of books for my Books to Uplift Publishing Company. They are the best at offering sage book-publishing advice, and they are two of the most wonderful people I've ever known.

My special readers with appreciation and thanks for allowing me to be part of your lives. I hope you have at least half as much fun reading this book as I did in writing it.

And my constant companions—God, Christ, and my guardian angels—for guiding me in how to live each day with more faith, joy, tenderhearted-ness, and peace, and to find God everywhere—in everyone and everything. This Divine romance is truly exquisite.

She is clothed with strength and dignity;
she can laugh at the days to come.
~ PROVERBS 31:25

Once you make a decision the universe
conspires to make it happen.
~ RALPH WALDO EMERSON

The world is extremely interesting to a joyful soul.
~ ALEXANDRA STODDARD

In any given moment, we have two options:
to step forward into growth or to step back into safety.
~ ABRAHAM MASLOW

Foreword

Treat others the way you wish to be treated.

~ MATTHEW 7:12

*Give me health and a day, and I will make
the pomp of emperors ridiculous.*

~ RALPH WALDO EMERSON

The day Susan asked me to write the foreword for this book, I felt completely chuffed. As a resident of both England and West Los Angeles, I've had the pleasure of knowing Susan and spending time with this wonderfully compassionate, kind, funny, and smart lady for almost fifteen years, and we have even started a few businesses together.

One thing is for certain regarding this Los Angeles native, lover of nature, who's always tenderhearted and filled with enthusiasm: Susan is the real deal, by which I mean that she is a lady who definitely walks her talk. She is a living, breathing, and shining example of what living a healthy, joyful, faith-filled, God-centered lifestyle is all about. I've had countless opportunities to be inspired by her, either through her magnificent array of books, her highly informative website, her inspiring radio and TV interviews, her motivational talks, and her personal counseling and friendship that has helped me enormously. Truly, Susan never fails to leave me or others I know uplifted in her wake.

When she asked me to read the manuscript, there was no title on it, and she asked me to search my mind for the perfect title, the result of which is the title you now see on the cover of this book. How gratifying this is to me to know that this timeless, heartwarming book features my suggested title with words describing what, in our heart of hearts, we all truly desire in our lives. This book has taught me so much about how to enrich my life with more love and kindness, faith and hope, positive thoughts, enhanced exercise program, improved nutrition, healthier foods, and so much more.

In a TV interview I saw Susan participate in recently, I heard her say that . . . *in our being, we hold the ability to have vibrant physical health and to create a gracious life intentionally filled with blessings.* That comment resonated deeply with me as do countless more insights she shares through the pages of this book.

Uplifted: 12 Minutes to More Joy, Faith, Peace, Kindness & Vitality offers us the keys to achieving our heartfelt goals through sound healthy living suggestions and motivation as well as the positive steps Susan calls the "12-Minute Action Steps" that will bring us closer to the ideal life we've always dreamed of having. It also offers Susan's renowned 21-day favorable program to foster more positive habits and let go of self-sabotaging habits, foods that bolster and deflate mood, and a life-enriching Workbook as a way to get to know ourselves better and help us get on the fast track to a successful, peaceful, and joyful life.

Uplifted can mean so many things—floating along on a transparently golden summer day, an inner lightness that buoys us up through any mood, or a sense of being lifted along by a higher power in which we have complete trust. In this instructive manual, written from the heart and based on scientific research, Susan shows readers how to achieve this enlightened state of upliftment by attending to the whole-person trinity of mind, body, and spirit. Through diligently applying the principles set out in this magnificent book, the result gives us an indescribable feeling of buoyant inner power and confidence.

If we are honest, most of us want to continuously improve our lives; we want to learn the art of living and find our own unique path on a quest to live a more effective and enjoyable life as we seek deeper answers to problems we encounter and question large philosophical issues we wish to better understand. By drawing from the great minds of history, as well as a range of literary, spiritual, and contemporary sources, Susan presents the reader with nuggets of wisdom to savor, first by opening every chapter with two intriguing quotations, and then by closing each chapter with more thoughtful insights.

This book isn't meant to just feed the mind and help you feel uplifted in some temporary fashion—it's a practical plan for daily action to create an enduring result in your life. In other words, the book is full of recommendations that are all created to leave you in a healthier, more vibrant state of mind, body, and spirit. By considering the foods you eat; by being kinder and more compassionate to all you meet; by watching the words you speak and write; by keeping your word with yourself and others; and by assessing your higher consciousness, while simplifying your life, and returning to a connection with nature, you will feel stronger, more relaxed, and eager to take on the challenges in your life. This book is supremely insightful in explaining the subtle wisdom that supports all these life changes and enrichments to bring you to peak living.

Busy lives inevitably create a hectic pace of life. Experiencing beauty, feeling wonder, and breathing in deeply of nature's blessings often fall to the bottom of our to-do lists. Susan's inspiring book helps us reconsider our objectives and priorities, our aspirations and ambitions, and our goals and dreams; it also helps us reassess how we use our time and what we value in order to live a more fully realized life. The secret to creating these transforming changes is that they're made one step at a time and in 12-minute practicable segments and 21-day commitments; they build on one another, so that nothing becomes a burden. They become manageable steps to take your life forward, until their cumulative effect manifests major changes of significance.

It's not easy to start a new life-changing program or to give up old habits. Fortunately, *Uplifted: 12 Minutes to More Joy, Faith, Peace, Kindness & Vitality* is a nurturing guide with wonderful stories from Susan's work with her clients worldwide and even two Humor Time Intermissions with really funny jokes and stories. Before you finish Chapter 1, you will be captivated by this book and won't want to put it down. Following Susan's advice reminds us of listening to an old friend reaching across the kitchen table to share both common sense and uncommon wisdom. This book is practical to read and delightfully pleasant to follow. I am keeping a copy on my bedside table to read from before I go to sleep each night. If we commit ourselves to the wise guidance that Susan proffers us on each page of this book, we will find that in a short time we'll feel stronger, happier, healthier, more serene, restored, ready to soar, and totally uplifted!

David Craddock, MA (Oxon)
DavidCraddock.com
BooksToUplift.com
ChristianLifestyleMatters.com

*Health is the first muse and sleep
is the condition to produce it.*

~ RALPH WALDO EMERSON

*Always do right. This will gratify some
people and astonish the rest.*

~ MARK TWAIN

Preface

Your life is really part of an unfolding plan, a charted voyage, an exquisitely executed work of art.

~ THOMAS KINKADE

*If one advances confidently in the direction of his dreams,
and endeavors to live the life which he has imagined,
he will meet with a success unexpected in common hours. . . .
If you have built castles in the air, your work need not be lost;
that is where they should be. Now put foundations under them.*

~ HENRY DAVID THOREAU

Stress is a major problem in modern life. Technological advances have increased the pressure to keep busy, even during leisure hours. We talk on the telephone and text while we drive, watch television while we read, and conduct business while we listen to the radio.

We are continually overstimulated, receiving more information from television, computers, radio, and satellites than our ancestors of several generations ago ever could have imagined! This year alone you will probably make more appointments, meet more people, and go more places than your grandparents did in their entire lives. All this manic rushing around creates a life filled with stress.

Given our current pace, we have little time to relax and cultivate relationships with our spouses, children, friends, and nature. Is it any wonder that stress-related diseases are now on the rise? Some studies even suggest that 80 to 90 percent of all doctor visits are for stress-related complaints.

Stress-related illness is implicated in our rapidly escalating health-care costs, and health problems attributed to job stress are estimated to cost U.S. businesses $150 billion every year.

I see unrelenting stress as a sickness of epidemic proportions—a "busyness" or "hurry" sickness. But you don't have to let it overwhelm you. You can *choose* to slow down and feel uplifted—create a life of more joy, faith, peace, kindness, and vitality. I'll address this throughout the pages of this book, but for now, let's see if you can find any of the following signs of "hurry" sickness in your daily life.

1. Do you eat in a rush, eat while standing or walking, or eat while driving?

2. Does your busy life prevent you from spending much time at home? And when you finally get home, are you too tired to do much beyond collapse and "veg out" in front of the television?

3. Do you routinely drive too fast, run yellow lights, constantly change lanes, and jockey for position? Are you impatient with other drivers?

4. Do you talk fast, have problems communicating how you feel, and lack the time to give emotional support to your family and friends?

5. Is your life so full of undone chores and responsibilities that relaxing has become almost impossible?

6. When you're not doing something productive, do you experience anxiety and guilt?

7. Have vacations become more trouble than they're worth?

8. Do you often feel tired and run-down, cry easily, or have trouble sleeping?

9. Do you frequently get sick with colds or the flu, or find yourself experiencing one of the many prevalent diseases of Western society?

10. Do you make everyone and everything in your life more important than taking loving care of yourself?

What causes our need to rush and discount our own physical health needs? We can blame it on economics—and the need to make enough money to pay for our chosen lifestyles. We can blame it on the fact that everything's moving so fast, and we have to, too. But I believe the real cause is something deeper. By crowding our schedule with "more"—more socializing, more eating, more work, more activity, more appointments—we may be trying to fill the emptiness we feel inside ourselves.

When you constantly direct your attention and energies outward, it's easy to lose the sense of inner wonder, calmness, balance, and beauty where true happiness, joy, and peace originate. By slowing down and redirecting your energies inward, not only will you train your brain to relax, you will begin to reestablish the wholesome sense of self-worth necessary to positively change your life.

When you're under stress, your blood sugar levels can be affected. The stress response activates the adrenal glands' release of adrenal hormones. If the stress is continuous, the adrenal glands may not be able to generate enough adrenaline to raise blood sugar when you need it. Hypoglycemia, or abnormally low blood sugar levels, may result. Irritability is one of the symptoms of hypoglycemia.

Stress often produces anxiety, defined as "a state of being uneasy, apprehensive, or worried about what may happen." According to the National Institute of Mental Health, anxiety disorders affect more than 20 million people in the United States.

How do you know when stress is getting the best of you? According to the latest edition of the *American Medical Association Family Medical Guide*, physical symptoms of stress include headache, heart disease (two symptoms are atherosclerosis and high blood pressure), insomnia, absence of periods in women, impotence or premature ejaculation in men, digestive tract disturbances (such as ulcerative colitis, irritable bowel syndrome, gastritis, and peptic and duodenal ulcers), back pain, frequent colds, shallow breathing, racing heart, herpes virus breakouts, slow wound healing, and tight neck and shoulders.

Behavioral symptoms of stress include an increase in smoking in smokers, an increase in alcohol consumption in drinkers, grinding teeth, compulsive eating, an inability to get things done, and bossiness. Emotional symptoms include edginess, loneliness, nervousness, crying, and a sense of powerlessness. Cognitive symptoms include forgetfulness, inability to make decisions, trouble thinking clearly, thoughts of escape, incessant worrying, and lack of creativity.

Most people work so hard at living that they forget how to live fully. Okay, you may not be able to change your boss's tendency to favor weekend workdays or control the bumper-to-bumper traffic to and from work, but you do have access to some powerful stress-busting tools that I write about in the pages of this book. The simple fact that you are perusing this book tells me that you may be feeling out of balance and stressed out in one or several areas of your life. As a holistic lifestyle coach and counselor for more than forty years, I've worked with thousands of people around the world. I offer my clients simple, yet essential, choices to bring purpose, harmony, and vitality back into their lives. Stress may be a fact of modern life, but you don't have to let it become your *way* of life. You can become the master of your life, create a lifestyle of vitality and joy, and keep noisome stress to a minimum. *The path to contentment is in choosing to have your life in balance.*

As my mom always reminded me when I was a young girl and throughout our decades together (her wisdom will go a long way to help you live a more stressless life, too): Never lose your childlike wonder, live by the Golden Rule (treat others as you wish to be treated), dream big, cultivate kindness, don't complain, follow your heart, and never give up. These are wonderful words to live by, which I have strived to do. She would always remind me that when we are experiencing ennui, or in times of struggle, when our faith is tested, to be strong and trust that's when we need to harness our inner strength, to trust, and to be hopeful. Mom would have loved and been inspired by two of my favorite current books, which I've read three times, by Shannon Bream, *The Mothers and Daughters of the Bible Speak: Lessons on Faith from Nine Biblical Families* and *The Women of the Bible Speak: The Wisdom of 16 Women and Their Lessons for Today,* with inspiring stories about strength, faith, and courage.

NAVIGATING THIS BOOK

For easy reference, I've divided this book into three parts. In Part One, we'll look at how to live a halcyon life with vim and vigor and to derive the health benefits of kindness. In Part Two, we'll explore ways to fill your life with youthful vitality and experience more joy and true aliveness . . . no matter your age. In Part Three, you'll learn more about yourself with the Workbook and also about how to use nature's foods to heal your body. As well, I give you many suggestions on what you can do for 12 minutes or fewer to help you fly higher in life.

For many people these days, with how hectic life can be, it may be impossible to carve out a day, a couple hours, or even 30 minutes of time to call your own. But I am confident that you can allocate 12 minutes to do something that will enrich your life, and you will find lots of my recommendations. And the cumulative effect of these "12-Minute Action Steps" as time goes by will definitely and wonderfully enhance your whole being—physically, mentally, emotionally, and spiritually.

My hope as you read this book is for you to feel that I'm writing directly for you and that you feel like we're friends now—as though we are sitting across from each other at my kitchen table visiting over a cup of delicious tea. (In Chapter 13, I recommend some delicious herbal teas to help relax and calm your body and mind.) One of the true, uplifting elixirs of life is humor, and I laugh often as I notice all the incongruities of daily living that don't make sense and all you can do is laugh as much as possible. So, as you'll see in this book, I have added in a couple Humor Time Intermissions, if you will, where you'll have some funny jokes and stories, which I hope will tickle your funny bone and help you to not be so serious about things.

Notice the quote below by J. D. Salinger about wishing the author of the book was your friend. That's my goal. When you finish this book, I hope that you wish we lived on the same block so we could visit often over tea or during early morning walks or hikes.

I encourage you to read the book through once in its entirety and then read it a second time more slowly and see which of the tips and "12-Minute Action Steps" you can adopt in your life right away. Remember, it's not what you read that makes the difference. It's what you assimilate and put into practice in your life. And it's simply a matter of choice. Choose to create your best, uplifted life, and start to live with balance and joy today!

Do not go where the path may lead. Go instead
where there is no path and leave a trail.

~ RALPH WALDO EMERSON

What I like best is a book that's at least funny once in a while. What really knocks me out is a book that, when you're all done reading it, you wish the author that wrote it was a terrific friend of yours and you could call him up on the phone whenever you felt like it. That doesn't happen much, though.

~ J. D. SALINGER

 ## Today's Affirmation

When I feel the pressures of life, I take time out to slow down and turn to the presence of peace within me. I live in an abundant universe. I give thanks for the good I have received and thanks, in advance, for the good I desire. I am nourished by the bounty of the earth that sustains me physically and by the spiritual teachings that feed my soul. I use, share, and bless all that I have been given, and I give thanks to God. I know that life flows from the inside out. I develop a rich inner life. Strength and courage have always been within me. It's up to me to tap into my inner power, a font of goodness and peace. I trust in who I AM.

 ## 12-Minute Action Step

Find a quiet place to sit down and take in some long, slow, deep breaths. Now, write down three things for which you feel immensely grateful today. Next, write down three goals you have that you want to achieve in recording-breaking time. Then, in your mind's eye, see these three goals as already achieved in your life, and, in addition to this enjoyable mental movie, feel the emotions of joy, satisfaction, and bliss you would feel if this vision were your current reality—as it will be soon. Finally, end with giving thanks to God by affirming, "This or something better I now accept in my life."

Introduction

Every beauty which is seen here below by personas
of perception resembles more than anything else
that celestial source from which we all come.

~ MICHELANGELO

Of all the beautiful truths pertaining to the soul which have been
restored and brought to life in this age, none is more gladdening
or fruitful of divine promise and confidence than this—that
man is the master of thought, the molder of character, and the
maker and shaper of condition, environment, and destiny.

~ JAMES ALLEN

Dear Reader,

Hello, and thank you for picking up this book and joining me through the pages on a life-enriching adventure that we'll take together. I hope you will feel like we are visiting over a cup of tea or fresh juice at my kitchen table. While I won't know much about your life, you will get to know me very well and I do know, since you are reading this book, that you are eager to create a healthy, happy, and rewarding life.

As I travel the country and the world giving motivational talks—whether in person or during radio and television talk shows (in person and virtual)—I meet countless people who all seem to be experiencing the same thing, what I refer to as a "busyness" or "hurry sickness," as elaborated in the preface. Everyone seems to be rushing around—from the moment they wake up until they go to bed at night—and it just seems to be getting worse. I read an article recently in the *New York Times* disclosing that one-third of all Americans are always in a state of rush. Where are we all going?

In one of my favorite books, *The Little Prince* by Antoine de Saint-Exupéry, there's a section where the little prince is in the railway station and asks where all these people are going back and forth all over the place. And someone replies, "Even the engineer doesn't know where he's going." Can you relate to this in your life, too?

When you reach the end of your life, I guarantee that you will not be wishing you had led a more stressful, harried life and spent more time rushing around. My mom, June, and my grandmother, Fritzie, were always right; they often reminded me that it's the simple pleasures that make life worth living—being with your friends; laughing much and often; celebrating the sunrise and sunsets; enjoying your children, grandchildren, and pets; carving out time to stroll in nature and appreciate its bounty, and so on—these are what bring sweetness and pure joy to living. These are the things that you'll remember with great fondness and that will bring a smile to your face. This is what living a sacred life is all about. We all need to create space in our days to experience the true sacredness of life and feel the joy of living fully. This is what being uplifted is to me.

Ask yourself the following questions:

§ Am I feeling physically, emotionally, and spiritually off-kilter?

§ Have I lost some joy of living?

§ Have I lost faith in myself and my life?

§ Is chaos consuming me more these days than serenity?

§ Do I feel overwhelmed by life and too much daily stress?

§ Or, perhaps, have I ever experienced, or wish to experience, the true sacredness of life?

Because you are reading this book, I have a feeling that you've answered yes to many of these questions. Well, you've come to the right place because my goal in this book is to gently and lovingly guide you back to your true nature—your sacred heart center where each day and each moment can be worth celebrating, even in the midst of stress and chaos. This door to your upliftment center, which by now might be rusted shut for lack of use, is simply waiting for you to open it. All it takes is your willingness to turn the knob and enter, surrendering to the gifts and miracles waiting for you. These gifts and miracles are already inside you, where they have always been. You can achieve this enlightened state by attending to the trinity of mind, body, and spirit, as I write about in the pages of this book. The result gives us an indescribable feeling of buoyant inner power and upliftment.

Accessing it is not, it should be noted, something you do just once, say on January 1 when you're all psyched up and motivated to make personal change. It's a process you can choose to engage in each and every day, preferably early morning as you awaken and greet the day.

Living an uplifted life involves a blending of body, mind, and spirit. Remember, the body reflects the mind, and the mind reflects the spirit. It doesn't matter whether you start with the body by choosing to upgrade your diet or exercise daily, or you start with your mind by choosing to think more positively, or if you simply focus on spirit and add in some special prayer or meditation time each day. All these endeavors will lead to the same place— your uplifted center and a life rich in joy, vibrant health, faith, peace, and soul-satisfaction. Prayer, as I see it, is the way we reconnect with our sacred essence, and this oneness with the Divine, with God, and our Christ Light is our lifeline to endless inspiration and vitality.

Hummingbirds are some of my favorite teachers and shining examples on how to live sacred lives. It's why I included this gem of nature, along with a butterfly, on the cover of this book. In a Papyrus card store on a greeting card, I read that "legends say that hummingbirds float free of time, carrying our hopes for love, joy, and celebration." The hummingbird's delicate grace reminds us that life is rich, beauty is everywhere, every personal connection has meaning, and that laughter is life's sweetest creation. So, my hope for all of us is that we become like hummingbirds, savoring each moment as it passes, embracing all that life has to offer, and celebrating the joy of every day. That's true upliftment to me.

With each chapter in this book, your understanding will grow on how to live more fully and bring positive enrichment and balance back into your body and all areas of your life. This moment can be a fresh start for you—a new beginning and a whole new way to create your very best life.

Let's start fresh right now. If you are willing to move forward and embrace a new way of living, then let's begin this journey together. I will be with you every step of the way, holding your hand and giving you encouragement.

Right now, you have the power and ability to transform and enrich the quality of your life and life on this planet. You can be all you were meant to be. No one has ever stopped you but you. Yes, you can live a luminous, munificent life, glowing with self-esteem and verve and radiating strength. But it requires that you make a conscious choice to do so. This moment—right now—can be a new beginning. No longer do you need to repeat the past, worry about the future, or struggle through life as a victim of circumstance. For if you begin to live today, absorbed in the present moment, letting your heart-light shine, being responsible and accountable for who you are and what you want to become, you will begin to experience every day a life more splendid, more wondrous, and more magical than you ever dreamed possible. You will experience a truly uplifted life.

... you can live a luminous, munificent life, glowing with self-esteem and verve and radiating strength

Taking responsibility and knowing that the responsibility is squarely on your shoulders is the first step. You cannot blame something or someone outside yourself for your own failure to live your vision. It's simply a matter of choice and creating what you want.

Of course, it isn't easy to accept that you have the power to choose, because you have probably been taught, as I was, to seek answers outside yourself. We can all learn something from outside sources, whatever they are, but the true teachers teach us to look within. The answers to the really important questions, the spiritual ones, can be found only by turning inward. Life, love, and peace dwell within each of us. If we really look, we find that we are never alone. Not only that, but we are the gift and miracle we've been seeking, and when we start to live a fully uplifted life, we inspire excellence in all who touch and share our lives.

We must start by remembering that we have a body. We take good care of our body by feeding it healthy foods and exercising regularly. We also have a mind, and most of us nurture that by thinking, reading, writing, and communicating with others. But we are a soul above all, and if we don't shepherd the soul by bringing sacredness and balance into our body and life, we won't be complete.

In this new century, I believe that the ones who will thrive are not necessarily those with the most accolades, achievements, or material possessions. Having a smartphone, a high-speed computer and printer, a GPS, and a PDA may make you *feel* plugged into the world of the future, but the only thing you may really be is wired. It's the people who are internally plugged in, the people who are deeply connected to their inner sacredness and spirituality who will thrive and be champions in the twenty-first century. Of this, I am sure.

The way to heal disharmony in your life and body and to reconnect with your sacred, uplifted nature is to realize that, first and foremost, you are a spiritual being. Vibrant health and healing stem in large part from embracing your inner self, from the mental caress of meditation, from prayer rich with belief, from the soulful stirrings of human touch, from knowing you are unconditionally loved by God's Divine Light within you, and from the resolution of conflict, anger, resentment, and hopelessness. Your Christ Light within you is like your soul's pilot light: it can choke in the face of deadlines, stress, traffic, days scheduled minute by minute, not telling the truth, not honoring your feelings, and not following your heart. You must choose to take ownership of your own soul and become the master of your life by harnessing the sacred within you and bringing it out into everything you do and create.

I believe that all endeavors toward attaining better health are feckless unless the healthy body is seen and used as a temple in which Spirit dwells. Because of my belief, my emphasis is on:

- Physical exercise
- High thinking
- Proper diet
- Simple living
- Time in nature
- Heartfelt prayer

As mentioned previously, the body reflects the mind, and the mind reflects the spirit, hence the motivation to attain better health. Henry David Thoreau once said, "How prompt we are to satisfy the hunger and thirst of our bodies; how slow to satisfy the hunger and thirst of our souls." If we want to nourish both, we see the body not as a lump of flesh but rather as a noble instrument; within is the source of all power. All we have to do is tap into it. Wisdom, light, and love are within each of us and make up the ribbon that unites us all together.

Life teaches us how to live. I am often asked if today's busy world can put one's spirituality at risk. Yes, it's easy to get caught up in the intense pace and stress of today's hectic lifestyle, especially if we've forgotten the truth of our being. The life force within us is diminished by misguided or pernicious attitudes about pain and growth, by our limiting beliefs and destructive self-definitions, and by judging others far more frequently than it is by disease or debacles. We have a tendency to approve or disapprove of others and ourselves, according to superficial standards and labels of acceptability and achievement, when we should be learning to love. Finding the way to honor the sacredness within and around us heals and enriches life. We must come back to and embrace our authentic selves—a sometimes difficult thing to do.

> *When we take our highest dreams seriously and focus on what we want, the natural pull of the universe will serve as a co-creative force that leads us to any goal we truly feel worthy to receive.*

Actually, we are all more than we know. Wholeness is never lost; it is only forgotten. We all need a strong foundation of practical spirituality based on the realization that we are co-creators with God, with the ultimate source of power and creativity. We all have access to the universal creative power. We are tied directly to it. When we take our highest dreams seriously and focus on what we want, the natural pull of the universe will serve as a co-creative force that leads us to any goal we truly feel worthy to receive. With that type of partnership, I believe that anything is possible.

What I see happen with so many people is that they give up easily when their quest is challenged (refer to Chapter 7: Intuitively Persevere with Determination). I have found in my own life that stumbling blocks and challenges are just opportunities to learn and grow. Nothing keeps us from going ahead but our own thoughts and self-imposed limitations. We must stop vying with other people and judging from the appearances of so-called reality and have enough faith to choose a loftier perspective on life. Then we can move toward what we want by taking action. Each chapter of this book is devoted to a certain kind of life-enhancing action, and many can be done in 12 or fewer minutes. At the end of each chapter, you will find a "12-Minute Action Step" you can take right away to put you on the road to upliftment.

Through decades of research into Eastern philosophies and Western medicine, I've come to understand and appreciate how much the lines of demarcation between science and spirituality are diminishing. It is an irrefutable fact that we can't separate body, mind, and spirit. Science corroborates that when we live with a positive attitude, with faith, hope, calmness, and love in our hearts, we boost our immunity, have more energy, look younger, and stave off disease. Furthermore, scientists now agree that those people who meditate regularly not only handle stress better but look years younger than those people who don't meditate. It's that simple. Especially in these "uncertain" times in which we live, we can't afford not to meditate. (Please refer to my two detailed chapters about the history and science of meditation, how to implement it easily and effortlessly, and the myriad benefits from meditating regularly in my book *Wired for High-Level Wellness: Simple Ways to Rejuvenate, Meditate & Prosper.*)

For more than forty-five years, I have practiced meditation and studied how cultures around the world throughout history have used meditation in their lifestyles and cultures. The more I meditate, the more I seek out and relish plain living and high thinking. I want my life to radiate my devotion to God and my loving reverence and concern for all fellow beings, creatures, and life itself.

I believe that spirit speaks to us daily through our intuition and what we call "coincidences" (aka "Godwinks"). Throughout our lives, coincidences lead us toward the attainment of our life's purpose. By increasing our awareness and remaining connected to our Creator, to God, we can see coincidences happening all around us when we ask the right questions. The answers are easy—it's the questions that are sometimes difficult. We must keep our energy at maximum level to be receptive to the messages that come to us through intuitive thoughts, daydreams, night dreams, and especially from people who show up on our path. And we must consciously develop our intuition.

Intuition is knowing something without thinking about it. I believe it's the voice, the whisper, of God within us. Too often we run away from ourselves, filling our lives with constant activity. We don't take time to be still, forget outside activities, and quell mental chattering. But intuition can be nurtured in a variety of ways, which I also describe in Chapter 7. The more you act on your intuitive hunches, the stronger and more readily available they become. As you grow more sensitive to your oneness with God and life, you will become more intuitive. Receiving those inner messages clearly comes when you learn to give up the analyzing, reasoning, doubting, and limiting part of your mind. The best way to strengthen intuitive power is to just sit still and listen. Turn within and pay attention.

If you don't like your current circumstances—if you want to lose weight, tone your body, have more energy and faith, live a more prosperous and peaceful life, and create vibrant health—you can do it. When you invite and allow Christ to be the guiding force in your life, as mentioned in the books *The Case for Christ: A Journalist's Personal Investigation of the Evidence for Jesus* and *The Case for Heaven: A Journalist Investigates Evidence for Life After Death*, both by Lee Strobel, you become empowered and uplifted, and this connection with your inner light creates miracles in your body and life as well as in the lives of others. And changes that are loved into being are permanent.

Once we discover the sacred connection with God, we come to realize that we are all magnificent spiritual beings having a human experience here on spaceship Earth. We can choose to see this glorious universe as alive and mysterious, ultimately benevolent and orderly. Intention, consciousness, discovery, and synchronicity are magical and all around us. Every day the world presents us with miracles waiting for our awareness. Life-giving colorful fruits and vegetables are miracles. So are hummingbirds, butterflies, horses, sunsets and sunrises, shooting stars, the fragrance of roses, puppies and kittens, and our remarkable bodies that house the loving Spirit within. Hidden beneath the wrapping of every experience is a new opportunity to know the joy and wonder of love.

One of the most important lessons I've learned is that if I'm facing a challenge—whether it's pertaining to health, relationships, finances, or whatever—all I need to do is to turn my focus from the challenge to God and let the divinity reveal the hidden gift within it. We're given the circumstances we require for our awakening.

Loving all aspects of your life, regardless of the challenges that inevitably come along, opens doors and lets in light, energy, and joy. Love yourself out of sheer gratitude for existence. Love the mystery of life and the process of creating what you want. Here's a wonderful commonsense quote from Joel Osteen: "Don't ever criticize yourself. Don't go around all day long thinking, 'I'm unattractive, I'm slow, I'm not as smart as my brother.' God wasn't having a bad day when He made you... If you don't love yourself in the right way, you can't love your neighbor. You can't be as good as you are supposed to be." And it was Elizabeth Barrett Browning who gives us this succinct, lovely passage: "Light tomorrow with today!" You need to be a light for yourself and others and the luminescence of your inner Christ Light is strengthened by love—love for God, love for yourself, and love for others and all life.

The more you love, the more you come to realize you don't need to force things. Jesus's teachings emphasize the importance of living from the love that is always within each of us. And it was Thomas Carlyle who so wisely tells us, "A loving heart is the beginning of all knowledge."

When you practice love and forgiveness on a daily basis (see Chapter 18 on love, oneness, and forgiveness), you discover that when you are uplifted and courageous, you will want to spend more time being, rather than doing, a paradigm for nonaction, the purest and most effective form of action. You learn that you don't need to force and manipulate things. One of my favorite maxims for decades has been "Let go and let God." Be your own best friend and be a light unto yourself. This is where we start this process of upliftment. Be the kind of friend to yourself that you wish another person would be with you.

Uplifted offers practical ways of living a more sacred life filled with joy, faith, peace, kindness, and vitality, an achievable goal. This is how I've done my best to live for over forty years, and I know this way of living works. Of course, I haven't always been a paragon, but every time I've fallen off my path, I've learned valuable lessons that I share in my books and workshops and with clients. We can all learn from one another. I've taught my holistic health and lifestyle program to thousands of people around America and the world, and I receive countless letters each year highlighting their positive results.

It all begins with getting back to the basics—things our grandmothers probably told us that we didn't really want to hear about back then. Simple things like eating more fresh fruits and vegetables (Chapters 13 and 14), spending more time outdoors in nature (Chapter 14), being more positive and enthusiastic (Chapter 6), giving joyfully to others (Chapter 1), showing gratitude and trust (Chapter 2), watching the words your think, say, and write (Chapter 10), and having faith in love and God (every chapter).

If you're still not convinced that the journey to vibrant health is simple, here is what I say to you (and it is something I always tell people in my workshops, too): The time you feel least like starting something is precisely the time to forge ahead. Just the physical act of beginning will create the momentum and energy that will allow you to develop beyond your fear and toward your greatest accomplishments. Every step you take is on sacred ground. Everything about your life is sacred. The path to the sacred upliftment is your own body, heart, and mind, the history of your life, and the relationships and circumstances closest to you. Don't place limitations on your dreams or your Creator by doubting that you can reach your soul's desire and live a sacred life. If not here, where else can we engender joy, compassion, and happiness?

When we choose to create upliftment and vitality for ourselves, we are enriching the quality of life on planet Earth as a whole, for at one level we are all connected; each person is a wave in this ocean of life. When you or I choose to be a responsible, loving, forgiving, healthy, happy person, living from integrity and oneness, I believe that this has a positive influence around the world, adding to the light. By the same token, choosing the opposite decreases the world's light and wholeness. Each of us makes a difference by how we live and especially how we treat other people. Dennis Prager puts it beautifully, "Goodness is about character – integrity, honesty, kindness, generosity, moral courage, and the like. More than anything else, it is about how we treat other people."

So, if you take responsibility, acknowledge the sacredness of your body and life, and walk a path with heart, greater world harmony will be created. Have faith in your vision, and your experience of living will become all the more magical and fulfilling. You will know what it means to be as you were created to be. Life will become an adventure, filled with celebration and joy. Wisdom, love, and light will be your constant companions. You will know serenity and powerful faith. You will become peace itself. You will be *uplifted*. It's your choice.

To see the world in a grain of sand
And heaven in a wildflower
Hold infinity in the palm of your hand
And eternity in an hour.

~ William Blake

Live in the present. Do the things you know need to be done.
Do all the good you can each day. The future will unfold.

~ Peace Pilgrim

 ## Today's Affirmation

I turn my attention from the challenges in my life and put my focus, instead, on my dreams and goals, and zero in on those things in my life for which I am grateful. I start with my miraculous body—the home where I live—and I choose to take loving care of myself and to be a shining example of vitality so I can inspire everyone in my life.

 ## 12-Minute Action Step

Take an important goal in your life, such as a desire to lose weight and get healthy and fit, and write down how your life would be different if this goal was already achieved, how you would feel with this success in hand, and how you would live differently if this goal were your current reality. End with thanking God and your angels for this success. Next, breathe slowly and deeply and see this goal in your mind's eye as already achieved and commit to doing what it takes to achieve this heartfelt goal. Writing down this goal as though it's already achieved and visualizing it as your achievement-come-true will help fast-track you to total success.

Part One

Choose a Halcyon Life of Vim & Vigor

Chapter 1

Are We Too Busy to Be Kind?

*Of course I love everyone I meet. How could I fail to
do so? Within everyone is the spark of God. I am not
concerned with racial or ethnic background or the color
of one's skin; all people look to me like shining lights!*

~ PEACE PILGRIM

*To find your own way is to follow your own bliss.
This involves analysis, watching yourself, and seeing
where the real deep bliss is—not the quick little
excitement, but the real, deep, life-filling bliss.*

~ JOSEPH CAMPBELL

I could hear the frustration in her voice the moment I picked up the telephone. My friend Rose called me because she was on the verge of quitting her job, even though she loved her work. She needed some guidance.

Rose is a very talented window dresser for a popular store on Rodeo Drive in Beverly Hills. She loves what she does, but she had been having an extremely difficult time with her boss. During our telephone conversation, she told me how often she felt that some of her best work was rejected and unappreciated by her supervisor. Not only were most of his criticisms unjustified, she said, but she was convinced he was deliberately rude and unfair to her. Because I believe we always attract to ourselves the equivalent of what we think, feel, and believe, I lovingly suggested to my friend that maybe she, rather than her boss, was the one in need of an attitude adjustment. Besides, she couldn't change him; the only one she could change was herself. Hardening of the attitudes we harbor—being inflexible in our thinking and seeing the world through judgmental eyes—can block our perspective on everything and foil discovering our bliss. I asked her how she felt about him.

Rose confessed that her mind was filled with criticism and unkindness toward this man and that she rarely felt positive in his presence because of the way he treated her. She even revealed to me that every morning as she walked to work, she would visualize the entire scenario of how badly he would act toward her that day. Rose confirmed my observation about the law of correspondence. I explained to her that he was merely bearing witness to her conception of him.

When Rose realized what she had been doing, she agreed to change her attitude and think of her boss only in a kind, loving way. I recommended that before drifting off to sleep at night, she visualized him congratulating her on her fine designs and creativity and that she sees herself, in turn, thanking him for his support and kindness. To her delight, after she had practiced her visualizations for only seven days, the behavior of her boss miraculously reversed itself. Rose proved the power of imagination and kindness. Her commitment to replace unkindness with love and openheartedness influenced his behavior as much as it did hers and reshaped his attitude toward her. And if he hadn't changed his behavior toward her, I know that Rose would have eventually found another job that utilized her creative gifts and talents in an environment where she was validated, appreciated, and cherished. We don't know we have this power until we try it, but it is always the same—as within, so without.

Humans are powerful spiritual beings who can create good on the earth. This good isn't usually accomplished in bold actions but in modest acts of kindness and love between people. The little things do count because they are more spontaneous and show who we truly are. Whatever amount of love and good feelings we feel at the end of our life is equal to the love and good feelings we put out during our life. It's that simple. "What a splendid way to move through the world," writes Jack Kornfield in *A Path with Heart*, "to bring our blessings to all that we touch. To honor, to bless, to welcome with

Humans are powerful spiritual beings who can create good on the earth.

the heart is never done in grand or monumental ways, but in this moment, in the most immediate and intimate way."

THE RELIGION OF KINDNESS

Antoine de Saint-Exupéry wrote in *The Little Prince* that what's truly essential is invisible to the eye—it can only be seen and felt with the heart. "When strangers start acting like neighbors, communities are reinvigorated," says Ralph Nader. Acts of kindness send out a positive ripple into the world and help bring us back to the feeling that people are basically good and kind. The love you give never runs out, for *the more you share with others, the more you have to give.*

The Dalai Lama would wholeheartedly agree. He says, "My religion is very simple—my religion is kindness." Kindness is an integral part of the choice to live fully. Not just kindness but gentleness. To my mind, they go hand in hand. *Gentle* means kindly, mild, amiable, not violent or severe. Gentleness also implies compassion, consideration, tolerance, calmness, mild temper, courtesy, and peacefulness. But the word I like to think of in connection with gentle is *tenderhearted.* I feel instantly at home with people who are tenderhearted. What about you? Think about those people you love to be around the most, with whom you feel the most enthusiastic and positive and able to be yourself. You'll probably say they're loving, supportive, uplifting, optimistic, kind, and maybe even tenderhearted.

To be treated with tenderheartedness and kindness, you must first offer those qualities to other people. Think that others deserve exactly the same treatment you would like for yourself. No one likes to be belittled, ignored, vituperated, or unappreciated. *Everyone* warms to kindness, patience, and respect.

I'll never forget the morning of January 17, 1994. It was 4:31 a.m., and I was in my home in Brentwood, Los Angeles, meditating on the floor in front of my altar. All of a sudden everything was in an uproar, and my first reaction was that God was speaking to me! Then I knew it was the biggest earthquake I had ever felt. I will never forget the terrifying sensation of hanging on to the corner of my bed while everything in my home crashed over and off the shelves. It felt and sounded like the end of the world, and I was certain

I was going to die. For almost everyone who went through the experience, it seemed as if the epicenter was right under their own home, and as if the duration was four minutes rather than forty seconds. For those seconds and the hours that followed, I was living totally in the present moment.

But what's germane and important here is the response from the community. Adversity always brings gifts and powerful lessons. Our indomitable, munificent spirit rears up and unites us with one another. After the earthquake, families, friends, and strangers, too, reached out to one another with true tenderheartedness and kindness. Sharing the same experience brought people together on common (if shaky) ground and opened our hearts to one another. Los Angeles was invigorated with a new spirit of compassion, which is exactly what is needed more of in this city now—compassion, kindness, and upliftment.

September 11, 2001, also brought the entire United States and much of the world together in feelings of loss, compassion, and generosity, and our sense of oneness with those who suffer from any natural or man-made catastrophe become stronger. So many have discovered that simple acts of kindness, in and of themselves, have amazing power to heal both those who receive them and those who perform them. Certainly, this was true following the 1994 earthquake, when the crime rate in our area went to its lowest level in years. We were forced to slow down and to see more clearly what is really important in life: not the things we possess or even the work we do, but the people in our life, the heart-to-heart connection we have with others, and the love we give.

Acts of kindness connect our heart with the heart of another person and create bridges over which our love can flow. Sometimes they are anonymous and sometimes not. Either way, they change us. When we give of our highest selves, purely out of love, our body, our heart, and our environment change, and for an instant, we realize that loving and being loved is the one true human vocation. We feel connected to the love in ourselves and the love in others.

Don't ever underestimate the power of kindness. "Random acts of kindness" may only be a slogan, but it has caught on all around the country for a reason. Doing lovely things for others for no reason has so many rewards. In an instant, the best of our humanity and heart come forward. These gestures aren't expected, but every time we seize the opportunity, we are transformed. We become, in a sense, an angel for a moment and touch the Divine. By giving someone else pure love and joy without expecting something in return, we become twice blessed, for in blessing another we also bless ourselves.

Every day presents us with hundreds of opportunities to practice kindness toward our fellow humans. Seize these moments and discover how wonderful it feels.

Several years ago, I was moved by a gesture of love at the airport. I was leaving Portland, Oregon, to fly to Los Angeles. Because of stormy weather, most flights were delayed, and some were canceled. The airport was crowded with unhappy travelers wanting to get someplace the weekend before the Thanksgiving Day holiday, so I was delighted that for some reason my flight was scheduled to leave on time. As they announced the final boarding, I noticed a harried man running up to the counter with his briefcase in one hand and his ticket in the other. The ticket agent said that unfortunately his reservation had been cleared and his seat given away. She told him politely and kindly that she would do everything she could to get him a seat on a later flight.

Well, he went ballistic. Everyone in the terminal could hear the din of his frustration. He had an important meeting in Los Angeles, and he had to get there. I couldn't help but feel for him, because I've been in similar situations where I couldn't afford to miss a flight, but everybody felt sorry for the ticket agent, especially when in his tirade, he yelled out that he wanted to see a supervisor.

All of a sudden, a woman who appeared to be in her late seventies walked up to this man and said that she wasn't in a hurry and would be happy to give him her seat. As you can imagine, the man stopped right in his tracks. It almost looked as if he was about to cry. He apologized to her, to the ticket agent, and to everyone around for his behavior and thanked the woman for being an angel in his life. He boarded the flight smiling, relieved, and much wiser! What a blessing for the lovely woman, too. The man never knew it, of course, but the airline got her on another flight just three hours later and also gave her a free, first-class, round-trip ticket to any destination served by the company. So, she was truly twice blessed.

As Mother Teresa once said, "Spread your love everywhere you go." Walk the path of love and kindness, and joy will be your constant companion.

LET YOUR HEART-LIGHT SHINE

Sometimes we get so caught up in our responsibilities and commitments to family, friends, work, and doing what's expected of us that there's little left to give to others, let alone ourselves. That's when we need to step outside the ordinary and enter into the realm of the extraordinary and magnificent. With willingness and a little effort, you can create miracles in your life and the lives of others. *You can become an angel, transforming the lives of others simply by giving with love.*

Something as simple as reaching out with a kind act or word of praise or appreciation can mean so much to others, and yet so often, we seem to assume that others have it all together and don't need our kindness. Wouldn't it be better to move beyond our assumptions and offer the kind of thoughtfulness we would appreciate receiving—a compliment, a smile, a hug, a pat on the shoulder, a note of thanks, or just a question that shows concern? Even if your kind gesture goes unnoticed or is refused, it doesn't matter, because in giving to another, you give to yourself.

If you need a place to start, begin by smiling. Everyone can do it. If you're not used to smiling, practice in the mirror by pulling up on the corners of your mouth! It's so simple and yet so effective. Learn to smile sincerely, from your heart. Did you know that it takes more muscular effort to frown than it does to smile? Smile at family and friends, at strangers, at everyone you meet or pass during the day today. Do you realize how many lives you can touch simply by smiling? You give a smile to one person, and he or she catches the good feeling and smiles at another person, and so on until your smile has indirectly affected the lives of several thousand people in one day. *Smile at everyone today and set off a wave of good feeling.*

Or how about writing a note of thanks or appreciation? You don't need a special occasion to send a card or note to someone. You think you're too busy to write something on paper, but it really doesn't take much time. It may even be quicker than a telephone call. I love to send "thank you" cards and letters and do so very faithfully, as most of my close friends will attest. Sometimes I'll go to a card store and purchase several dozen cards to have on hand, because it's a very harmless addiction! Isn't it fun to receive a card from a friend for no reason at all?

Random acts of kindness that involve money can be satisfying, too. Last week a friend and I were having dinner at a local restaurant. It was early evening, and the restaurant wasn't busy, so we had the opportunity to visit with our server. We found out that she was a single mom in her early twenties, with two children, and that she was putting herself through college by working at two jobs just to make ends meet. In spite of all her challenges, she was sanguine and a joy to be around. When we got our bill, my friend and I decided to do something special, just because we could. Even though the bill was under $30, we left a $100 tip. What a great feeling to see the look on our server's face when she discovered her good fortune and rich blessing!

COMPASSION IN ACTION

Sometimes the kindest gestures may not even be noticed. When I walk down the street, I love to put coins in parking meters if I see any that have expired. The drivers of the cars may never know, but it makes me feel good that I may have spared them a parking ticket. From time to time, I put a few dollars in an envelope and send it anonymously to someone I know is in need. It takes so little to do so much.

Sometimes gestures are very much noticed. When I was in Oregon many years ago, back before carrying cell phones was the norm, my wonderful, dear friend Helen accompanied me to a radio station, where I was scheduled to do an interview from 11 p.m. to midnight. After the interview was over, the radio station closed, and everyone left. Helen and I walked to my car, only to discover that it wouldn't start. I lifted the hood to see if anything looked out of the ordinary. Helen reminded me that we were not in the safest area of town and blocks from a telephone. It was cold and beginning to rain. I told Helen that we needed to imagine and affirm that an angel would help us out of this dilemma.

As we were getting back into the car to see if an angel would start the engine, a cab drove by. The driver stopped and asked if we needed any help. Helen whispered to me to have faith, even though he didn't look like the angel she had imagined. I agreed. The cab driver looked under the hood and immediately checked the battery. It was out of water. He had a jug of water in his cab and filled the reservoirs. He also told us an interesting story. He had just dropped off a passenger several blocks away and was heading home, since his shift was over. Something inside him guided him to take a totally different route that evening, one he had never taken before. He thought it was odd but did it anyway. That's when he saw Helen and me looking under the hood and wondered if we needed help. When we told him that he was the angel we had imagined, his delighted smile warmed our hearts. He followed us in his cab all the way back to my home, to make sure the car didn't stall, then said goodbye.

That's not the end of the story. The next day I found a book about angels left "anonymously" on my doorstep. But Helen and I both knew who left it. Were these random acts of kindness, or were they specifically the work of angels? I don't believe it matters, because they blessed us, and they blessed our "angelic" cab driver.

In his book *Joy Is My Compass*, Alan Cohen writes that "the difference between a saint and a sourpuss is that the sourpuss sees his daily interactions as a nuisance, while the saint finds a continuous stream of opportunities to celebrate. One finds intruders, the other angels. At any given moment we have the power to choose what we will be and what we will see. Each of us has the capacity to find holiness or attack all about us." By our intentions and through our attitudes we can choose to see heaven or hell. Choosing heaven has so many advantages.

THE HEALTH BENEFITS OF SMALL PLEASURES

Even though Chapter 3 is totally devoted to the health benefits of kindness, I will briefly touch on an interesting clinical study here about being more joyful day in, day out. Being kind and gentle begins with how we treat ourselves. So many of us excel at being tough on ourselves. We beat ourselves up when we make a mistake, choose incorrectly, or repeat the past. Try being kind and understanding with yourself. Be especially kind to yourself if you behave in a way that you dislike. Always talk kindly to yourself, and be patient when you find it difficult to be a "holy" person. Forgive yourself, and when you do not act as you would like, use your actions to remind you where you are and where you want to be. Be your own best friend. This is the most important step on the path to joy and health.

A clinical study uncovered a surprising physical benefit from working small joys into our day-to-day schedule. It can help give our immune system a boost. Researchers in the Department of Psychiatry at State University of

New York at Stony Brook asked one hundred volunteers to fill out an evaluation of daily ups and downs. They then compared this information with antibody activity in the participants' saliva, a test that indicates immune system fluctuations. They found that *the stress of a negative event weakens the immune system on the day it occurs, but a positive event can strengthen the immune system for two days or more.*

"In other words, positive daily events help immune function more than upsetting events hurt it," says Arthur Stone, PhD, the psychologist who conducted the study. Among the everyday events that boosted subjects' immune systems were pursuing leisure activities, such as gardening or walking in nature, and spending time on a favorite hobby or special interest. Take time to be kind to yourself with life-affirming pleasures and activities.

THE HEALTH BENEFITS OF LOVE AND KINDNESS

Often in today's society we are tempted to put our selfish interests first, before loyalty or integrity or commitment to higher values. Since what emanates from us will come back to us at some point, this is ultimately not a winning attitude. We must do what is right for the sake of doing what is right. True friendship can be one of the rewards. The love shared between two people is the most precious gift we have. I love what Sir Hugh Walpole said, which I found online: "The most wonderful of all things in life, I believe, is the discovery of another human being with whom one's relationship has a glowing depth, beauty, and joy as the years increase. This inner progression of love between two human beings is a most marvelous thing, it cannot be found by looking for it or by passionately wishing for it. It is a sort of divine accident."

I am reminded of my beautiful friend Molly. Well into her seventies when I met her, she certainly knew how to celebrate life and how to be kind and loving; it was evident in her many friendships. The times we spent visiting together will always be special to me. A vibrant, alive, positive woman, Molly spent her days swimming, walking, doing yoga, and volunteering at the UCLA hospital. When she was diagnosed with terminal cancer, the shocking news darkened her sunny disposition for the first three days. Then she adjusted to it and decided to make the most of whatever time she had left. She continued her routine and seemed as radiantly alive and cheerful as ever.

The last month of her life, Molly was a patient in the hospital where she had volunteered for so long. I was away on a lengthy speaking/media tour, and when I returned, I immediately went to visit her. I wasn't prepared for what I saw. During my absence she had lost nearly half her body weight, all her teeth, and most of her color but, astonishingly, not her cheerful attitude. Although she was physically unrecognizable, her spirit shone through when she said, "Sunny, I know I've looked better. Let's see if you can perform your magic and fix me up." I brushed her hair, washed her face, and applied a drop of her favorite perfume. Although she could barely move and had difficulty speaking, she still told me a couple of jokes. She also spoke with great appreciation about the flowers in her room and the birds singing to her from the tree outside her window.

She then asked me to lie down next to her because she needed to talk and didn't think she had much time. In that final hour, she spoke to me about the light and colors she saw and about the peace and joy she felt. She was ready to cross over to the other side and was actually eager to make her transition. Just before she died, she said to me, "Life is meant to be joyful. Don't ever get too serious about life. Laugh every day and live each day as though it were your last. Continue to find ways to give love to others like you have always done with me. Follow your heart and let the beauty of life into your spirit." And then she passed on.

My experiences with Molly taught me so many precious and invaluable life lessons that have taken up permanent residence in my heart such as this one:

> *One of the greatest hungers of every human heart is to feel understood.*

Molly also reminded me that we must embrace all of life and live every day as though we were born anew. Erich Fromm said, "Living is the process of continuous rebirth. The tragedy in the life of most of us is that we die before we are fully born." My experiences with Molly also make me think of something Elisabeth Kübler-Ross said in her book *Death: The Final Stage of Growth*: "What is important is to realize that whether we understand fully who we are or what will happen when we die, it's our purpose to grow as human beings, to look within ourselves, to find and build upon that source of peace and understanding and strength that is our individual self. And then to reach out to others with love and acceptance and patient guidance in the hope of what we may become together."

A single act of kindness throws out roots in all directions,
and the roots spring up and make new trees.

~ AMELIA EARHART

SHOWING KINDNESS DAY TO DAY

Practice makes us better at recognizing those daily opportunities to show kindness toward ourselves and others. If you're looking for new ideas, here are some to add to your list and some of these will take only **12 minutes or fewer**, such as picking up trash as you stroll down the sidewalk or giving another person your parking spot at the grocery store:

- Go to your local shelter and adopt a pet.
- Offer a ride to a friend who can't get around.
- Volunteer at your local library.
- Pick up some trash as you walk down the sidewalk.
- Ask your friends and coworkers to tell you their stories of simple acts of kindness. Have a party just for that purpose.
- Give another person your parking spot, or let another driver get in front of you if they want. Wave and smile at them, too!
- Surprise a forgotten friend or relative with a phone call.
- Give a present to an underprivileged boy or girl, or to someone you know, for no reason at all.
- Take the clothes you haven't worn in a year to a homeless shelter. Organize neighbors on your block to do the same.
- Wave hello to pedestrians when you're in your car, even if you don't know them. It will lift their spirits, as well as yours.

- ۞ Let the person behind you in line at the grocery or hardware store go in front of you. Pay for their purchases, too, if you can. If they are hesitant, just tell them it will make you feel terrific.

- ۞ When you're in line for a movie, anonymously pay for the ticket of someone behind you in line. Then watch their face when they receive the news.

- ۞ Order a gift anonymously for someone you know who needs to be cheered up, or slip a $20 bill into the pocket or purse of a needy friend or stranger.

- ۞ If you drive on a manned toll bridge, pay for the next few cars after yours.

- ۞ Laugh out loud and smile often. Even when you're not in the mood to smile, do it. It will lift everybody's spirits.

- ۞ If you know someone who's having a difficult day, do something special for them without telling them you did it.

- ۞ Tell your family and friends often how much you appreciate them and how blessed you are to have their presence in your life.

- ۞ Tell your boss or employees the same things. Everyone wants and needs to feel appreciated.

- ۞ If you have children, get them to go through their toys and select some to give to those less fortunate. Let the children go with you to take the toys someplace they will be appreciated.

- ۞ Plant a tree or flowers in your neighbor's yard or somewhere they are needed—with permission, of course!

- ۞ Take a beautiful plant to your local nursing home, fire station, hospital, police station, or doctor's office.

- ۞ Make sandwiches, drive by a city park, and give them to homeless people.

- ۞ Leave a flower anonymously on someone's windshield.

- ۞ Look in the mirror every day and tell yourself how beautiful and wonderful you are.

- ۞ Compliment others whenever you can.

- If you see someone who appears stressed or unhappy, visualize them surrounded by light and love.

- Be loving and kind to yourself every day, knowing you deserve to live a happy, joy-filled, wonderful life.

Spread your love everywhere you go.

~ MOTHER TERESA

It isn't enough to talk about peace. One must believe in it.
And it isn't enough to believe in it. One must work at it.

~ ELEANOR ROOSEVELT

 ## Today's Affirmation

Peacefully and gently, I relax and feel the love in my heart. I let go of any thoughts of unkindness or unforgiveness toward myself and others. In everything I think, feel, say, and do, I let my gentleness and my kindheartedness shine through.

 ## 12-Minute Action Step

One of the easiest ways to show kindness is by being present, physically and mentally. Put your phone away, and give people your full attention when you're with them. Be intentional about eye contact, and share the gift of a smile. Other things I like to do include the following: Check in with a friend or family member you haven't heard from to make sure they're doing well. Write an encouraging note with sidewalk chalk outside to brighten the day of people who see it. And/or compliment a loved one in the morning to make their day bright as it starts.

Chapter 2

Flying High with a Tender Heart & Gratitude

Only a life lived for others is worth living.

~ ALBERT EINSTEIN

What do we live for, if not to make life easier for each other?

~ GEORGE ELIOT

Gentleness and kindness are usually in tandem. As I touched on in the last chapter, the word "gentle" means to be kindly, mild, amiable, and not violent or severe. It means being compassionate, considerate, tolerant, calm, mild-tempered, courteous, and peaceful. But I think that the best synonym for being gentle is tenderhearted. I love that word. And I love being around people who are tenderhearted.

To be treated with tenderheartedness, we must first offer this quality to other people. Respond to others exactly as you would want to be treated. No one likes to be rushed or belittled, ignored, or unappreciated. Ephesians 4:32 advises, "Be kind to one another, tenderhearted, forgiving one another." And throughout the Gospels, Jesus teaches, "As you have believed, so let it be done unto you" (Matt. 8:13). Gandhi said that the pure loving kindness of one gentle soul could nullify the hatred of millions. Now is the time for all of us to live more tenderheartedly.

If you need a place to start, begin by smiling. Everyone can do it. It takes seventeen muscles to smile and forty-seven muscles to frown. That means that it takes more muscular effort to frown than it does to smile. It's so simple and yet so effective. Learn to smile sincerely, from your heart. Smile at family and friends, at strangers, at everyone you meet or pass during the day today. Do you realize how many lives you can touch simply by smiling? You give a smile to one person, and he or she catches the good feeling and smiles at another person, and so on until your smile has indirectly affected the lives of several thousand people in one day.

How about writing a note of thanks? A real note, sent in the postal mail, rather than through e-mail. It doesn't take much time. Sending notes is becoming a lost art form, and it's such a simple, considerate act of kindness. I learned about this from my dear friend Alexandra Stoddard whose wonderful book *Gift of a Letter* changed my life.

Another act of kindness I always appreciate is a hug or simply the touch of another person. Since I was a young girl, my mom, June, was always my shining example on how to treat others with kindness. She encouraged me to be loving and kind to others, to offer a gentle yet appropriate touch to another, such as on the shoulder or arm, or even a thoughtful hug. She would always tell me that her prescription to health and happiness was "to keep the doctor away, give three hugs each day" and would encourage me to do the same. Of course, that was before the global pandemic, and it's important to be cautious these days. However, I've been known to give hugs in important business meetings, even when I've just met the person. I've had my share of awkward looks, but it's how I like to be, and unless someone specifically says to me that he or she doesn't like to be touched, I will continue following my heart and doing what feels right to me.

Touching does so much. Studies at the University of Colorado Medical School have shown that *touching increases hemoglobin, increases immune functioning, decreases tension in the body, and accelerates healing.* Yes, there is great power in our hands.

About three years ago, I visited a friend in the hospital. When I walked into her room, she began complaining about her male nurse acting forgetful and rude. When my friend left the room for her therapy, her nurse came in to change the sheets. I could see the pain and anguish on his face. So I offered a few kind words about how much I appreciated his hard work and dedication. That opened the way for him to reveal the incredible hardship in his life. His wife still lived in South Africa and his two children had recently died from medical complications. He was working a double shift just to make ends meet. When I heard all this, I felt a deep, loving-kindness for him. Before he left the room, I gave him a big hug. He started to cry. You know how that can be sometimes? All it takes is a hug or kind word and the emotional floodgates open.

Over the next couple weeks, whenever I visited my friend, I took the nurse some of my homemade organic granola, muffins, cupcakes, cookies, or bread, which he loved and appreciated. Both my hospitalized friend and I learned a valuable lesson during those two weeks about how important it is to reach out to others with tenderheartedness even though you have no guarantee of what you'll get in return.

Sometimes the kindest gestures can go unnoticed. As mentioned previously, I love to put coins in parking meters when I walk down the street if I find some that have expired. The drivers of the cars never know what I have done, but it makes me feel good. Sometimes I send a note anonymously with a kind word or a few dollars when I know the recipient is in need. It takes so little to contribute, and you receive so much in return.

Each of us can make a difference in the world. It is a strong person who is gentle. We always feel at peace with such a person. When we relax and are centered in the divine flow, we express this gentle kindness toward ourselves and toward others.

To be gentle and kind to others, we must first be gentle and kind with ourselves. There's no need to be hard on yourself when you make a mistake. Just as God forgives us, we must forgive

To be gentle and kind to others, we must first be gentle and kind with ourselves.

ourselves. Through love and forgiveness, we can live from our hearts and live in the heart of Love. And when we live in the heart of Love, of God, we can let our tenderheartedness shine through in everything we think, feel, say, and do.

CULTIVATE GRATITUDE & REAP THE HEALTH BENEFITS

You can spend thousands of dollars changing your physical features, but that will do little good until you cultivate a positive relationship with yourself. Gratitude can really influence your attitude. Take a minute to think of everything for which you're grateful. If you are mindful of the positive in your life, you'll create more positive thoughts, energy, and events.

Any time of the year is the perfect time to cultivate the health-giving benefits of gratitude. Regardless of the circumstances of your life or the losses you've suffered, gratitude can help you.

When you find one thing, however small, to be thankful for and you hold that feeling for a little as 15 seconds, many subtle and beneficial physiological changes take place in your body:

1. Coronary arteries relax, thus increasing the blood supply to your heart.

2. Heart rhythm becomes more harmonious, which positively affects your mood and all other bodily organs.

3. Stress hormone levels of cortisol and norepinephrine decrease, creating a cascade of beneficial metabolic changes, such as an enhanced immune system.

4. Breathing becomes deeper, thus increasing the oxygen level of your tissues.

So think of it in this other way. If all this happens when you focus for just 15 seconds on something that brings you pleasure, joy, or a feeling of gratitude, imagine what would happen to your health if you were able to cultivate grateful thoughts and feelings regularly, at least once per hour throughout each day of the year.

The health benefits of gratitude (which is really the same thing as love) are an amazing example of how connected the bridge between the mind, body, and emotions really is and how simple it is to put this connection to work in your own life. But, as you well know, simple isn't necessarily easy.

Like maintaining strong muscles and bone, cultivating gratitude takes discipline and will. That's right. It takes practice to feel gratitude and reap its physical and emotional benefits. There are valid physiological reasons why focusing on gratitude isn't easy. Physically, we humans evolved along with a nervous system wired to ensure our survival by keeping us alerted to possible danger from the occasional wild animal or violent storm—events that were relatively infrequent within a life span.

Now fast-forward that same nervous system to our current era of mass media, when all the possible dangerous events from the entire planet are beamed into our living rooms day and night. No wonder so many people feel anxious and can't sleep! Our primitive nervous systems are being given the message to stay on "alert" 24 hours a day, something our bodies were never designed to do. There's only one way out of this dilemma, and that is to change our habitual reactions to uncertainty.

One of the most powerful ways to do this is to cultivate the habit of gratitude. No matter what's going on in the world, the economy, or the news, you have the power within you to create the biochemistry of gratitude right now.

Take a moment to feel gratitude in your heart and in your body. Create some gratitude "touchstones" that will evoke physiological benefits within seconds.

GRATITUDE TOUCHSTONES

Write your favorite memories or peak experiences on index cards to keep close at hand as gratitude touchstones. This is something my mom and grandmother both taught me to do. You could take just 12 minutes and write on a few cards and then add to them over the day or week as you think of more. Here are a few examples:

1. A child you love. Whether it's your child, grandchild, niece, or nephew, or even your neighbor's child who brings you joy and happiness, write down a few words about your gratitude to uplift you whenever you think about these loving memories.

2. A beautiful place in nature. I hike often in the Santa Monica Mountains early mornings and see luminous sunrises, animals like deer and rabbits, insects like butterflies and dragonflies, birds like hummingbirds and hawks, and so much more. Just visualizing these hikes and experiences in the mountains is refreshing and uplifting.

3. Enjoy the company of your furry friends. Petting your cat or dog or brushing your horse, or even sitting and observing fish in a fish tank while breathing deeply would be a special moment for you.

4. An event that was special to you. I was blessed to have a 30-minute swim with a school of dolphins in the Santa Monica Bay. You glean physical benefits from one perfect moment by reimagining it over and over again.

5. A museum with glorious works of art. I am blessed to live minutes from both the Getty Center Museum in Brentwood and the Getty Villa in Malibu, and I am a frequent visitor to both places. How could I ever tire of viewing the masterpieces of Claude Monet, Sir Peter Paul Rubens, Édouard Manet, Pablo Picasso, Leonard da Vinci, Vincent van Gogh, Paul Cézanne, and thousands more? Fostering and appreciating the joy of magnificent art is of one of my favorite hobbies. I often write down on cards what I experience when viewing these timeless, resplendent artifacts so when I read them again, the experience comes back to life in my mind and body as though I am standing in front of the art at the museum. I am never stressed out at a museum. You may be interested to know that when you view art in a museum, studies have shown that it can lead to a decrease in cortisol, the stress hormone. Visiting a museum actually reduces stress! Looking at art gives us greater empathy as we strive to understand the context of the artwork and the events and emotions surrounding the piece.

Don't let your fears overshadow the beauty in your life. It takes practice to turn it around. It takes practice to notice what gratitude feels like in your body. It takes practice to notice when you get off track and into a downward spiral by consciously deciding to focus on something that feels better. Pay attention to your thoughts and choose to think, speak, and write in a positive light. (Refer to Chapter 10 for more information on the importance of what you think, speak, and write.)

SHOW GRATITUDE AND RESPECT FOR YOUR WALLET AND THE MONEY INSIDE

This may seem like a total digression to you, but I also believe it's very important if you want to grow your prosperity, to show kindness, gratitude, and respect for your money. This is one of the many simple, surefire ways I recommend to grow your money. Here's what I mean:

Don't simply throw your money into your wallet, purse, or other receptacle. Money needs to be respected. Always keep it aligned without creased corners, wadded up, or messy. I even take this a step further. In my wallet, my paper bills are all lined up and placed in descending order and all facing the same direction. For example, my wallet might have two 50-dollar bills, followed by three 20-dollar bills, followed by two 10-dollar bills, followed by three 5-dollar bills, and, lastly, nine 1-dollar bills. As I align the money, I also feel a deep sense of gratitude that I have money in my wallet.

Keep your credit cards in alignment, too, and have as your goal to pay them off *in full* monthly, or at least every 90 days. If my money gets too old, I make a visit to the bank to trade it in for new money. If you show gratitude for your money and respect your money in this simple, yet practicable way, it will return the favor by multiplying and growing for you.

Here's a quick example of how this idea played out for one of my friends and how you are a stronger magnet for blessings and miracles when you live with gratitude. Sarah called me up and asked if she could take me to lunch in Brentwood (Los Angeles) near where I live because she needed some of my prosperity guidance. A year earlier, she had taken my workshop "Choose to Thrive." I hadn't seen her in about five months.

Over lunch, she told me that a month prior, they phased out her job at her company so she was out of work. And after sending out multiple résumés to different companies, she hadn't gotten so much as a nibble of interest from anyone. She was at a loss for what to do next. When our lunch bill arrived, she took out her wallet, opened it up, and wrinkled paper money was falling out all over the table. The bills were creased, ripped, folded, and a total mess.

I reminded Sarah that in my workshop a year prior, I taught everyone the importance of treating our money with thanksgiving and respect and then it would grow for us, and even showed them my tips on organizing one's wallet. She admitted that this key point was the one thing she hadn't done yet. So I told her that there was no better time than the present, and together we organized all the money in her tattered wallet. She felt deeply grateful for my assistance and support.

Next, I excused myself, saying I was going to use the restroom and, instead, went next door to a lovely gift shop and purchased a beautiful new wallet for Sarah to hold all of her unwrinkled and organized money. Before I gave it to her, I reached into my wallet and pulled out a new $50 bill and slipped it into her wallet. When I gave her the present, she was overjoyed and so grateful. She loved the wallet in her favorite teal color (and even said she had admired it before I arrived for lunch in the gift shop window and wished she could buy it); she even told me that this gift shop was her favorite store in Brentwood. In fact, three years earlier, I learned that she had applied for a job to be manager at the store but someone else got the position. We talked for about two more hours while sipping tea, and I shared with her again some of the prosperity and health suggestions I included in my book *Wired for High-Level Wellness*.

Well, that's not the end of the story. After I treated Sarah to lunch, we went together to the gift shop and looked around. While she was trying on scarves, I was near the front counter and overheard the store's manager on the telephone telling someone that she needed to find a replacement for her position because her husband just got a promotion and a new job in another state, and they needed to move quickly. I rushed over to Sarah to share with her what I had heard and she was gobsmacked and a little nervous at the idea of talking to this manager about the position.

We walked over together, and I told the manager that I couldn't help overhearing her news about moving, and Sarah told her she would like to apply for this position again. This store manager was now also astonished at how quickly everything was happening. It turns out that Sarah got the job that same day, the manager was able to move quickly without worrying about how to find a replacement, and I was delighted that everyone was so happy.

Okay, I know what you are thinking. Did simply feeling gratitude for her new wallet and organizing the unwrinkled bills (showing great respect to the money) in the new wallet get Sarah the new job? We won't really ever know for sure, but I've seen things like this happen too many times to refute it as just a coincidence. You must always respect your money and how you carry it in your wallet, and it will respect you by growing and multiplying.

It's also a great lesson to learn about timing and how we are always at the right place at the right time. The more grateful you are for each day and the more you choose to live by the Golden Rule and show kindness to others, I know for certain, the more you will find yourself in the right place at the right time. If we arrived only a couple minutes later at the gift shop, I would not have heard the manager on the telephone talking about needing to find someone to replace her quickly. Trust more and live with faith and gratitude. Know that everything is working for your highest good.

And, yes, I now get to visit Sarah more often during her breaks from the gift shop at our favorite restaurant in Brentwood. She never lets me pay for lunch anymore when we meet at the restaurant next to the gift shop, which, by the way, is now doing better than ever before since Sarah is at the helm.

Dare to be naïve.

~ BUCKMINSTER FULLER

Kindness is the language we all understand. Even the blind can see it and the deaf can hear it.

~ MOTHER TERESA

 ## Today's Affirmation

Today I sing a song of praise and gratitude. I see each person in my life as God's gift to me. In each encounter of this day, I learn, grow, and deepen my awareness of God's wonder and blessing. I dedicate my life to doing God's will and to creating my best life. Today I think only loving, kind thoughts.

 ## 12-Minute Action Step

Send a note of kindness to someone today for no reason at all except to say, "I appreciate you. You bless and enrich my life." While you're at it, send a love note to yourself, too. Or sometime before you go to bed tonight, write down at least ten things for which you are grateful. If you can write more in 12 minutes, go for it! Write as many as you can and feel the joy and thanksgiving you have for each blessing on your list.

Chapter 3

The Health Benefits
of Kindness

Gratitude is not only the greatest of virtues,
but the parent of all the others.

~ WINSTON CHURCHILL

How beautiful a day can be when a joyful heart,
hearty laughter, and sincere kindness touch it.

~ DAVID CRADDOCK

The saying that "it's better to give than to receive" is not just a platitude that your mother used to tell you when you thought life was being unfair. It's now actually a saying you might find on the lips of scientists; studies show that the benefits of kindness are greater for the performer than for the receiver. If kindness is actually having a positive effect on our physical health, and research proves that it is, then clearly, it's much more than a platitude. To me, genuine kindness is a gift of rare beauty to give others and ourselves every day. Being kind to and helping others reveals the best version of ourselves. And as you'll read throughout this book, living by the Golden Rule, and always being kind to others, was one of the most import-ant and sacred life lessons I was taught by my parents and grandparents, and often by their examples.

In the two previous chapters, you learned about my perspective on gratitude and kindness and why it's so important to let our heart-light shine in our daily lives, and you read some of my stories about seeing or per-forming acts of kindness in person. In this chapter, to motivate you to keep

36

kindness your daily default position in life, here's some uplifting research and scientific information on all the many ways that kindness can benefit us physically and mentally, whether it's some kindness that you show others or that you personally witness from someone else. So, let's start boosting our health with this empowering information.

KINDNESS IS OUR DESTINY

It feels good when you do something kind for someone else, right? This isn't a secret. But you probably weren't aware of the fact that your brain's pleasure and rewards center are lighting up like a Christmas tree when you do something kind. A chemical reaction is taking place, releasing the neurotransmitters serotonin and dopamine, the feel-good chemicals that combat anxiety and depression. Also elevated through acts of kindness is the hormone oxytocin, which is often known as the "love hormone" since it increases feelings of intimacy. Not only that but these chemicals are essential to certain aspects of maintaining a healthy body. Endorphins are another neurotransmitter that is released during acts of kindness and that means that you may even find physical pain alleviated.

That's a lot of bang for your buck for something that might be as simple as opening a door for a stranger. But that's how powerful kindness is. From a biological perspective, it makes sense, because human survival depends on cooperation and the good will of others. And when we take care of others, we strengthen bonds, helping to ensure that they'll reciprocate and take care of us in return. Kindness benefits ourselves as well as the receiver of the kindness. And since kindness is infectious, it can benefit an entire community as the effects ripple outwards.

human survival depends on cooperation and the good will of others.

So, let's learn a little about these chemicals and just what they can do for us.

SEROTONIN

Mental Health

In people with depression, signals in the brain are misinterpreted, causing the brain to fail to release the amount of serotonin necessary for well-being, leading to depression. Low serotonin levels are also responsible for OCD-related behaviors, anxiety, and suicidal behavior. Antidepressants are designed to alter these signals so that proper serotonin levels are restored.

Many people see modern society as complicit in affecting neurochemical activity and causing depression. Ours is a society that values independence, competition, and getting ahead. It's possible that we've created a world that doesn't encourage good mental health because of our failure to prioritize cooperation, intimacy, and kindness. So, is it possible that we could change our brain chemistry by shifting our values? Studies say yes.

A University of British Colombia study had several people with high anxiety perform at least six acts of kindness a week. After just one month, they reported experiencing less social anxiety and overall felt an increase of positive feelings. It's why mental health practitioners often incorporate mindfulness meditation into therapy. Mindfulness focuses on gratitude and kindness, and clients of these therapists are encouraged to include acts of kindness into their daily lives. What this can offer is a natural increase in serotonin levels in the brain. Moreover, other studies identified an increase in a sense of self-worth, a result of increased serotonin, when regularly behaving compassionately. Along with other personal changes, this could be a recipe for good mental health and, ideally, a reduced dependence on antidepressants.

Physical Health

It comes as a surprise to many that serotonin affects physical health since in most people's mind it's so inextricably linked to mood. But the mind-body connection is indisputable, with the body affecting the mind and vice versa. And if 90 percent of serotonin receptors are in the gut, then we should definitely expect that it's going to affect our appetite and digestion. But it even affects bowel movements and also helps to control nausea. This explains why people with clinical depression struggle with nausea and diarrhea. Also, dependent on healthy serotonin levels, surprisingly, is blood's ability to clot. This means that healing depends on serotonin as well, another reason why maintaining healthy serotonin levels is so important.

DOPAMINE

Mental Health

The brain's reward center is something you may have heard of. You may have also heard dopamine mentioned in reference to this area. That's because this is the neurotransmitter associated with reward and pleasure, the one that encourages us to seek out experiences that are needed to sustain ourselves. Like serotonin, dopamine is released when engaging in acts of kindness. Dopamine deficiencies alone do not generally cause depression. When the relationship between serotonin and dopamine is regulated, it keeps us feeling stable.

Dopamine in itself is associated with things like motivation. When you feel good about accomplishing something, dopamine is the factor and will continue to keep you seeking the rewarding feeling. To be depleted in dopamine means that you'll likely be lacking in motivation and may even feel hopeless and helpless. In other words, dopamine is really necessary for an overall sense of well-being. Dopamine also works to control cortisol levels, the chemical your body produces when you're stressed. Increased cortisol is associated with feelings of isolation and hopelessness and can also cause us to feel irritable and have trouble with concentration.

Physical Health

To get a little more technical about how dopamine functions, let's consider how it works. Our bodies produce natural pain relievers and mood lifters called endogenous opioids. Yes, our bodies create our own opioids, and they're created through the release of dopamine. You may be familiar with opioids if you've ever had surgery or chronic pain because it's likely that they were prescribed by your doctor. And you've also probably heard about how addictive they are and the widespread issue with their abuse. This is a testament to how powerful they are. So, it's incredible to think that we have the ability to produce our own opioids that can control and neutralize pain. And it's astounding to think that this complex neurochemical process can be stimulated simply by acts of kindness.

What you'll also get from dopamine is a reduced sense of stress. Stress is harmful to our health, as I discussed in the Preface, because it increases the production of cortisol. Besides the mental health implications of increased cortisol, there are a myriad of physical issues associated with it. One, not surprisingly, is high blood pressure, the main physical ailment associated with stress. But cortisol also is what causes people to store belly fat, a particularly stubborn type of weight gain that's known for its defiance against efforts to remove it. High cortisol levels also cause injuries to heal less expeditiously and can cause headaches, fatigue, muscle weakness, and thinning skin.

Although you may not have the ability to quit your job and move to a tropical island, you can still control your stress levels. There are many ways to offset some of the unavoidably difficult aspects of life, and kindness is a significant one. Kindness to yourself is an important part of that equation too. And when you kindly set aside enough time to get a good night of sleep, you'll find that the kindness you've shown others throughout the day pays off. That's because dopamine is a key factor in helping us to get a good night sleep because of its ability to reduce stress. Combined with the increase of serontonin from your kindness adventures, you can count on sleeping like a baby.

So go ahead and do it—take your busy friend's sick cat to the vet, help that elderly gentleman on to the bus, or even just give a stranger a big smile. Active compassion can help us to stay positive and optimistic in addition to optimizing our physical health.

OXYTOCIN

Mental Health

Oxytocin is considered both a neurotransmitter and a hormone. Maybe it's the two titles that make it extra powerful in terms of the benefits. When oxytocin is released, it causes the production of nitric oxide in our blood vessels. When this occurs, our blood vessels dilate, thereby reducing blood pressure, which, as we know, is good for heart health as well as for mood. In terms of mood (we'll get into physical health shortly), oxytocin produces, as mentioned earlier, a feeling of closeness and connectedness.

Oxytocin is produced by caregivers when caring for their children, particularly breastfeeding mothers. It's also associated with romantic feelings toward a partner. And it's recently been determined that pet owners as well as their pets (mostly dogs) experience the release of oxytocin when spending time together. It produces a sense of being loved and cared for. And even though you may be performing the act of kindness, you're receiving a feeling of being loved. Furthermore, oxytocin makes us feel more confident and even more optimistic.

Physical Health

As mentioned, oxytocin promotes the feeling of social bonds by causing the release of nitric oxide, which dilates blood vessels, lowering blood pressure, an important aspect of cardiovascular health. Oxytocin is actually known as "cardioprotective," because by lowering blood pressure, it's protecting the heart. This also leads to more optimal metabolic functioning. In fact, giving to others is said to be twice as effective as taking aspirin daily to protect against heart disease. Also, reduced blood pressure leads to reduced cortisol levels as well, which is important because high cortisol levels are complicit in causing a host of health complaints. Believe it or not, people who are regularly kind are said to have 23 percent less cortisol. And, finally, oxytocin can increase pain thresholds while also helping to promote healing.

ENDORPHINS

Endorphins are the body's natural painkillers, also endogenous opioids, and acts of kindness affect their production as well. Studies have found that people who volunteer experience fewer aches and pains. Furthermore, people over age 55 who volunteer for at least two organizations have almost half (44 percent) the chance of dying early than others do. That's an impressive statistic. And endorphins also have a role in creating an overall feeling of well-being.

Here are some more uplifting quotations to inspire you to be a kinder person.

Try to be a rainbow in someone's cloud.
~ Maya Angelou

Love is patient and kind; love does not
envy or boast; it is not arrogant.
~ 1 Corinthians 13:4

*He that has done you a kindness will be
more ready to do you another, than he
whom you yourself have obliged.*

~ BENJAMIN FRANKLIN

*Three things in human life are important:
the first is to be kind; the second is to
be kind, and the third is to be kind.*

~ HENRY JAMES

THE RELATIONSHIP BETWEEN KINDNESS AND HAPPINESS

If you've not already inferred it, let me make it crystal clear: kindness really is a recipe for a happiness, better health, and thus, a greater sense of well-being and fulfillment, which is ultimately what we're all striving for, right? However, we frequently get lost in the details of life and are convinced that acquiring more things or doing more will deliver the satisfaction we're seeking. Bewilderment and disappointment set in when we find ourselves still feeling a void in our lives after accessing the things we thought would lead to happiness. But instead of reevaluating, we often just jump right back on the hamster wheel, believing that *more* money, *more* status, *more* things, *more* friends, more whatever *it is*, will finally fill the void.

Searching outside of ourselves will never yield the results that connection with family, friends, and especially self can provide. The kindness we extend to self, family, friends, and even strangers can produce much more substantive results than buying a new sweater. Shopping does indeed feel good, and we do actually get some brief benefits in terms of extra serotonin and dopamine in the brain when purchasing something new. And although you may be "in love" with that sweater and it may keep you warm, the feeling its purchase provides is fleeting (not to mention that the feeling is not mutual since sweaters are notoriously aloof wardrobe items). And there's no oxytocin involved since you can't quite bond with a sweater in the same way you can with a loved one.

THE HAPPIEST COUNTRIES IN THE WORLD

Analyzing what causes Nordic countries to frequently appear at the top of the "happiest country in the world" lists can offer some insights about how to augment our own levels of happiness. Although we can't change governmental policies that could make daily life more pleasant, like the ones they have in Scandinavia, we can try, at a more micro level, to create some of the conditions that positively affect the Nordic folks.

One characteristic of these countries is the significantly lower levels of corruption in public institutions. This ripples out to affect every level of society, causing people to be more trusting and kinder. It's also an effect of living under more compassionate governments, which pay fair living wages, provide low-cost childcare, and offer paid yearly five-week vacations. It seems that by generously extending benefits that improve the quality of life, sort of state-sanctioned acts of kindness, the citizens feel that their well-being is valued, and this leads to increased feelings of contentment and happiness. We might see this as a state-run "serotonin/dopamine" social program. And the fact that some of those countries allow citizens to leave work to pick up their kids at school and thus develop better bonds with their children might be viewed as a state-run "oxytocin" program!

Scandinavians are known for being compassionate and looking out for one another. Low crime rates and the fact that children under age 10 often take public transportation all alone make them feel that they can trust those around them. This, as well as everything discussed above, are all factors that lead to a happy populous, and thus, their top spots on world happiness lists. And remember, these countries are cold, not to mention without sunlight for much of the year, something that is actually known to cause depression. The fact that, despite this, these countries citizens are the happiest is a powerful testimonial to the power of kindness, compassion, and social connectedness!

OPTIMISTS VERSUS PESSIMISTS

If kindness can flood our brains and bodies with so many feel-good chemicals, then we're more likely to have a positive attitude about life, which not surprisingly can lead to better health and therefore increased longevity.

Studies have proven that there is a strong correlation between health and optimism. For example, one study that evaluated patients' psychological states after heart surgery found that those with positive attitudes were half as likely to be rehospitalized.

Studies evaluating men without heart disease who were tracked for a ten-year period revealed that those they'd determined had pessimistic attitudes were twice as likely to develop heart disease. Studies have found similar correlations between pessimism and increased hypertension and higher rates of infections. And studies on overall health have shown that higher levels of optimism are associated with better general health, better mental functioning, and increased feelings of well-being. You don't have to be a scientist to deduce that higher life expectancy will result.

Another study found that participants who were taught a technique to help them reframe negative thoughts developed more of a sense of compassion for others. The evidence is pretty stark. All of us, whether the recipient or performer of an act of kindness, benefit in a multitude of ways through kindness. Please refer to my book *Wired for High-Level Wellness* for the chapters on how to meditate to bring the best results, including higher self-worth, peace, joy, faith, and vitality.

THE NITTY GRITTY OF THE KINDNESS-HAPPINESS CORRELATION

The kindness-happiness connection seems undeniable based on everything we've already discussed, but in case you're still having doubts, you should know that studies have actually been done that prove that there is indeed a connection. In a study published in the *Journal of Social Psychology*, 86 people, divided into three groups, were given different instructions for a ten-day period. One group was given no instructions at all while another was told to engage in a novel activity each day. The third group was told to engage in a daily act of kindness. Before they began though, the participants took a life satisfaction survey. This survey was repeated after the ten-day period; what it revealed should come as no surprise since we now know how beneficial kindness is to our health and well-being. Indeed, participants found an increase in the reports of happiness levels in both the groups who tried new things and who performed acts of kindness daily.

Other studies show similar results. In one, researchers gave participants money and asked them to spend it on themselves or someone else. When they later reflected on their feelings, participants reported that they felt happier when they remembered buying something for someone else. Researchers also determined that this increased feeling of happiness results in the search for more of this mood boosting sensation and leads to a positive feedback loop, which keeps people continuing to engage in acts of kindness.

FINAL THOUGHTS

It should be mentioned that to really enjoy the benefits of kindness we've been discussing, you should make kindness a way of life. A one-off act of kindness will make you feel good temporarily. But if you get into a pattern of behavior that prioritizes kindness to others, you're likely to find yourself becoming a happier, healthier, and a more optimistic individual. And, of course, this produces its own positive feedback loop because when you feel good, you attract more positivity into your life.

And get this! Studies actually show that random acts of kindness increase empathy for others. It's true that we can train ourselves to become more compassionate. This was even verified in brain scans. Researchers compared the brain scans of people who had been trained to be more compassionate with those who had not. When they all viewed pictures of people suffering, the empathy trainees' prefrontal cortexes, the area of the brain most associated with empathy, was activated, unlike the control groups'. On the syllabus of this training, of course, had been random acts of kindness.

At the beginning of the chapter, you may recall that I called kindness our destiny and mentioned its biological purpose. Humans couldn't survive without being able to trust and rely on others. As social creatures, we depend on one another for both physical and emotional support. Society these days, however, often seems to value competition and materialism, things that can alienate us from others and lead to depletions in the important health and happiness sustaining neurotransmitters and hormones. This causes us often to become self-absorbed and diminishes our capacity for empathy and compassion. When prioritizing cooperation and intimacy, however, we tend to focus less on ourselves and our problems, and get out of our own way, creating the conditions that can lead to a much more fulfilling life.

Kindness is exactly what the world needs right now as an antidote to some of the anger and hostility, which, unfortunately, seems to be on the rise these days. And how empowering it is to know that simple acts can be so transformative to both ourselves and others. The people in our orbits will benefit from our compassion, making it more likely that they'll feel uplifted in ways that may radiate beyond our immediate locations, crossing cultures and generations, so that we can build bridges and, ultimately, a better world.

LIVE BY THE GOLDEN RULE
EVEN WITHOUT GUARANTEES

I'd like to end this chapter with a personal story about a man I tried to help. Of the many valuable lessons taught to me by my mom and grandmother, one was to live daily by the Golden Rule, and that's why I always seek to treat others the way I wish to be treated myself. Sometimes, however, you can have the best of intentions in treating others with kindness, but it doesn't turn out as expected.

Recently, I was out and about doing errands in the Santa Monica and Brentwood areas of West Los Angeles. Pulling up to a red light on Wilshire Boulevard and another busy cross street, my car was right at the crosswalk, and I was waiting for the light to turn green so I could get on with my activities. I noticed a homeless man attempting to cross the bustling street right in front of my car, but he was walking so slowly that three red-then-green-then-red lights came and went, and he wasn't even halfway across the busy Wilshire crosswalk.

Many people passed him by as they were walking across the street. Moreover, the cars were all passing only inches by this homeless man, who seemed to be in a daze and not fully functioning mentally. So I turned off my engine (so no one could get into my car and take off in it), got out, and walked over to this disheveled man to help him get to the other side of Wilshire so no one would accidentally hit him with their cars.

I said to him, "Hello, my name is Susan, and I would like to assist you in getting to the other side of the street." I kept talking to him slowly, lovingly, and kindly, hoping he would comprehend what I was saying to him and permit me to assist him.

He just stared at me as though he didn't understand me. At the same time, dozens and dozens of cars where rushing by us, coming only inches from us and honking their horns for this man and me to get out of their way. I was beginning to feel very stressed out and even somewhat afraid. After taking only about five steps together in two minutes, I wondered if I should get back in my own car but didn't want to leave him. Just then, this homeless man swung back his arm to literally punch me in the face, and, fortunately, I was right there with him rather than looking in the other direction, so I was able to quickly duck down and get out of the range of his strong-arm swing. This was the first time in my life anyone had ever tried to attack or punch me.

Somehow this man's attempted punch stimulated him to walk more quickly to the other side of the street and back onto the sidewalk, much to my relief. I was a little shaky after this had happened. When pondering the thought if I would ever do this again, I thought, *Of course I will. I know that this man's heart and soul recognized, on some level of his being, my gesture as a kind and loving one and maybe one day he will understand. But I also know that God put me at that intersection at that exact moment so, perhaps, I could help him, or maybe show other drivers how essential it is to be kind on the road.*

I don't try to figure things out that way anymore; I just think, *What would Jesus do in this situation?* And I try to emulate His words or actions. I felt great that, at least, I tried to set a positive example for all the people rushing by in their cars to reach out and help others and, maybe, also made a positive difference to the man who was living a very difficult life.

Even though you might not get the outcome you expect, you can never go wrong with showing kindness to others as well as yourself.

*Whenever there is a human being,
there is an opportunity for a kindness.*

~ Lucius Annaeus Seneca

*Whoever pursues righteousness and kindness
will find life, righteousness, and honor.*

~ Proverbs 21:21

Today's Two Affirmations

1. Kindness is my middle name. Throughout this glorious day full of potential, I find opportunities, large and small, to bestow kindness on myself and others. Just thinking about being kind brings joy to my heart and a smile to my face.

2. To be kind with others, I must first be kind to myself. I honor God when I take care of myself. All the ways I can care for myself—with rest and nutrition, quiet moments with family and friends, and fun doing my favorite things—are not only good for my physical and emotional health but also nurture my spiritual health. The more I care for myself, the more beautifully and completely I realize my divine nature and the more fully I can be the hands and heart of God in the world. Renewed and refreshed, I shine the light of God with kindness for myself and others wherever I go.

 ## Two 12-Minute Action Steps

1. Find someone in your life today—maybe someone you know or even someone you encounter during the day whom you can see is having a difficult, stressful day. Find a way to brighten his or her day with a beautiful, thoughtful act of kindness. Maybe an elderly person needs help lifting bags of groceries from the shopping cart into his or her car. Or maybe it's raining, and you are walking across the street in the crosswalk with your umbrella and someone else is getting soaked without an umbrella. Share your umbrella with that person and tell him or her that you are so delighted to help them. Or perhaps you are in your car on the way home carrying take-out food and you see a homeless person on the street. Give him or her your food (and maybe even your shoes and/or your jacket), since you are on the way home where you have these comforts in excess at home. It will make you feel wonderful for days and weeks.

2. Today when someone shows you kindness, don't hesitate to say thank you. If someone lets you in front of them in traffic, always say thank you. You can simply lift up your hand, and they will see it in the car behind you. And this includes saying thank you to your own divinity. If you get a great idea about something that seems to pop into your mind, say thank you to God and your guardian angels for bringing you the idea, answer, or solution you needed. Or perhaps you write a thank-you note to someone who has blessed you in a special way. Being thankful and demonstrating that you are thankful is a ripple in the lake of life that goes out and touches countless people, thus changing the world in a small way by making it a more positive place to live. By your thoughts and actions, you can make a profound difference in the world.

Chapter 4

Unleash Your Inner Compassion

In wilderness I sense the miracle of life, and behind
it our scientific accomplishments fade to trivia.

~ CHARLES LINDBERGH

I think that I cannot preserve my health and spirits unless I
spend four hours a day at least—and it is commonly more
than that—sauntering through the woods and over the hills
and fields, absolutely free from all worldly engagements.

~ HENRY DAVID THOREAU

Are people really getting meaner or is it just your imagination? From the halls of Congress to the main streets of small-town America and big cities everywhere, it seems like no one is capable of civilly listening to others whose viewpoints are different.

I believe that we are in the midst of an epidemic in which few people have the time to be kind. This rampant form of business is nothing short of a sickness—a form of self-centeredness brought about by people rushing around trying to make ends meet and cope with mounting stress and numerous health issues.

Do you feel overwhelmed in your life and less compassionate than you did years ago? As I counsel people around the country, and even worldwide, it's been my experience that most people are burning the candle at both ends—daily, most people are experiencing severe sleep debt, most people have no time to call their own, and most folks are living in what I refer to as a spin-cycle lifestyle. Can you relate to any of this?

World peace must develop from inner peace.
Peace is not just mere absence of violence. Peace is,
I think, the manifestation of human compassion.

~ DALAI LAMA

Computers have sped up our lives. We want to do everything, and we want to do it all at once. If you understand the speed of life, you can slow it down by enjoying it more and by making a conscious choice to be more compassionate. Start with yourself.

The more you rush around without keeping your life in perspective and in balance, the more you lose compassion for others and yourself, too. People are in such a rush these days, living on the fast track—talking fast, eating fast, and moving fast. What a difference from fifty years ago.

Given our current pace, we barely have time to relax and cultivate relationships with our spouses and children, friends and nature, much less with God. Is it any wonder that stress-related diseases are on the rise? We are under pressure to keep busy even in our leisure hours.

Did you know that you'll probably do more in this year—with appointments, people to meet, and places to go—than your grandparents did their entire lives?

William Penn described well the importance of not putting off acts of kindness when he wrote, "If there is any kindness I can show, or any good thing I can do to any fellow being, let me do it now, and not deter or neglect it, as I shall not pass this way again." What's more, the Dalia Lama avowed: "World peace must develop from inner peace. Peace is not just mere absence of violence. Peace is, I think, the manifestation of human compassion."

Do you feel your compassionate nature slipping away? Want to be a more compassionate person in your daily life? While you will find more details in the pages of this book, here are some highlights to help make compassion more a default position in your daily life.

SLEEP

Getting only six or fewer hours of sleep nightly makes you feel more stressed, depressed, and impatient; increases blood pressure; and makes you more irritable. It's hard to feel compassionate when you are just trying to get through the day with a short fuse and not enough time to accomplish all you need to do. Studies reveal that when you get more sleep on a regular basis, your stress level abates and you become a more compassionate person. In my book *Wired for High-Level Wellness*, you will learn details about the one thing you should never do before bedtime if you want a good night's sleep, which is to not use your cell phone because of its deleterious effects on brainwave activity, as well as more information on the role sleep plays in our mood.

MEDITATION

You don't have to be a Buddhist monk to know how to meditate. As a disciplined meditator for more than thirty-five years, I know of its benefits personally. **Here's one way to meditate:** find a special, quiet space your home. Spend at least 15 minutes there first thing in the morning and, if you can fit in a second session, also before going to bed. Sit and close your eyes and focus on your breathing. Inhale and exhale slowly and deeply, focusing on the sound and rhythm of your breathing. Mentally visualize peace and calmness. Your day will start and end on a stress-free note. According to recent studies, *practicing meditation daily will change your brainwaves in a positive way, and make you feel calmer, less anxious, and more compassionate.* Additionally, other studies show that compassionate people are healthier, happier, and more successful at work—*and earn more money!* When I meditate regularly, I am constantly reminded that the world is on my side, even if appearances may show something different. Affirm this daily: **The world is on my side.**

DIET

What you eat affects your mood as you'll read more about in Chapter 13. That's right. If you want to be more compassionate and kinder, you must eschew foods made with white sugar and white flour, and also avoid foods made with artificial flavorings, colorings, and preservatives. Choose to eat foods as close to the way nature made them as possible—food with natural colors and with an emphasis of plant-based foods, which are teeming with antioxidants, nutrients, and fiber. *Make at least 60 percent of your diet from living (uncooked foods) because these are calming foods.* You will find many correlating studies (in *Wired for High-Level Wellness* and *Kitchen Gardening*) that support how the foods (and which foods, herbs, and spices) you eat can make you a kinder and more compassionate person. Also, keep your body hydrated with purified water, too. I use the Ionizer Plus water-filtration system. (Refer to my website for articles about water hydration.)

EXERCISE

Mens sana in corpore sano is a Latin aphorism, usually translated as "A sound mind in a sound body." Researchers are finding that there's even more to the adage than might first appear. In a four-year study on 200 people, Dr. Malcolm Carruthers found that *most people could ban the blues with a simple, vigorous 10-minute exercise session—three times a week.* He found that just 10 minutes of exercise doubles the level of norepinephrine in the body, a chemical key to happiness. It was also discovered in another study that people became more compassionate after exercising outdoors as opposed to indoors. Being in nature calms us and reduces anxiety. I prefer to hike in the mountains or jog on the beach to working out indoors. For loads of information on how to get the most from your exercise program, or how to start one and stay motivated to continue, please check out my upbeat, informative, full-color book *Invest in Yourself with Exercise.*

NATURE

Here's a simple and inexpensive way to become more compassionate. View a photo or image, such as a poster, of a nature scene. You can put it in your home or office and look at it a few times a day. In one study, it was revealed that those people who spent a few minutes a day viewing images of nature, especially expansive views of nature such as an ocean scene or the mountains, became more compassionate. There are many nature photos on my website for you to view and help you become more relaxed, calm, and compassionate. And I have a variety of nature sounds there, too.

Even better than *viewing* images of nature is *being* outdoors in nature and experiencing it firsthand. In my private practice, I talk about a disease I call **Nature Deficit Disorder** (NDD). When you have the choice, exercise outdoors—take a hike in the mountains, walk in your local park, enjoy a brisk walk on the beach, or ride your bike. Not only does too much time away from nature drain our body's energy and throw off our "physical-mental-emotional balance," it also wrinkles our soul and deprives us of a cost-free "visual valium" experience. The more time we spend outdoors in nature on a regular basis, the healthier and more balanced we become. Our moms were right when they said, "Go outside and play." To this, I will add, **Go outside to play and pray!**

When you invite kindness to be your default position each day, and compassion to be your constant companion, your daily path in life will be brimming over with more light and joy. As my mom and grandmother always used to say to me, "Susan, always remember above all else to live by the Golden Rule." I know my grandmother and mom were guiding me the day that I met Melissa, whose personal story totally uplifted me and reminded me to treat others with loving-kindness.

Melissa's Story: Commit to Excellence

A few years ago, I gave a talk in Los Angeles on "Stressless Living: The Power to Be Your Best," during which I shared the whole-body upliftment choices you're reading about in this book. One of the points I emphasized was the importance of putting inspiration back into your life, because when you feel inspired, you also feel purposeful and empowered. I also addressed the fact that many people are experiencing a crisis of the spirit, feeling disconnected from their authentic selves—the spiritual self within each of us and its connection with God, who is the source of love and, yes, is Love. I believe what we need is a revolution of the spirit, a renewal of the spirit, one that unfolds naturally when you begin taking loving care of yourself, choose a more balance lifestyle, and honor the love of God that is within you.

After my presentation, I went into the ladies' room and found a woman crying. I recognized her. She had been sitting in the front row of the audience and had cried through much of my talk. Since I had no plans for the evening, I asked if she would like to join me for dinner. She was surprised by my unexpected invitation, but she smiled, wiped away a tear, and nodded yes.

Melissa's story was heartbreaking. Her husband recently had left her for a much younger woman. She was almost one hundred pounds overweight, had no job, was living temporarily with her sister, and needed to find a new home for herself and her children. She was so depressed that she was actually considering suicide. One morning, when she was feeling at her lowest, she took a walk and noticed a flyer for my talk in the window of a natural food store. Something inside her told her she had to attend—even though she had never attended a motivational talk before.

Melissa believed in the ideas I discussed but wasn't sure how to implement them in her life. She knew she was falling downhill, but she didn't know how to climb back up. She wanted more than anything to turn her life around—to find a job and a decent place for her children, to lose weight and get back into shape, and to live a balanced life. After listening to her story, I asked her to consider the possibility that the universe was taking everything away from her so that she could and would, for the first time in her life, put *herself* first. Like most women, she was so accustomed to putting everyone else's needs before her own that she took no time for herself. She was learning the hard way that you can't run on empty forever. She was being forced to learn that she had to take loving care of herself first, before she could nurture, love, and take care of others.

I told Melissa that if she were willing to make a real commitment to do whatever it took to live her highest vision, I would be happy to work with her. For the rest of that evening, I asked her to share with me her highest vision and to answer questions like I offer you in Chapter 20, the Workbook: "If you couldn't fail and if you were living your best life—right now—what would that look like?" At the end of the evening, I gave her copies of a few of my books and wrote out a walking and meditation/prayer program that she could start the very next morning.

Over the next month, I designed a nutrition program for Melissa that included cleaning out her refrigerator and cupboards and removing all the processed (and junk) foods that didn't align with her new vision of herself. I taught her how to shop for healthy foods and nutritional supplements, how to make fresh vegetable juices, and how to create meals that emphasized organic, raw, colorful whole foods. I also customized a cardio-weights-stretching routine for her that she could do at home or at a gym. Lastly, I taught her how to visualize her goals and practice deep breathing and meditation.

Melissa's favorite stress release was aerobic dance, but she was always too tired to participate when she got home from the very strenuous part-time job she found. So we found a lunchtime class, offered at a gym in an office building near where she was working, as well as some video programs she could do at home early morning. She took an aerobic dance three to five times a week. As I told Melissa, researchers found that a 60-minute aerobic dance class improved the mood of participants, particularly those who were feeling depressed. And according to the National Institutes of Health, regular exercise (even 20 minutes daily) benefits mental health by reducing stress and increasing confidence. Melissa's entire attitude about work changed for the better when she scheduled in her dance classes during her lunch break or alternately in her living room with the help of an aerobic dance video.

Melissa was an inspiration. Her dedication and commitment created miraculous results. Three weeks after getting her part-time job, she applied for and was hired for a full-time one at a florist shop. Within four months, she had saved enough money to move into a large, new apartment with her very happy children.

Today, Melissa is down to her ideal weight, works out regularly, frequents natural food stores, and manages the florist shop. She now lives with a sense of freedom, control, and power over her life. She learned, firsthand, that breakthroughs and miracles occur when you are willing to live a balanced life—one that minimizes stress and maximizes joy.

A few months after he divorced her, Melissa's ex-husband said he wanted to get back together again. But she knew it wouldn't be for her highest good and said no. Soon afterward, she met a wonderful man who supports her positive vision, and they are engaged to be married. Needless to say, Melissa is feeling empowered, compassionate toward herself and others, and peaceful.

Inner peace is what we feel when our body, mind, heart, and soul are at rest. Instead of striving to control or resist ourselves and others, we feel a sense of profound acceptance, forgiveness, love, and compassion, just as

Melissa did when she made a commitment to create healthy, happy, and peaceful life. Inner peace is synonymous with being in touch with your true nature or soul and knowing that your life is on purpose and that you are following your heart on your path's journey. And above all, inner peace can only ever occur in the present moment (which is all we truly have). One of the most effective ways to cultivate inner peace and compassion is to book-end your day with some quiet and peaceful prayer and meditation, something Melissa took to like fresh avocado slices on organic, homemade whole grain toast (one of my favorites!). (Refer to my book *Wired for High-Level Wellness* to learn more about the health benefits of prayer and meditation and how to get the best results.)

The manner of giving is worth more than the gift.

~ SUSAN WISE BAUER

A hero is no braver than an ordinary man,
but he is brave five minutes longer.

~ RALPH WALDO EMERSON

 *Today's Affirmation*

I am a compassionate presence. I now see the people in my life with new eyes. Beholding the divinity of each one I meet, my heart overflows with empathy as I respond to their troubles and celebrate their triumphs. I am patient. I listen with intention. I recognize their divinity as I recognize my own. I welcome the flow of divine love as it blesses me as well as those with whom I am sharing my compassion.

12-Minute Action Step

Do something special today to take care of yourself in a loving and kind way. Maybe you put a hydrating beauty mask on your face and neck for 12 minutes and then wash it off. Or perhaps you cut some flowers from your garden, or that you picked up at your local nursery or market, and arrange them in a vase to put in your home where you can see them often. Or maybe when you're sitting and watching television, make it a point during the commercials to stand up and get in some exercise movement with stepping in place, reaching to the floor and up to the ceiling a few times, or using some dumbbells to work out your upper body. Do this for you, and while you are doing the activity of your choice, make sure to breathe in deeply and slowly and focus on what you are doing—in the present moment.

Chapter 5

The Path to Forgiveness & Courage

One kind word can warm three winter months.

~ JAPANESE SAYING

When you hold resentment against anyone, you are bound to that person by a cosmic link, a real tough mental chain. You are tied by a cosmic tie to the thing that you hate. The one person, perhaps in the whole world, whom you most dislike, is the very one to whom you are attracting yourself, by a hook that is stronger than steel.

~ EMMET FOX

Forgiveness changes lives. Choosing to forgive unlocks the gate to healing and health, prosperity and abundance, joy and happiness, and inner peace. As we learned in previous chapters, patience can be essential to this process, but with faith, you can always come to a place of new understanding and forgiveness. Jesus said, "Father, forgive them for they know not what they do" (Luke 23:34). He also told His disciples, "Whenever you stand praying, forgive, if you have anything against anyone, so that your Father who also is in heaven may forgive you your trespasses" (Mark 11:24–25). The Master always reinforced the need for forgiveness.

Forgiveness is the central teaching of many of the world's religions. Forgiveness can heal our minds, dispel our pain, and ultimately awaken us from the confines of time and space. It's the vehicle that helps us to release fear and the past. To forgive is to let go. Forgiveness lightens our hearts and reunites them with the Divine. Through forgiveness miracles occur.

In the field of psychoneuroimmunology, there is an indication that lack of forgiveness can contribute to disease. That's right. Medical researchers are also coming to the conclusion that an unforgiving nature may be one of the major culprits in human disease. If we condemn, criticize, or resent, if we feel guilty, shameful, or angry toward another, we are only hurting ourselves.

As so aptly stated by Emmet Fox at the beginning of this chapter, you become linked to another person when you don't offer forgiveness. You also give away your power by creating a charged, emotionally active connection. But *when you forgive, you take back your power and can no longer be controlled by the other person.* Some say that forgiveness is a sign of weakness. I disagree. It takes strength and a generous spirit to understand that people do not always hurt us because they choose to, but more because they couldn't help it. People do harm to others when they are in pain or are out of alignment with their source. If you give back to another person the same pain that person has given you, you are making it impossible for a miracle to occur.

You can transform any negative emotion into love. Though you can't control another person's feelings, you can choose what you want to experience, and how you want to be. Let kindness and tenderheartedness be your goal. Jesus tells us to love our enemies. I understand how difficult this can be, especially when you believe someone has wronged you. Maybe you ask yourself, "How can I forgive what this person has done to me?" The secret is to get out of the way and let the loving presence within you forgive through you. "To err is human, to forgive divine," wrote Alexander Pope. When you choose to live your life more internally, your heart softens and your life changes. Resentments, anger, guilt, and hurt are released. But you can't release these negative emotions yourself. In my prayer time every day, I ask God to show me how to forgive the past, forgive others, and forgive myself.

Forgiveness has to start with the self. Be gentle. When we forgive ourselves, that doesn't mean we condone everything we have done. It means we claim it and own it. We accept that we made some mistakes and now it's time to let go and to move on. Let go. Release all the pain and replace it with God's love. When you forgive yourself, you move more fully back into your heart.

Forgiveness is also an essential ingredient in any healthy, successful relationship. Communication is the key. Be aware of your feelings and allow them to come to the surface for you to own. Share these feelings with your partner. Never go to sleep feeling angry, resentful, or upset. Offer forgiveness, let go, and let love purify your emotions.

What if you can't contact another person or that other person has passed away? It doesn't matter. Forgiveness means a change of heart. It was about twenty years after my dad had passed away that I forgave him for what I believed he had done to me as a child. I also forgave myself for having unloving thoughts about my dad. God showed me the way to do these things. I wrote my dad a letter. I visited his gravesite. And I brought my dad to my mind's eye and talked with him. As a result of practicing forgiveness with my dad, miracles occurred—in my relationships, in my career, and in my health. And from this forgiveness, I experienced a profound peace. There's no doubt in my mind that forgiveness is the greatest act of healing; it transforms lives and creates miracles. Choose to forgive.

Here's an affirmation you can memorize and repeat out loud or silently to yourself when you need the reminder:

Forgiveness is a gift I offer others and myself. It acts as my heart's paintbrush and can color anything bright and luminescent. I let the purifying wash of forgiveness cleanse all of my past mistakes and wrong thinking. I now have an inward sense of peace and tranquility.

It's not an easy journey to get to a place where you forgive people. But it is such a powerful place because it frees you.

~ TYLER PERRY

Never lose an opportunity of seeing anything beautiful, for beauty is God's handwriting.

~ RALPH WALDO EMERSON

 *Today's Affirmation*

I forgive others in my life who I feel have treated me unkindly in some way. I understand they were either having a bad day and have never been taught how to forgive themselves and others. Offering my forgiveness to someone else builds a bridge over which love, kindness, and joy can flow.

 12-Minute Action Step

Offer forgiveness to someone in your life today. You might choose to do it in a note or telephone call or in person. If this person is no longer living, you can still extend forgiveness in the form of a letter. It will release you from the darkness and lift you up into the light of love and peace. Think forgiveness today.

CULTIVATE COURAGE IN EVERYTHING

Life is either a daring adventure—or nothing. To keep our faces toward change and behave like free spirits in the presence of fate is strength undefeatable.

~ HELEN KELLER

Live your life while you have it. Life is a splendid gift.

~ FLORENCE NIGHTINGALE

It takes daring just to live, but it takes courage to live your vision. Is it possible to be in touch with your true courageousness without being in touch with your divinity? I don't think so. We can soar to the top of the mountain and beyond when we know that the courage we want is already part of us; it's our trust in Love. Trust in God's loving presence, which will help you destroy the fear that stifles our efforts.

Fear means looking through our human eyes and mind rather than through the eyes and the heart of God. When we face our fears, and act from the awareness that we are one with Spirit, we learn and nurture courage. Goethe said, "Whatever you can do, or dream you can, begin it. Boldness has genius, power, and magic in it." When we face our fears head on, they begin to evaporate. When we embrace what scares us, we find that we are endowed with a level of courage that we never knew existed.

Every day we have so many opportunities to act courageously. Committing to a 21-day program or 12 minutes a day takes courage. Putting fresh ideas on paper each day takes courage. Getting up each morning to face the day as a willing participant takes courage. Become enthusiastic about your life. Muster the courage to live your life with gusto. It was Thomas Edison who said, "When a man dies, if he can pass enthusiasm along to his children, he has left them an estate of incalculable value." Let courage be the shield that protects you. In the end, most people don't regret the things they do. They regret what they failed to do.

With so much negativity in the media and around the world these days, it takes courage to see the good and the positive. When I was in college at UCLA, I acquired the nickname of "Sunny" because I always had a sunny disposition and, like Pollyanna, chose to look beyond negativity, with the eyes of my heart.

Why do you defend limitations? Why let fear paralyze you? Choose differently. Let Spirit be your guide, with courage at the reins. My mom taught me to be courageous. She would never allow me to defend my limitations.

What is courage to you? To me, courage means moving through uncertainty. Courage means changing when that's the hardest thing in the world to do. Courage means being responsible for what you've created in life and relinquishing blame. It's making difficult choices when, in this fast-paced, overstimulated world, we're overwhelmed with information. Courage is choosing to live simply when everything seems to teach the opposite. Some people think that, if you have courage, you don't have fear. Not at all! Courage is being fearful but doing it anyway, and courage is admitting you don't know all the answers. Courage is trusting again in a relationship, even when you've been hurt or disappointed. Courage is living up to the promises we've made to ourselves and to others. Courage is when we do what we have to do even though we might not want to.

True courage enables us to live in the present and make choices rather than being a victim and settling for what life gives us. Sometimes we just need to make the choice to move in the direction of our dreams. Movement is powerful. The American dancer and choreographer Martha Graham, a premier figure in modern dance who lived to ninety-seven, always advocated movement. She said, "There is a vitality, a life force, an energy, a quickening that is translated through you into action, and because there is only one of you in all time, this expression is unique. And if you block it, it will never exist through any other medium and will be lost." I love that thought.

AN UNFORGETTABLE TRIP TO THE MOUNTAINS

As I write about in more detail in Chapter 9, becoming more childlike will help to foster a courageous joy in your life, and this principle came to life during one of my nature trips. Several years ago, I went alone to the Sierra Nevada Mountains for a few days of quiet and prayer, and just to be out in nature. On this particular summer trip, I had a cabin next to a beautiful placid lake. My last day there, I decided to take an all-day hike in the mountains. I left at around dawn and hiked uphill for most of the morning.

Around two in the afternoon, I decided to sit down, relax, and meditate by a tree. It was unusually quiet that day; I passed only five people on the trails. Sitting cross-legged, with my eyes still open, I could see paradise—several lakes and most of the Sierras. With each breath, I felt more peaceful, relaxed, and connected with the spirit of life. I closed my eyes and began to concentrate on my breath, slowly inhaling and slowly exhaling. It felt wonderful. In a few more moments, I was totally absorbed in my inner world, not at all distracted by my surroundings, except for one minor thing. I thought I could hear some leaves moving.

Often, when I'm meditating outdoors, I'm extra sensitive to nature's sounds. I figured I was in tune with the leaves and their musical dance. After a few more minutes, however, the sound of the leaves rustling got louder. Slightly curious, I opened one eye. What I saw made my heart jump so that I thought it was on the outside of my body. No more than about twenty feet in front of me was a bear.

My first reaction was unbridled fear. The bear just stood there and stared at me. My second reaction was to ask God what to do. The answer was instant and, as I look back on the situation, somewhat off the wall. Or should I say tree? I was told to breathe slowly and deeply—as best I could. I was also told to smile at the bear and to say some kind words from my heart. I gave it my best shot. I told the bear—in a voice three octaves higher than I use for speaking—that he was beautiful, his fur was shiny, and that I didn't intend on being his lunch. By talking to him, I actually began to feel relaxed. As I acted with courage, the fear slowly began to disappear. For about five minutes, I spoke to the bear.

Then something really amazing occurred. I sensed that the bear was talking with me and responding to my comments. He even seemed to smile. Yes, part of me was still scared, but not paralyzed or mentally frozen. I paid attention, felt all my emotions fully, and actually enjoyed the experience. Then the bear started to move in my direction, but I wasn't quite ready to hold out my hand to pet him. Before he got to me, he turned around and shuffled away. As I watched him meander off into the forest, I reflected on my extraordinary experience, one in which I learned that courage is inside of us all just waiting to rear its beautiful head.

We strengthen and develop our courage by using it. Don't let it go to waste. Trust in who you are and be all you were created to be by living a courageous life. That's exactly what Mary June did in her life. With courage and commit-

Trust in who you are and be all you were created to be by living a courageous life.

ment, she broke through her depression and major challenges, became a magnet for miracles, and was such an inspiration to me. I shared this story in one of my previous books, but in case you never read it, it's worth high-lighting again here.

Mary June's Transformation

As the sun was shining over Santa Monica Bay, with its panoply of luscious colors illuminating the sky and the water, I was in-line skating on the bike path, oblivious to people playing on the beach or passing by me. Alone and pensive, caught up in the fluid motion of my body and mind harmoniously in sync, I felt a palpable peacefulness—so often fleeting in today's stress-filled lives—infusing every cell in my body and permeating my thoughts. The melodious syncopation of the waves caressing the sand accompanied each stride.

And then it happened. What felt like a gigantic rock—actually it was only a quarter-sized stone—caught a wheel of my in-line skate and down I went, slamming into the cement. Fortunately, at that moment, no one was there to see my less-than-graceful descent, except for a woman sitting on a bench about ten feet away. She immediately came over to make sure I was okay. Her gentle kindness and amiable countenance immediately comforted me. She helped me to the bench, where I removed my helmet. Seeing the jagged lacerations on the helmet, resulting from my skid on the walk, I was feeling overjoyed and grateful that I had worn protection and that nothing in my body was broken—just a few minor scratches and abrasions on my arms and legs and some major bruises to my ego.

As I got myself under control and determined that I could skate back to my car, I focused my attention on the sympathetic woman by my side and noticed from her swollen, bloodshot eyes that she had been crying. Feeling I could help, I invited her, after exchanging a few niceties, to have lunch with me, and she acquiesced. So I skated to my car, and we met a few minutes later at a nearby restaurant.

We all have difficult and sometimes heartbreaking stories to tell, and Mary June (MJ) was no exception. Over a three-hour lunch I learned, in a nutshell, that MJ's two children had been killed by a drunk driver less than a year before. Soon thereafter she discovered that her husband was having an affair with his assistant, twenty-five years his junior, and he had recently served her with divorce papers, only weeks after they had learned she had breast cancer. Then, a couple of days before we met, she had been let go from her job because of all the time she had been absent from work, owing to the necessity for medical care.

Through all the twists and turns of her recent life, MJ had kept a remarkably optimistic attitude and ability to rise above her challenges and had been able to hold on to a childlike trust and belief that there had to be some Divine order to it all. I learned that only minutes before my fall, sadness had overcome her and she had been crying, grieving the loss of her family and husband, her breast, her job, and everything about the normal life she thought was hers only a year before. It would have been easy to see herself as a victim and sink into despair, and most people she knew would not have blamed her, but MJ believed there was another, better way.

Fortunately, MJ had enough money to live for a few months without needing to work. Her only goal now was to create a healthy, balanced life-style and find ways to nurture her body, mind, and spirit. She told me that she wanted to lose weight and get back into shape, simplify the clutter in her house and beautify her surroundings, learn to meditate, plant a garden, and find some good books to read to nurture her new holistic lifestyle, but she didn't know where to start.

At that moment I discovered why my angels had made me fall practically at her feet. Until then, she was not aware of my work, books, and passion for motivating others to live their highest vision. When she found out about what I did and that I was giving a three-hour workshop that same evening on "Celebrate Life: Rejuvenate Body, Mind, and Spirit with Empowering Disciplines," we both laughed until we cried. What a providential encounter it was, and what a powerful lesson for both of us that we're always in the right place at the right time and are constantly being guided and cared for by a loving Presence. *Only minutes before I crashed into her world, she was asking God for the right direction to take and the best person to guide her in living a more healthy, balanced lifestyle.*

Over the next three months, I was MJ's holistic lifestyle coach. We started by writing out her goals and dreams and creating affirmations to support her highest vision for herself. She immediately implemented a well-rounded exercise regime, which included aerobics, strength training, and flexibility exercises. In her home, we started with the kitchen and cleaned out anything and everything that wasn't for her highest good, nearly emptying the cupboards, pantry, and refrigerator. We went shopping at the local health food store and the supermarket so that she'd have healthy foods in her home from which to choose.

Next, we cleaned out every drawer and closet in her home (my passion for simplifying, organizing, and beautifying our surroundings has resulted in a fulfilling side business I call "Simply Organized"), added cheerful shelf paper here and there, and brightened some walls with new paint. We extended the theme of brightening and adding more color by creating two lovely gardens in the front and back of her home, where nothing but weeds had grown.

As an amateur horticulturist and landscape designer, I relish getting my hands in the soil, planting a variety of greenery, flowers, and trees, and working with the nature angels to create a natural, celestial environment that will attract birds—especially hummingbirds—and butterflies. I even persuaded MJ to add a fountain to her yard and bring a couple more into her home as a way of fostering tranquility and serenity. Finally, I taught her how to meditate, a discipline that she took to like a butterfly to buddleia (a butterfly-loving plant!).

MJ made a conscious choice to surrender her life to God and commit herself to being the best she could be. Within six months, she was down to her ideal weight, having lost thirty-three pounds, and was fitter and healthier than she had ever been in her life. After taking a few classes in interior design, a dream of hers since she was young, she started working part-time as an assistant to a prominent designer in Santa Monica. Because of her courage and assiduity, her healthy diet, a positive and balanced lifestyle that nurtures her body, mind, and spirit, and a support team of doctors and friends, MJ feels confident that neither cancer nor any other degenerative disease will ever be part of her life again. And when she least expected it, as she was working out in the gym, she met a loving, upstanding man who shares many of her interests and has asked her to go with him on a long trip to Europe.

I have no doubt that our meeting was divinely guided for our mutual empowerment. I helped her transform and enhance her life with many of the principle, tips, and suggestions I've detailed in this book; MJ profoundly inspired and motivated me with her integrity, willing spirit, and devotion to making her life better. She realized that "if it's to be, it's up to me" and took responsibility for her own happiness and fulfillment. She has discovered her purpose, followed her heart, and begun living with authentic power and passion. MJ and I both learned firsthand that breakthroughs and miracles occur when we're willing to live our vision and commitment.

Here are a couple uplifting quotes that I've memorized and think about often:

> *Courage is the first of human qualities because it*
> *is the quality which guarantees all others.*
>
> ~ WINSTON CHURCHILL

> *The last of human freedoms—to choose one's attitude in*
> *any given set of circumstances, to choose one's own way.*
>
> ~ VIKTOR FRANKL

Remember, we strengthen and develop our courage by using it. Don't let your courage go to waste. Trust in who you are and be all you were created to be by living a courageous life. Cultivate courage in everything.

Kites rise highest against the wind—not with it.
~ WINSTON CHURCHILL

You have power over your mind—not outside events.
Realize this, and you will find strength.
~ MARCUS AURELIUS

 ## Today's Affirmation

Courage is my middle name and is part of my very nature. I am courageous in all my activities today and trust that the spirit of Love, of God within me will show me what to do and what to say. I have the courage to face anything and everything, including myself. I trust the whisperings of my heart to lead me to my very best life.

 ## 12-Minute Action Step

Is there something you've wanted to do but haven't had the courage to take the first step? Do it today. Whatever it is that you can do in 12 minutes or fewer, such as calling someone, writing page one of your novel, joining a gym or crafts group, seeking therapy or counseling, or simply going to a movie for the first time in your life—alone (at least the decision to do this will take a few seconds), do it. Don't put it off another day. This step of courage you undertake today will springboard you into a more extraordinary, uplifted life. Think courageous thoughts today.

Chapter 6

Buoy Up Your Enthusiasm & Confidence

Nothing great was ever achieved without enthusiasm.

~ RALPH WALDO EMERSON

The more you praise and celebrate your life, the more there is to celebrate.

~ OPRAH WINFREY

*M*any years ago, I made a decision about my work that has had great consequences. I decided that I would do only work about which I could be enthusiastic. Instead of accepting writing assignments simply because the payment was generous, I chose to write articles about which I felt great passion. It was a frightening decision for me, since at that time I lived alone and was dependent on my writing as a major source of income. But I never regretted the decision; not only did I start making more money than ever before with my chosen assignments, but I also learned a valuable lesson about enthusiasm. Enthusiasm isn't something you find out in the world; it's a God-given quality that you must choose to bring to whatever you do.

The word "enthusiasm" comes from the Greek *entheos,* meaning, "to be filled with God." Isn't that fantastic? We must identify with and call forth that which is already within us. Charles Fillmore, cofounder of Unity, was in his nineties when he declared, "I fairly sizzle with zeal and enthusiasm." Regardless of our age, our line of work, or our purpose in life, we can be enthusiastic.

Dale Carnegie gave this advice: "Act enthusiastic, and you'll be enthusiastic!" In his lectures across the country and in his books, he told people not to wait for circumstances to transform their indifference into enthusiasm. "Even if you feel uninspired, act as though you were overflowing with enthusiasm," he advised. He often gave examples of people who had been failures early in life, but who persevered by having an enthusiastic outlook. Albert Einstein, Charles Darwin, and Thomas Edison all did poorly in school. Yet each possessed a great deal of enthusiasm for his work and, eventually, each one's genius became known. *When you take on an attitude—when you become it—it then becomes you.* The action itself is a kind of affirmation.

Several months of the year, I travel internationally (or virtually) giving workshops, seminars, and keynote addresses and doing television, radio, magazine, and newspaper interviews. One question I am frequently asked is: "How do you manage to stay so positive and enthusiastic in the face of so many local and global problems?" And I usually respond, "If I chose to be negative and unenthusiastic, that would just add to the problem. I know I can be most effective if I remain positive, optimistic, and enthusiastic."

The Bible says to be of a happy heart. I've discovered that I am the master of my life, cocreator with the loving presence within me. I can choose to live fully and to make a difference. Health is a choice! Happiness is a choice! Peace is a choice! And enthusiasm is the elixir that generates change, nourishes the body, and feeds the soul. As you age, your skin may become wrinkled, but without enthusiasm, your soul will wrinkle up.

Many years ago, I spent several days in Switzerland where I presented a workshop on "Wellness Lifestyling" at a local hospital in a charming town outside of Zurich and gave the Sunday services at the church. While there, I stayed at a bed-and-breakfast owned and run by a beautiful soul named Sarah. Sarah taught me that enthusiasm, positive thinking, and happiness are the main ingredients in being energetic and staying youthful.

Eighty-five-years young, Sarah greeted each day with enthusiasm and lots of energy. After making mouthwatering, healthy breakfasts for me and the other guests, she would then take me hiking for a good part of the morning, knowing how much I delight in this way to exercise and experience the local vistas. After that, she would spend most of her day working on tidying up her inn, writing her life story down for her family, or working in her organic garden. When I asked Sarah her secret for staying so enthusiastic, she responded, "Never think of your age, always look at the bright side of everything and, if something bothers you, talk it out. Don't ever hold in small grievances with a friend or spouse because they just fester and grow and create much bigger problems." I loved being around Sarah because she brought out my enthusiasm and zest for life.

During my time in Switzerland, I stayed a few extra days after finishing my work. While jogging in a park, I noticed several children playing a game that was new to me. Their parents and nannies were sitting quietly, not talking or paying much attention to the children. The kids were having a fantastic time laughing, running, touching, being silly, and enjoying one another's company and were personifying enthusiasm to the max. It looked like so much fun. After watching for a few minutes, I felt compelled to join them. Through hand signals I asked if I could play, and an hour later I was exhausted.

Although I couldn't speak their language, we laughed a whole lot. There was a special bonding and love, a respect and sharing, that transcended the need for words. Laughter can be so freeing and so uniting at the same time.

The very next day, toward the end of my walk, I saw a boy and girl down on all fours, looking keenly at the ground next to a beautiful flowering tree. I stopped to see what was so captivating. In intermittent English, their mother told me that for nearly thirty minutes the two children had been engrossed in watching some ants as they made their journey from the tree to a scattering of breadcrumbs a few feet away. Then and there I got down on my hands and knees, too, and for several precious minutes, I joined the children in their enthusiastic adventure, becoming totally involved with them and the ants. It was delightful.

Enthusiasm resides in your heart, so you must bring your heart to everything you do.

Enthusiasm resides in your heart, so you must bring your heart to everything you do. Let that heart-light shine with the rays of enthusiasm permeating everything you think, feel, say, and do.

Enthusiasm and confidence are intimately connected. When you trust in something greater than yourself, enthusiasm and confidence become your natural expression. I have always admired Oprah Winfrey. No matter what, she exudes enthusiasm and confidence. She brings her heart to everything she does. And, as a result, she is successful, loved, and supported by millions of people around the world.

My favorite movie of all time is *The Sound of Music.* I've seen it more than twenty times. Playing the role of the governess, Julie Andrews personifies enthusiasm. Filled with God's presence, her character radiates enthusiasm in everything she does—climbing mountains, playing with the children, singing in the abbey, or talking to God. That enthusiasm strengthens her confidence. Do you remember the song she sings called "I Have Confidence"? Its lyrics include: "I have confidence in sunshine. I have confidence in rain. I have confidence that spring will come again; besides which, you see, I have confidence in me."

SETTLE FOR GOODNESS

My mom used to remind me often that "When you settle to find goodness, then goodness finds you." And my grandmother taught me that we live in a friendly universe that is always saying "yes" to us. Our responsibility is to identify and transform those beliefs that have been sabotaging us from accepting and receiving the good that is our birthright. We must learn to trust and love ourselves as much as we are loved by God. When you remove all the blockages to God's presence and align with the love that you are, then abundance, prosperity, peace, enthusiasm, and success will be yours.

Trust God. Believe in yourself. Have faith that nothing is impossible. We are always in the right place at the right time. I trust that unexpected changes in my daily schedule is simply God making necessary adjustments to help my day and life unfold swimmingly and to help miracles flower up in my life. So I choose to believe in unlimited possibility before I can even see the results of what I am visualizing and dreaming about in my mind and heart.

THE RING AND MY DREAM COME TRUE

Here's another story that reminded me to trust, have faith, live with enthusiasm, and believe that "You are always in the right place at the right time."

One day many years ago, I had a cancelation in my work schedule and decided to drive to Westwood near the Brentwood community of Los

Angeles where I live to attend a sing-along of the movie *The Sound of Music*. From time to time, they have this event at the movie theater where everyone in the audience sings the songs out loud. It's really fun, but I always choose to go alone and sit in the back row where I sing my heart out; I even stand up if no one is around me. It's almost like my own personal karaoke, and I have a great, enthusiastic time all by myself.

After the movie was over, I drove back to Brentwood to get something to eat at a local café. Driving back, I kept wishing I could meet Julie Andrews and tell her in person how much this movie, and her appearance as Maria in the movie, made such a positive difference in my life over the decades. In fact, I have often referred to that movie in my talks worldwide because virtually everyone has seen the movie and most people appreciate it as I do. So, in the car, while driving, I was visualizing meeting Julie Andrews and was having a great time with these mental movies. (Yes, I was also simultaneously focusing on the road and traffic!)

I arrived at the café, ordered my salad and tea, and then, with my eyes closed, while waiting for my order to arrive, I continued visualizing an encounter with Julie Andrews. I'm sure the other customers at the café were probably wondering why I was smiling so much with my eyes closed. The meal was delicious, and I was about to leave. Something inside me told me to stay a bit longer to outline the details of an article I needed to start writing for a magazine when I got back to my office. So I pulled out a pad of paper and pen and created the perfect outline for the article, which was about "How Enthusiasm Builds Hope, Faith & Vitality."

After I paid the bill, I went outside, and as I was walking to my car, I passed by a jewelry store with some beautiful selections in the window. One ring in particular caught my eye. It was a stunning sapphire, one of my favorite stones, with yellow diamonds flanking it on each side. I couldn't take my eyes off of it. Similar to when you watch a fire crackling in a fireplace on a cold day, and you just want to stare into the captivating flames, my eyes were locked on the beautiful, resplendent ring, and I was wondering if I should go in and ask to try it on.

Just as I was thinking those sweet thoughts, someone walked out of the jewelry store door while my eyes where still zeroed in on the ring, and I didn't look up. Suddenly, someone said to me, "That is certainly a beautiful ring, and we were watching you from inside the store as you were completely enthralled by it and smiling the entire time." In a split second, my mind thought I was hearing the voice of Julie Andrews, and I thought it was because I had just watched and sang along to the movie. But I looked up to acknowledge this kind person talking to me, who also appreciated the ring, and I almost fell down in front of the store.

As you have probably guessed, it was, indeed, Julie Andrews standing there in front of me—talking to me. It brought tears of joy to my eyes. I told her I was just at the nearby movie theater in Westwood singing along with her in her movie and had been visualizing meeting her in person ever since. Well, this brought tears of happiness to her eyes. Then I told her I was sitting at the café next door and was going to leave about 20 minutes earlier, but I got this intuitive hunch that I should stay longer to outline an article about enthusiasm I needed to start that evening. Julie commented that if I didn't honor my inner guidance, I would have totally missed her because she only made a quick stop at the jewelers to clean a couple rings. We both smiled and laughed and said to each other that this serendipitous experience brightened both of our days. And, as you can probably imagine, to this day, I still smile and am deeply enriched each time I think of our providential encounter.

There are many people who would write off the Julie Andrews experience to coincidence. I don't believe in coincidence. Coincidence (aka "God-wink") is when God decides to do something but prefers to stay anonymous.

With the right attitude, enthusiasm, and confidence are always available. Look at everything you do as service to your Creator, as a way to do Love's work, and to establish a closer relationship with God. When your life has that purpose, you become filled with enthusiasm and confidence. The smallest tasks take on new meaning. Everything you do becomes special. It's almost as though you're growing new eyes and ears. Acknowledging and living in the presence of your inner heart-light brings peace and a whole new dimension to life.

I'd like to end this chapter with a lovely essay by Collin McCarty that I have posted in my office:

24 Things to Always Remember . . .
and One Thing to Never Forget

Your presence is a present to the world.

You're unique and one of a kind.

Your life can be what you want it to be.

Take the days just one at a time.

Count your blessings, not your troubles.

You'll make it through whatever comes along.

Within you are so many answers.

Understand, have courage, be strong.

Don't put limits on yourself.

So many dreams are waiting to be realized.

Decisions are too important to leave to chance.

Reach for your peak, your goal, your prize.

Nothing wastes more energy than worrying.

The longer one carries a problem, the heavier it gets.

Don't take things too seriously.

Live a life of serenity, not a life of regrets.

Remember that a little love goes a long way.

Remember that a lot . . . goes forever.

Remember that friendship is a wise investment.

Life's treasures are people . . . together.

Realize that it's never too late.

Do ordinary things in an extraordinary way.

Have health and hope and happiness.

Take the time to wish upon a star.

And don't ever forget . . .
for even a day . . . how very SPECIAL you are.

With confidence and enthusiasm infiltrating your daily life, you will find that you are feeling more uplifted by the day. To help you in this process, here are some things I encourage you to always remember that will bring you upliftment:

- Find ways to love one another, offering a helping hand, a smile, a hug, a word of encouragement, or maybe just listen.

- Live your life for something bigger than yourself. If you do, your life will become a great adventure and will be extraordinary.

- Remember, we can make all kinds of outer changes, but these will mean little unless we can become more childlike, unclutter our life, and surrender to God and the spirit of life. In surrender, we find everything we are seeking.

Enthusiasm is the mother of effort,
and without it nothing great was ever accomplished.
The successful person has enthusiasm.

~ RALPH WALDO EMERSON

Once we believe in ourselves, we can risk
curiosity, wonder, spontaneous delight, or any
experience that reveals the human spirit.

~ E. E. CUMMINGS

 *Today's Affirmation*

I greet this day with enthusiasm and confidence. It feels like I am walking on air and totally uplifted. With enthusiasm, I can be happy and successful at whatever I choose to do.

 12-Minute Action Step

Today, take a normal, mundane activity and infuse it with loads of enthusiasm. If you're driving to work in bumper-to-bumper traffic, sing aloud songs that resonate in your heart. If you're doing the dishes, pulling weeds in your garden, or changing the baby's diapers, make a conscious choice to bring your enthusiastic heart into each moment of that activity. Be enthusiastic!

Chapter 7

Intuitively Persevere with Determination

Let us be silent that we may hear the whispers of God.

~ RALPH WALDO EMERSON

*The mind's internal heaven shall shed her dews
of inspiration on the humblest day.*

~ WILLIAM WORDSWORTH

*H*ave you ever been thinking of someone you haven't heard from in a long time when suddenly that person called? Did you ever have the feeling that a friend was in trouble, contact him, and find out that he needed your help? Or have you ever met someone and somehow known that this person was going to be your spouse? Some call it a sixth sense, a hunch, a gut feeling, going on instinct, or just knowing deep inside. Psychologists call it intuition—an obscure mental function that provides us with information so that we know without knowing how we know. I refer to it as God's whispering to us and giving us direction.

How tuned in are you to this voice within? I have found from countless experiences that the more we pay attention to our intuition, the more we'll find ourselves in the right place at the right time. Here's a case in point: A few years ago, I was driving around Santa Monica doing some errands. I passed by a quaint little café and, although I wasn't hungry, I felt I should go in and get something to eat.

The café wasn't crowded; only four other tables were occupied. I ordered a salad. Just as it arrived at my table, I noticed the man sitting next to me grabbing his throat. His face was turning red. I knew he was choking. Since

I am trained as an emergency medical technician, I quickly went over and asked if he could talk or breathe. He said no and gestured to me that some food was lodged in his throat. I immediately stood him up and performed the Heimlich maneuver. Out popped the food. While all this was happening, the other patrons of the café just watched in disbelief. They applauded when it was over. I think I received more hugs that day than I usually do in a week. Most important, however, I learned how valuable it is to pay attention to and then act on your intuition. I have no doubt that God was making sure I was in the right place at the right time.

The key here is not just getting the message but listening to it and acting on it. According to one study I perused recently, divorced couples were asked when they first realized the relationship wasn't going to work out, and an astounding 80 percent replied, "Before the wedding." Although something told them that the marriage was foolhardy, each couple stood together at the altar, either because they wished too strongly that their intuition was wrong or they didn't identify the messages as a kind of knowing they could trust.

I consider myself very intuitive because I have worked for years on developing that faculty. There are a few people in my life who afford me the opportunity to see my intuitive side in action. My dear friend Ginny Swabek, who lives in another state, is always picking up on my energy. We might not have talked for several days when I'll sit down to write her an e-mail. Before the note is complete, she'll call to say hello. Or I'll get an inner signal to call her just when she's thinking of something she needs to ask me. It was the same way with my mother, who was my best friend. We were always picking up on each other's thoughts and feelings, even though we were thousands of miles apart when I was away on media tours. I'd get a signal that Mom was nonplussed about something, and I was supposed to call her. When I did, I'd usually find out she was hoping I'd call.

It can be quite enjoyable to let your intuition be your guide. People often change their lives not based on what they know but based on what they feel. When we listen to that inner voice, we are never wrong. The key is really tuning in and paying close attention.

So how can we develop the intuitive side of our being? The best way is just to sit still and listen. Too often we run away from ourselves, filling up our lives with constant activity. Turn within. Creative geniuses often report that their "real world" discoveries are made from connecting to a deep silence within. When someone asked William Blake where he got his ideas, he replied that he stuck his finger through the floor of Heaven and pulled them down. And Michelangelo turned away the congratulations someone proffered him for turning a block of stone into a man, saying the man was in there all the time and just required a little help in getting out. Franz Kafka wrote:

"There is no need to leave the house. Stay at your desk and listen. Don't even listen, just wait. Don't even wait, be perfectly still and alone. The world will unmask itself to you; it can't do otherwise. It will rise before you in raptures."

Intuition can be nurtured in a variety of ways—through prayer, contemplation, walks in nature, or time spent alone gazing out a window and thinking. Part of receiving these inner messages clearly comes when you learn to give up the analyzing, reasoning, doubting, and limiting part of your mind. And the more you act on your intuitive hunches, the stronger and more readily available they become. As you become more sensitive to your oneness with God, you will become more intuitive.

Tuning in to yourself is the basis for becoming all that you were created to be—your best self. As Dag Hammarskjöld, former secretary-general of the United Nations, once observed, "What you have to attempt [is] to be yourself, to become a mirror in which, according to the degree of purity of heart you have attained, the greatness of life will be reflected."

GOD SENT A JEEP, BOAT & HELICOPTER

This is a story that's been around for a while, and it often uses a variety of vehicles. With enthusiasm and confidence, you can more readily distinguish your intuition inside you from less reliable chatter—your ego, your history, your doubt, or your fear. How will you know your intuitive whisperings? You'd probably like a signal that alerts you and says, "Okay, this is the real thing; listen up!"

As the story goes, the dam above a man's town has broken, and a flood is imminent. A jeep comes by his house, and the driver says, "Get in. I'll drive you to higher ground."

The man refuses, saying, "No, God will save me."

When the river rises, forcing the man into the second floor of his house, he looks out the window and sees a boat gliding toward him. But when the oarsman calls out, "Get in, and I'll tow you to higher ground," the man again replies, "No, no, God will save me."

As the water rises, he climbs to the roof, and a helicopter hovers overhead and drops a line. The pilot yells, "Grab hold, and I'll put you aboard."

The man still says, "No, no, God will save me."

Finally, the man drowns. When he arrives in heaven, he asks God in bewilderment, "Lord, why didn't you save me?"

"I tried," answers God. "I sent you a jeep, a boat, and a helicopter, but you turned them all down!"

Just because we have reached a point of crisis during which our inner voice can no longer be silenced does not mean we will necessarily act on its guidance. Old ways die hard. How many times, when questioning which way to go, have we heard the voice say, "Go this way!" but we choose to head in another direction? We ignore our inner voice and later say, "I knew I should have listened. I just knew it!" I could feel my inner voice talking to me and encouraging me the day I met Gloria, whose experience uplifted both of us.

Reach Out and Touch Someone

Many years ago, a friend and I went to see a play in Los Angeles. When it was over, we decided to get something to eat at a café down the street. It was late, and few people were in the restaurant. After a while I noticed a ragged woman, probably in her mid-fifties, who obviously didn't feel good about herself. The waitress told us that she came in every Saturday evening at the same time. While I was talking with my friend, I couldn't help but notice the woman's appearance. Her clothes were dirty, her hair was matted and greasy, and she carried a backpack as her purse. I could sense her sadness and loneliness and was keenly aware of my desire to reach out to her, but I didn't really know what to do.

My friend had to leave, but I decided to stay. I went over to the woman's table, touched her hand, and asked her to keep me company while I finished my meal. At that point, she started to cry, and I thought to myself, *Susan, you certainly misread your inner signals this time.* As I sat down to try to mend the situation, the woman, Gloria, told me I was the first person to approach her with genuine warmth and caring in months! We talked for an hour, and then she invited me to her apartment a couple of blocks away. In her cramped, disheveled one-room apartment, I listened through the night to her life story.

I found out that Gloria hadn't worked for months and that she had no family and rarely had visitors. As she spoke of her love for children, I remembered a telephone call I had received two weeks before. A friend who owns a day-care center had called, asking me if I could recommend someone for an opening as a teacher's aide. I will never forget the sparkle in Gloria's eyes when I told her the details of this possible job.

It was now eight o'clock in the morning. I suggested she take a shower, and then we could return to the café for breakfast. I also called the day-care center owner. The position was still open, and I arranged for Gloria to have an interview later that day. In the meantime, I helped Gloria curl her hair, showed her how to apply some makeup, and helped her pick out a clean dress to wear for the interview. It was wonderful to see her transform before my eyes. Gloria got the job and began work the next week.

After several weeks, I paid a surprise visit to Gloria at the center. I could hardly believe my eyes. She looked ten years younger and was aglow with enthusiasm. The children all loved her, and so did the center's owner. She invited me to her apartment for dinner that evening. I didn't recognize her home, either. She had cleaned and painted every inch and even had a couple of plants on her dresser. I was so touched. Gloria was radiantly alive and happy, as she was meant to be.

Life is not a spectator sport. Participate in the adventure of living.

From this experience, I truly learned the value of reaching out to someone, even though we have no guarantee of the outcome. I believe we have to try to live that way—person to person, heart to heart. Life is not a spectator sport. Participate in the adventure of living. You cannot induce positive change in someone by doing for them what they can and should do for themselves, but you can be a catalyst for change. With love in your heart and a willingness to risk and be vulnerable, you'll do all right.

Calmly, clearly, and without judgment, our inner voice is always ready to help us move toward our highest good anytime we choose to listen. We find ourselves navigated to our dream. As we increasingly listen to and follow our inner guidance, we gradually develop a deeper relationship with

Our intuitive nature is always working through us 24/7.

God. The voice gets clearer and louder because we pay attention, because we become attuned to its vibration. We don't have to wait for a crisis. We can communicate with our still, small voice every day, if we desire. Our intuitive nature is always working through us 24/7. We start finding the jeeps, boats, and helicopters in our lives the moment we choose to listen to our intuition.

Carve out quiet time every day to sit in silence and to turn your thoughts to the divinity that lies within you, waiting to guide you every step of the way.

I would like to end this section of the chapter with one of my favorite passages from Helen Keller. "The most beautiful things in the world cannot be seen or even touched. They must be felt with the heart."

The one essential thing is that we strive to have light in ourselves.

~ ALBERT SCHWEITZER

The intuitive mind is a sacred gift and the rational mind is a faithful servant. We have created a society that honors the servant and has forgotten the gift.

~ ALBERT EINSTEIN

 *Today's Affirmation* ─────────────────

I am a clear and open channel for the power of love to flow through me. In quietness and confidence, I wait for my guidance. I listen to my intuition and act on what I hear.

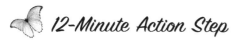 *12-Minute Action Step*

Take 12 minutes today to pay attention to your inner guidance system—your intuition. Sit quietly with your eyes closed and breathe deeply. See if you get a hunch about something, and, if you do, make sure act on it. The more you act on your hunches, the more intuitive whisperings you will get. Be quiet enough to listen to and honor your inner whisperings. Think intuitively today.

PERSEVERANCE & DETERMINATION

Our greatest weakness lies in giving up. The most certain
way to succeed is always to try just one more time.

~ THOMAS EDISON

The road to success is dotted with
many tempting parking spaces.

~ WILL ROGERS

One of the many life lessons given to me by my loving grandfather, Benny, was this: "The solution to a challenge always appears when your determination and faith don't disappear." He also reminded me often to focus on the present moment and told me, "If you spend too much time thinking about the past or the future, the present will slip through your fingers." Benny taught me that the present moment is a gift to each of us; in other words, he would say, "Each day you are given a present from God when you wake up in the morning, and this present is the present moment all day long." As I look back and remember his pearls of wisdom, I am so thankful; his guidance in my life has always meant the world to me.

Sometimes the answer to a challenge or the guidance we seek seems just beyond our reach. This is the time to "keep on keeping on." You can win the race no matter how far behind you are when you start. Perseverance and determination will see you through. Keep your goal clearly in sight, and don't get side-tracked. Here's another great quote by Thomas Edison: "The reason a lot of people do not recognize opportunity is because it usually goes around wearing overalls looking like hard work." So true!

Life can be complicated. It's easy to lose sight of our purpose in the midst of our daily lives. We often become wrapped up in the demands of our schedules, paying the bills, rearing children, or getting ahead at work. We live our lives from a rabbit's-eye view—our noses pressed up against the blade of grass right in front of us. Just as grasping the beauty of an entire tapestry is difficult if we view it too closely, we can, similarly, lose clarity. We must learn to take an eagle's-eye view. Soaring far above the ground, the eagle can see farther and with greater clarity than the earthbound rabbit. And as the eagle uses the wind to keep it aloft, you can choose to use determination and perseverance to keep yourself on course.

Through the decades of life experiences, and the joy of working with clients worldwide and learning so much from their life experiences, it's become crystal clear to me that we need to always follow our heart. Our intuition is always guiding us to walk in the direction of our dreams with courage, enthusiasm, perseverance, and determination. My mom used to tell me to "let your feet bring you to where your heart is." She also reminded me often, and I can still hear her voice in my heart and head telling me these sage words: *"You can wait for things to happen, or you can make things happen yourself,"* which is what she always encouraged me to do—to persevere and take action.

When I am faced with a challenge and am not sure what to do to move onward and upward—and I feel stuck in a spin-cycle of discouragement or lack of confidence, I will ask the right question, which usually brings me the solution I seek. Instead of asking, "Why is this happening *to* me?" I change out the preposition and instead ask, "Why is this happening *for* me?" It's been my experience, and that of countless people to whom I teach this lesson, that if we ask the right questions, we will get the answers we are seeking.

Don't be tempted to give up. Never give up. You are never given a dream from God without the ability to make that dream come true. Be enthusiastic about your dream, be determined to follow your heart and inner guidance, and when the going gets tough, have the courage to persevere and not be tempted to give up and take the easy road. It was Oscar Wilde who told us, "I can resist everything except temptation."

Recently, I read the book *Women Saints East and West* and was fascinated by Saint Teresa of Ávila, also known as Saint Teresa of Jesus. She grew up in the sixteenth-century Spanish town of Ávila and was intelligent, beautiful, sagacious, and charming. While she was still a teen, she began to realize that the things of the world did not have nearly so much appeal for her as the things of the spirit. She prayed for greater awareness, clarity, and strength to follow her heart. What was it that made her listen to her heart and follow that guidance? Determination. It's one of the qualities she emphasizes. "Those who have this determination," she reveals, "have nothing to fear."

How determined are you to live joyfully, healthfully, and peacefully? How determined are you to keep on going when the going gets tough? When I began writing nearly fifty years ago, I received more than a hundred rejection letters from magazines. There were times I felt like giving up. Even my close friends and some family members encouraged me to seek another profession. "You can't pay your bills on dreams," they would tell me. "Look for a job that offers security, a regular monthly paycheck, and normal hours," was something I heard regularly. Well, I'm glad to say I didn't listen to them. I was determined to be true to my vision and dreams. Now many years later, I've written more than 33 books and over 2,500 magazine articles. Editors now approach me to write articles for their magazines. Determination and perseverance always pay off.

I love the following words that appear in Richard Bach's insightful book *Illusions*: "You are never given a wish without also being given the power to make it true. You may have to work for it, however."

Are you willing to do what it takes to become master of your life? How much do you really want to reach the top of the mountain? Do you have the sheer will to give it your all, and then some, even when the odds of attaining your goal appear to be insurmountable?

I have great respect for world-class athletes who, against all odds, become winners. And I'll never forget the story about the cyclist Greg LeMond. In 1985, he finished second in the arduous Tour de France, a twenty-three-day 2,025-mile cycling race through France. Then in 1986, at the age of twenty-five, LeMond became the first non-European ever to win the race. With his prime competitive years still ahead of him, he was on top of the world.

Within a few months, however, his life turned upside down. In April 1987, LeMond was with his uncle and his brother-in-law on a hunting trip when he was hit by a shotgun blast. His brother-in-law had accidentally shot him. LeMond took approximately sixty No. 2 pellets in his back and side. He could barely breathe; his right lung had collapsed. His liver and kidney were hit. So were his diaphragm and intestines. And two pellets were lodged in the lining of his heart. LeMond thought he was going to die as he lay in the field waiting for the helicopter that would take him to the hospital. His main concern was whether he would ever see his wife and kids again.

While in the hospital, LeMond learned about real pain. A tube to draw blood out of his collapsed lung had to be inserted into his chest without anesthesia, and it remained there for a week. He had thought he was used to pain because he had pushed himself so hard in competition. But the pain he felt while racing his bike was nothing compared with the pain he felt as he fought for his life.

Miraculously, none of the damage was irreparable. Doctors left thirty shotgun pellets in LeMond, including the two in the lining of his heart. They doubted that LeMond would ever race again. Eight weeks later, however, with sheer determination and perseverance, he started the long road back. Before the accident, LeMond weighed 151 pounds, with a total body fat content of 4 percent. When he was able to start training again, he weighted 137 pounds, with 17 percent body fat. In an effort to survive, his body had consumed vast amounts of its muscle.

He had a rough two years coming back. Months after the accident, just when he was beginning to show signs of real progress, he had an emergency appendectomy. The following year, he had to have surgery to repair an infected tendon in his right shin, forcing him to miss the Tour de France for a second straight year. PDM, the Dutch team, with which LeMond had signed a two-year deal in 1987, wanted to cut his 1989 salary by $200,000. The team had lost all confidence in him. But he had not lost confidence in himself. LeMond entered the 1989 Tour de France, along with 155 other riders, and came out the winner. Determination makes all things possible.

Are you willing to do what it takes to become master of your life? Do you have the sheer will to give it your all, and then some, even when the odds of attaining your goal appear to be insurmountable? As a cocreator with God, you have the power and ability to achieve your heart's desire. Let your perseverance and determination fuel your mind and body into action. Know that the loving presence within you is your strength and power.

When you feel that connection, peace will be your constant companion and success will be yours.

People seldom see the halting and painful steps by which the most insignificant success is achieved.

~ ANNE SULLIVAN

Nothing is impossible, the word itself says "I'm possible!"

~ AUDREY HEPBURN

 ## Today's Affirmation

I keep my sights focused on my goal and refuse to be discouraged. Divine love, flowing through me, gives me the strength and determination to follow my heart and achieve my heart's desires. I persevere, for I know my success is assured. Anything is possible if I trust and believe.

 ## 12-Minute Action Step

During your exercise session today, just when you think you can't push any harder, do it for 90 to 120 seconds. Or if you have no plans to exercise, do something active for at least 12 minutes. Even if you're in your office, you can step in place for 12 minutes. Running errands? Park at the far corner of the parking lot. Take the stairs instead of the elevator or the escalator and climb—don't stand still on this moving ramp. Think about taking action and doing your best today in just a few minutes. Go the extra mile (pun intended!).

Chapter 8

Choose to Be
Self-Discipline

*To act magnanimously, to maintain high standards, to be
honorable, requires commitment to yourself. Make it.*

~ ALEXANDRA STODDARD

*Character isn't inherited. One builds it daily by the way one
thinks and acts, thought by thought, action by action.*

~ HELEN GAHAGAN DOUGLAS

*D*iscipline is a choice. If we are to live our highest potential, the way we
were all created to be, we must practice self-discipline in every aspect
of our lives. It's the only way to live on higher ground. The mountain of
soul-achievement and fulfillment cannot be scaled by anyone who lacks
control of body, mind, and emotions.

*Discipline of the mind
leads to discipline of
the body. And from a
disciplined body comes
an exhilarated mind.*

Discipline, to me, means the ability to carry
out a resolution long after the mood and enthusiasm has left you. It also means doing what you
say you're going to do.

Discipline brings freedom and peace to
your life. A disciplined person is not at the
whim or mercy of external circumstances,
but is in control of what he or she thinks, feels, says, and does. An undis-
ciplined person is lazy, undirected, and usually unhappy. Discipline of the
mind leads to discipline of the body. And from a disciplined body comes an
exhilarated mind.

We cannot discipline ourselves with the larger things of life unless and until we understand that discipline must be achieved with the smaller things. It's been my experience that through discipline in small things, greater tasks that once seemed difficult become easier. For example, it takes discipline to sit at my desk each day to write this book. As the days go by, however, the writing becomes more enjoyable, and I see my vision of a book come into fruition. Similarly, it takes discipline to eat healthy foods all the time and to exercise regularly. But if I take on this adventure of healthy living daily, I will reach the tenth, twenty-first, or thirtieth day more easily.

We can't address the topic of discipline without also venturing into the power of conditioning. The way we have been conditioned to behave affects all areas of our lives.

How often do you eat compulsively rather than from true hunger? Think of your eating behavior at social gatherings, at the movies, or when you're watching television or attending sports events. Discipline yourself to eat slowly and only when you're truly hungry.

When I've been out skiing, I sometimes notice a small ball of snow that begins to roll down from the top of the mountain. At that point, the snow is easy to stop. But if it continues to roll, it may grow steadily bigger until an immense mass weighing tons descends. At that size, it is impossible to stop. Our desires work the same way. They gain in power and strength through repetition. Repetition is the key to mastery, or to failure. When a negative desire first surfaces, we must nip it in the bud; we must eradicate it quickly and firmly. When you have a desire to eat junk food, don't give in. Exercise discipline. Choose something healthy to eat or abstain from all food.

. . . what you eat today, you crave tomorrow. Choose wisely!

Whether for food or something else, the difficulty in resisting sensory desire comes from the force of conditioning. Every time we are negatively conditioned, we lose a little of our freedom to choose. For example, if you eat unhealthy donuts or French fries, you strengthen your desire to eat them tomorrow. In other words, *what you eat today, you crave tomorrow.* Choose wisely!

In other words, when you repeat negative behavior, it develops into a bad habit. To eradicate your negative conditioning, make a 21-day agreement with yourself. It takes 21 days to form a new habit or break an old one. Let's say that you want to stop eating before you feel stuffed at mealtimes. Make an agreement with yourself to do that. Resolve to stick with your agreement every day for 21 days. If you skip a day, you must begin the cycle again. By the twenty-first day, your mind and body will stop resisting the change you're trying to make. Three weeks isn't a long time. If you find your mind coming up with excuses, as it will, you can maintain discipline by reminding yourself that you only have to continue for 21 days.

I have been incorporating this tip into my life for forty years. On the first of each month, I make an agreement with myself to give up some unhealthful habit or to reinforce a positive pattern. In this way, I make twelve beneficial changes in my life each year.

Honoring your agreements with yourself boosts your self-esteem. I know how I feel when I say I'm going to do something but don't follow through. I feel lousy. But when I stay disciplined and do what I say I'm going to do, I feel empowered. I have great respect for people who keep their word. And I lose respect for those who don't.

One of my favorite heroes and friends was John Wooden, basketball coach for UCLA. For twenty-seven years, he molded champions on and off the court. His leadership generated excitement all over campus and touched the lives of millions around the country. His unparalleled string of victories and National Collegiate Athletic Association championships remain the benchmark for basketball teams everywhere. One of the main ingredients in what Wooden called the "pyramid of success" is practicing discipline in every aspect of life and keeping one's word with oneself.

One way to begin to master this art of discipline and to see immediate results is to schedule time every morning to meditate. Even if you are not yet a committed disciple on the spiritual path, meditate for the practical health benefits. I have discovered that by being disciplined with my meditation, I have more discipline in other areas of my life. What's more, being disciplined brings me more peace. And it's from a more peaceful mind and heart that I am consequently able to welcome more discipline in other aspects of my life.

It also takes discipline to exercise every day or commit to your wellness program. And you may be wondering, "Where should I start in my life to become more disciplined and follow through on what I say I am going to do?" Maybe a place for you to start is with prayer-walking or prayer-hiking.

FOSTER SELF-DISCIPLINE WITH PRAYER-WALKING AND PRAYER-HIKING

I've been doing prayer-walks and prayer-hikes for over three decades. I find that these silent walks enrich my body, mind, and spirit. In other words, they keep me immensely uplifted. For those of you who are into multitasking and making good use of your oh-so-limited time, this concept of combining walking and prayer should be most appealing. I wrote about it briefly in my book *Invest in Yourself with Exercise*, but here are the juicy details on exactly how to do it and why it's so beneficial for our mental health and to bolster our mood.

Most of us are busy talking all day long. Just 20 minutes of walking in silent contemplation can slow down the mind, relax the body, and feed the soul. Besides, it's a practical and efficient way to preclude overloading the daily schedule!

When I teach this kind of walking, I tell beginners to start with 20 minutes at least three times a week. Make sure to walk fast enough to elevate your heart rate so that you will get a workout. Of course, if you're not a beginner, you can walk longer for more benefits. On days when, for whatever reason, you don't feel like walking fast, it's all right to go at a more leisurely pace.

Best Locations to Do Prayer-Walking or Prayer-Hiking

When I do prayer-walking, I select places in nature, whether in the mountains, by the ocean, in the desert, or at a botanical garden or local park. I try to find areas with the least noise and the fewest people, especially places where I won't run into anyone I know. It can be very disconcerting, when you've been prayer-walking for 20 or 30 minutes and are deeply into your inner reflection, to hear someone call your name and come over for a chat. If that happens, politely say that you're doing a special silent workout today and will be happy to give them a call later on. That usually works. If not, enjoy the encounter and then pick up where you left off, or try again another day.

What I've learned about prayer-walking is even truer of prayer-hiking. Prayer-hiking is the ultimate experience for me because I'm enveloped in the musical sounds of nature, the majesty of the trees, the fresh air, the fragrance of the surroundings and the subtle whisperings of the angelic forces all around. When I make my hike a prayer-hike, I choose paths I know well so that my mind won't deviate from its inner focus to figure out which way to go. Since I've hiked the Santa Monica Mountains for over four decades, and now many trails throughout Great Britain for years, I know the idiosyncrasies and nuances of all the different trails very well.

You can conduct a prayer-hike with a friend or two, knowing that you'll choose silence during the hike and catch up on things when the hike is over. If you can't resist conversation when a friend is around, however, you might choose to prayer-hike alone to garner the most benefits for body, mind, and spirit.

Turn on any news program or read any newspaper and you'll doubtless find information abounding on crime, terrorism, violence, viruses, war, and every kind of abuse. The information alone is enough to create within us fear, frustration, confusion, and disharmony. The most effective way I know to restore balance and foster serenity is to appreciate beauty. Of course, you can visit a museum, listen to a symphony, watch an awe-inspiring sunrise or sunset, or arrange some freshly cut flowers in your home, but I think simply being out in nature is the best.

The natural environment is the most fundamental form of beauty, and it's absolutely free. When you are "out of sorts" and need to be reconnected with your own true beauty and best self, nature will gently steer you in the right direction. Our hearts and minds resonate with the amazing colors and sounds of nature, and our cells actually begin to vibrate at a higher frequency that affords a deeper spiritual connection and a feeling of belonging.

Prayer-Walking and Prayer-Hiking for Life-Enriching Mental and Spiritual Discipline

By silently communing with what is around us, we can learn many things, and this is especially true when it comes to prayer-walking and prayer-hiking. Sometimes, instead of repeating an affirmation or mantra, I will simply stay in the present during the hike, breathe deeply and focus on and appreciate the beauty all around me. This is much harder to do than you might think. When I first started doing it, my mind seemed to wander every few seconds, like an untrained puppy, to every subject but the task at hand: appreciating the beauty of my surroundings.

It took about a year, prayer-hiking four to six times monthly, for me to be able to do an entire one- or two-hour hike absorbed in nothing but the present and the beauty around me. Like anything worth learning, prayer-hiking or prayer-walking takes disciplined practice, but the effort has made a positive, profound difference in all areas of my life. The physical and mental discipline brings spiritual discipline, and when all three are in harmony, all directed by the same desire and intention, I feel faith-filled, empowered, and invincible.

And, most important to me, I feel divinely guided and loved by God and connected to everything good and loving. And so will you! When can you plan your prayer-walk or prayer-hike?

Now is the time to become a disciplined person. Enrich every aspect of your life with self-discipline. You will discover, as I have, that discipline is the road to freedom, mastery, and peace. Choose to be self-disciplined today.

It is neither wealth nor splendor, but tranquility
and occupation which give happiness.

~ THOMAS JEFFERSON

Good habits are your best helpers; preserve their force by
stimulating them with good actions. Bad habits are your worst
enemies, against your will they make you do the things that
hurt you most. They are detrimental to your physical, social,
mental, moral, and spiritual happiness. Stave bad habits
by refusing to give them any further food of bad actions.

~ PARAMAHANSA YOGANANDA

 *Today's Affirmation*

I make self-discipline a way of life for myself. My mind is disciplined, which means my body is disciplined. Thank you, spirit of life within me, for letting your discipline shine through in everything I think, feel, say, and do.

 12-Minute Action Step

Whatever you say you are going to do today, do it. Keep your word with yourself and others. Also, make a special agreement with yourself to get something done about which you have been procrastinating. Maybe you clean out the junk drawer in the kitchen, or your makeup shelf, or one dresser drawer. You can get these done under 12 minutes if you focus. No excuses today. Get it done. As the famous slogan goes (and my favorite advertising slogan ever created), "Just Do It." Think self-discipline today.

Chapter 9

Lighten Up, Be Childlike & Live Faithfully

Cannot we let people be themselves,
and enjoy life in their own way?

~ RALPH WALDO EMERSON

The most wasted day of all is that on which we have not laughed.

~ SÉBASTIEN NICOLAS DE CHAMFORT

When we are anchored in God, no matter what comes our way, we can remain positive and look for the good in everything. Easier said than done, right? Attitude makes all the difference. A positive attitude doesn't just happen by itself; we must cultivate it. William James, the noted philosopher, put it beautifully when he said that the greatest discovery of our generation is that a human being can alter his life by altering his attitude.

Indeed, situations will arise in our lives that may seem difficult, but a positive attitude regards problems as opportunities for growth. I believe that nothing happens that does not afford us the chance to deepen our understanding of and appreciation for life.

A negative attitude functions like an insulator that inhibits the flow of creative energy. Criticism, gossip, anger, fear, envy, suspicion, jealousy, worry, hate, doubt, laziness, anxiety, guilt, and shame are all forms of negative thinking. Watch your thoughts. Make them obey you. Train your mind to think constructively at all times. A joyful, thankful attitude will carry you a long way toward the goal of bringing into your life the health, happiness, and peace that you deserve.

It's been my experience that if you laugh and smile more, your attitude will tilt toward the positive. And if, by chance, you feel you don't have any reason to smile, let me give you four: it firms your facial muscles, it makes you feel better, it makes people wonder what you've been up to, and it creates the quickest bond between two people. And here's a fifth reason from Mother Teresa: "A smile is the beginning of peace."

Humor and laughter have both been found to be important components of healing. William Fry of Stanford University has reported that laughter aids digestion, stimulates the heart, strengthens muscles, activates the brain's creative function, and keeps you alert. So make up your mind to laugh and to be happy. As Abraham Lincoln said, "Most folks are about as happy as they make up their minds to be."

Laughter also helps you to keep things in better perspective. When you laugh at yourself, you take yourself far less seriously. "Angels fly because they take themselves lightly," says an old Scottish proverb. Isn't that wonderful?

So with the right attitude, with joy in your heart, with a smile on your face, and a guard at the door of your mind, you can experience life as a great adventure, a celebration of spirit manifested everywhere. You'll come to realize that life is meant to be lived with a childlike sense of wonder and expectancy. It's not too late to experience life fully. As long as you're breathing, it's never too late.

With your new positive attitude, you will come to understand that it is not the times, complications of society, or other people that cause problems. It is only your inability to cope. Whatever is going on with you at the moment, choose to make it okay. Give up the fear of making mistakes and the need for approval from others. I see so many people living according to how others expect them to be. Live more from inner guidance. Understand that there is no absolute way to happiness. Rather, acting with happiness is the way.

BEING CHILDLIKE

So many of us are searching for the "fountain of youth"—the secret that will enable us to live long and healthy lives. We have tried special diets, supplements, and exercise. Yet the secret to living a quality life, full of vitality and celebration, comes from within—from our attitudes, our expressions, and how we view ourselves and the world around us.

Young children are my greatest teachers. They laugh, tell jokes, play, sing, dance, move, and live in their own magical world. They express pure joy. There are no masks when they relate to each other. When children meet for the first time, they often relate as if they were lifetime buddies.

Compare this to your response when meeting someone new. Are you trusting, comfortable, and enthusiastic? Or perhaps suspicious, reserved, and unwilling to be vulnerable? Our individual attitudes and feelings about ourselves are reflected in our actions toward others. Every day we have an opportunity to spread joy in this world by how we relate to other people. It could be something as simple as being a good listener or offering a warm hug. The other person receives your joy and will then pass it along to others. It's so simple and yet so profound. What you give always comes back multiplied.

Every day we have an opportunity to spread joy in this world by how we relate to other people.

From my point of view, natural childlike qualities are the true essence of life. They are the magic we should seek to recapture. To be childlike is to be innocent of all the strange, authoritarian ideas of what adulthood ought to be. Children are trusting and straightforward, honest and natural, free from the need to impress others. Being childlike means being more concerned with the experiences of life than with how others view you. You do not have to give up being an adult to become more childlike. You do not have to become infantile or irresponsible or unaccountable. The fully integrated person is capable of harmoniously blending the adult and the child.

Think about the adults you most like to be with. I'll bet they are genuinely happy, joyful people. From joyfulness flows laughter, a sense of humanness, and silliness. You don't always have to be orderly, rigid, serious, and adult-like. Learn to have fun and to be a little silly and crazy. In other words, lighten up. When you do this, the whole world will seem brighter and more beautiful.

Within each of us is a child waiting to come forth and express himself or herself more fully. What usually keeps us from getting in touch with the child within is our unwillingness to recognize and accept this child. We often feel that we have to act our age. Recover the vibrancy and spontaneity that may be missing in your life. Remember to laugh, simplify your life, slow down, take time to smell the flowers, talk to the animals, and watch the clouds.

In my life, I have noticed that when my judgmental self rears its ugly head, I tend to be more controlling instead of letting go and flowing with life. When I release my desire to be in control and to live more from inner guidance, I notice that struggle dissipates and I feel more peaceful.

The more I pay attention to how children experience and embrace life, and the more I release my fears about feeling uncertain, the better life becomes because the more gentle, tenderhearted parts of me come forward. As that happens, the oppositions within my life soften. My work becomes play; my challenges become wonderful opportunities to learn and to grow. My life takes on clarity and purpose as I move closer to becoming a master at the art of living.

According to James Michener:

"The master of the art of living draws no distinction between his work and his play, his labor and his leisure, his mind and his body, his education and his recreation, his love and his religion. He hardly knows which is which. He simply pursues his vision of excellence through whatever he is doing and leaves it to others to decide whether he is working or playing. To himself, he is always doing both."

Each day, make a point of doing something out of the ordinary that brings joy to others and to you. The results may surprise you. For example, I love teddy bears. Often when I take long trips in my car, my bears accompany me. I also take one when I fly. My bears help me keep my inner child alive and happy.

Children accept your good points and your not-so-good points. They don't care about differences, about different races, religions, or backgrounds. In a world in which so much conflict exists, the best bridge to understanding, peace, and joy is built through love and forgiveness. When we reach out to another and offer unconditional love and forgiveness, as children do, joy and peace are the result.

Living well means putting a big emphasis on having some fun.

~ ALEXANDRA STODDARD

Bless the good-natured, for they bless everybody else.

~ THOMAS CARLYLE

 ## Today's Affirmation

I let my inner child out today to help me orchestrate my day. I look for ways to have more fun, to frolic, and to be a little silly. Even though I am an adult, I can still act with a lightness in my heart and a bounce in my step. I am walking on air and let everyone with whom I come in contact today see my smile and feel my inner joy.

 ## 12-Minute Action Step

At some point, do something today that brings out your inner child and helps you to cultivate a sense of humor. For example, if you drive by a children's playground, stop and swing on the swing set. Or fly a kite, throw a Frisbee, or skip during your daily walk. As you're doing this out-of-the-ordinary activity, feel your inner child coming out to play. Be more childlike and sillier today.

LIVING WITH FAITH

*We could never learn to be brave and patient
if there were only joy in the world.*

~ HELEN KELLER

*Seeds of faith are always within us; sometimes it takes
a crisis to nourish and encourage their growth.*

~ SUSAN TAYLOR

Faith, as usually understood, is an elusive quality. The definition in *Webster's* reads, "unquestioning belief that does not require proof or evidence." I see faith not so much as trusting that events will always occur to our liking, but rather trusting that whatever life brings us, our inner resources will rise to the moment and we will be able to handle it.

You may have heard the saying, "I'll believe it when I see it." Easier said than done, right? It seems to me that, for our faith to truly take hold, we must trust in something greater than ourselves. We must put our trust in the Spirit of Love within us. It is an illusion to believe that any security can be found on Earth; the only security comes from trusting in the higher power within you. Through this trust, all things are possible. Trust and faith can work miracles. To reiterate what I wrote earlier, one of my most favorite passages is this one by Ralph Waldo Emerson: "The whole course of things goes to teach us faith." If you think about it perspicaciously, I think you, too, will agree with the profundity of his words.

In the relatively new field of science of psychoneuroimmunology, researchers are discovering that belief and faith play a major role in healing the body. It's an impressive nine-syllable word—*psychoneuroimmunology*. And, by the way, what a great word to bring up during a lull at your next dinner party or family gathering; you can ask people what they think of this science. I guarantee you will get some funny, inquisitive looks, as I did recently during a holiday meal. I was at a friend's home when everyone at the table was quiet and chewing their food, and I said, "Is anyone at this table as impressed as I am with how we are seeing the evidence of psycho-neuroimmunology almost daily in the news broadcasts." If you want every-one's attention, asking something like this is a surefire way to get it! And just think, when they ask you what the heck you are talking about, you will explain and, hence, increase everyone's IQ a point or two.

Psychoneuroimmunological studies show an undeniable link between the workings of the mind, the nervous system, and the body's ability to fight off disease. Studies also reveal that attitudes are based in biochemical real-ities. Medical research has demonstrated, for example, that panic, depres-sion, hate, fear, and frustration can have negative effects on your health. On the other hand, Norman Cousins presents evidence in his book *Head First: The Biology of Hope* that hope, faith, love, laughter, festivity, the will to live, and a sense of purpose can combat disease.

Faith will lift all sense of discouragement, defeat, and helplessness. Nurturing faith will change your consciousness so that the creative flow of life, love, and unlimited possibilities can fill your being. We cannot expect to see changes in our outer world, without first making changes within. We must stop looking outside ourselves for the answers, and instead put all trust in a higher power, in God.

We live in a friendly universe that is always saying "YES" to us. Our responsibility is to identify and transform the beliefs that have been sabotaging us from accepting and receiving the good that is our birthright. We must learn to trust and love ourselves as much as our Creator does. *When you remove all blockages to the loving presence within you and align with the love that you are, abundance, prosperity, peace, and success will be yours.* Believe in yourself. Have faith that nothing is impossible.

There are many people who write off amazing occurrences as coincidences. I don't believe in coincidences, as you know by now if you've been reading this book sequentially. Have you heard the saying that a coincidence is when God decides to do something but prefers to stay anonymous? I have a story to share with you that I don't think was simply a random happening.

> *When you remove all blockages to the loving presence within you and align with the love that you are, abundance, prosperity, peace, and success will be yours.*

In the 1970s, I ran my first marathon in December in Culver City (in the Los Angeles area). I had devoted a year to training. When the race day arrived, I had mixed emotions. On the one hand, I was eager and excited to run, although not quite sure what to expect since I had never done this before. On the other hand, I was feeling sad. The day of the race was the one-year anniversary of my grandmother Fritzie's death. Fritzie, as you know, had been instrumental in teaching me about my own spirituality, self-reliance, simplicity, and living fully. The morning of the race, I felt a tremendous longing to visit with her. I missed her so much. In the car, I was actually talking out loud with her as a way to soothe my heart. I even told her I was open to her spirit and energy. I asked her to let me know somehow if she could hear me. I asked her to help me through the marathon.

When I arrived at the race site, there were lots of people getting ready. I was wishing I knew someone so I wouldn't have to run alone. The gun went off and so did a few thousand runners. For the first three miles, I was alone and felt great—confident, relaxed, and energetic. Around the fourth mile, a young man who looked to be in his mid-twenties ran up next to me and we began talking. Before we knew it, we were at mile ten, then fifteen, then twenty. It's amazing the things you'll tell someone you've never met when you're running together. We talked about our lives, families, interests, dreams, and goals. I was extremely grateful to him because our conversation made the miles sail by.

Before we knew it, we were at mile twenty-five. At this point in our conversation, we started talking about where we lived. I told him I lived in Brentwood, and he told me he lived in Studio City. "That's interesting," I said. "My grandmother used to live in Studio City. What street do you live on?" When he told me the street, I gasped, for it was the same street as Fritzie. At this point, we were close to the finish line. I had just enough time to inquire about his exact location. We were crossing the finish line when he told me he had moved into his home eleven months earlier, and that the lady who had lived there before him had passed away. I could hardly breathe, not because I was tired, but because of what he was telling me. He had moved into Fritzie's house!

Coincidence, you say? I don't think so. Out of all the thousands of people in the race, how did I end up running with the man who lived in my grandmother's home? And how do you explain this happening only a few hours after I had asked Fritzie to give me some sign that she was receiving my communication?

GREEN SMOOTHIE ALL OVER

Bless the good-natured, for they bless everybody else.

~ THOMAS CARLYLE

Before I end this chapter, here's one more story about the importance of cultivating a sense of humor, good nature, and not taking yourself too seriously. David Craddock briefly wrote about it in his foreword in my previous book *Choose to Thrive*, but here's the entire story.

I was giving a cooking class to about twenty people in my home. I had just totally refurbished my kitchen and large adjoining family room with new cabinets, wood floors, shiplap on the walls, new paint everywhere, wood beam ceilings, new area rugs, etc.—everything was new and beautiful, and I was so excited for my guests to see how I had decorated it all.

It happened to be St. Patrick's Day and during this lunch-time class, everything was laid out on the massive marble island in the center of my kitchen and the guests were either seated around the island or standing behind it. All the foods we had made during the previous hour were displayed on the island for us to eat shortly. But first, I wanted to finish my cooking and nutrition demonstrations by making a healthy and delicious green smoothie.

So into the blender went fresh almond milk (that was just made earlier), frozen blueberries and raspberries, a frozen banana, one cucumber, a tablespoon of flaxseeds, some baby leaf spinach, celery, a dash of cinnamon, and ice cubes. I blended it all in the 72-ounce jar, which was filled to the brim with scrumptious, creamy, totally blended green smoothie. Next, I took the lid off the blender and was about to give everyone a sample when I realized that I forgot to put in some kale. So I asked one of the guests seated at the end island stool to get the kale from the refrigerator and finish making the smoothie while I went to use the bathroom and quickly changed my clothes before eating.

While I was at the far end of my home in my bedroom, this guest put some kale into the blender, and you've probably already guessed what was about to happen next. She forgot to put the lid on the blender after the kale went in and she pressed the start button that was already on high speed before anyone had a chance to tell her to put the lid back on top first. With the force of an angry volcano, this green 72-ounce smoothie shot up to the high ceiling above, drenching all the shiplap in "green goodness" and also covering the entire island with all the food, the floors, the area rugs, the walls, and most of the people watching, too. Everyone was in shock and didn't even know what to say so most of the guests were totally silently and, at the same time, very nervous because my kitchen and family room had just been refurbished and now everything was a vibrant green.

Oblivious to what had just happened, I danced out of my bedroom and down the hall singing the song "You Make Me Feel So Young" by Frank Sinatra and was eager to sit down with everyone and start eating. Then I saw what had happened, and everyone was staring at me (yes, I was partly in shock!). To the surprise and delight of everyone, I started laughing so hard that everyone else started laughing. It definitely relieved the tension in the room. But I couldn't stop laughing for about three minutes; in fact, I was laughing so hard that I was tearing up.

Then I said joyfully, "It's my fault, I forgot to tell you to put the lid on, and how beautiful is this! Today is St. Patrick's Day and now there's no need to decorate because everything is already green." Well, that made all the guests laugh even more. Everyone joined in to clean up, and I turned on some great music and ordered some food to be delivered from a local restaurant for everyone to eat together. (All the food we had prepared to sample was covered in green smoothie.)

I enjoy being lighthearted and not taking life too seriously, especially when unexpected things happen to me in my life. When your heart is filled with joy and thanksgiving, and you go through your days feeling thankful and uplifted, it's easy to cultivate a sense of humor and to focus on the bright side of life.

We must be willing to get rid of the life we've planned,
so as to have the life that is waiting for us.

~ JOSEPH CAMPBELL

In the best of times, our days are numbered anyway. So it would be
a crime against nature for any generation to take the world crisis
so solemnly that it put off enjoying those things for which we were
designed in the first place: the opportunity to do good work, to
enjoy friends, to fall in love, to hit a ball, and to bounce a baby."

~ ALISTAIR COOKE

Today's Affirmation

The spirit of God within is my source, supply, and support. I draw forth the kingdom into my consciousness, and the fullness of my blessings is now being made evident in my world. I stand firm in my faith. Miracles are a natural part of my life. I trust and I believe.

 12-Minute Action Step

Today, live with faith that everything is happening and unfolding for your highest good. As each hour arrives, say thank you for everything from the previous hour and for the upcoming hour because you live with a grateful heart and trust in the entire course of things. Living with faith is the gateway to miracles and feeling uplifted. Live faithfully today.

Humor Time

The most wasted of days is one without laughter.

~ E. E. CUMMINGS

If you could choose one characteristic that would get you through life, choose a sense of humor.

~ JENNIFER JONES

L aughing is one of the healthiest things for our mind and body! Research has shown that the health benefits of laughter are far-ranging. Studies have shown that laughter can help relieve pain, bring greater happiness, and even increase our overall well-being. Laughter reduces the level of stress hormones like cortisol, epinephrine (adrenaline), and dopamine. It also increases the level of health-enhancing hormones, like endorphins.

Laughter increases the number of antibody-producing cells we have working for us and enhances the effectiveness of T cells, a lymphocyte produced by the thymus gland that supports immunity. All this means a stronger immune system, as well as fewer physical effects of stress. Unfortunately, however, many people don't get enough laughter in their lives. In fact, one study suggests that healthy children may laugh as much as 400 times per day, but adults tend to laugh only 15 times per day or less.

All of us could use a little more laughter in our lives, considering how beneficial a good laugh can actually be for our stress levels and overall wellness. So, the following stories and jokes may tickle your funny bone and foster more upliftment in your day. Later in the book, you will find another Humor Time Intermission. Enjoy!

Sitting on the Cushion

Have you ever wanted to reveal your deep inner truths to the world? What if someone said that you knew the secret of life and put you on a stage to tell it? Well, a few decades ago, the *Totally Hidden Video* television show set up a convincing prank on precisely this theme.

For the gag, a FedEx driver was asked to deliver a package to a religious temple (fabricated by the television show). Unknown to the driver, the pranksters had taken a photo of him and replicated it as a painted portrait, depicting the young man dressed in the royal regalia of the fictitious sect.

When the delivery man arrived, the disciples (actors hired by the program) took one look at him and began buzzing excitedly. They ushered him to the front of the sanctuary and invited him to sit on a plush cushion of honor. Then they revealed to him that he was the chosen one, the long-awaited prophet foretold in their scriptures. To allay any doubts, a servant parted the alter curtain where, lo and behold, hung the majestic portrait of the deliverer, supposedly "painted by a visionary centuries ago."

"Please," begged a disciple, "give us some words of wisdom."

The driver surveyed the portrait and looked over the throng of expectant devotees. A hush fell over the assembly. He sat down on the pillow, took a deep breath, and spoke: "Life," the driver-turned-sage explained, "is like a river." The disciples *oohed* and *aahed* on the heels of his utterance, hanging fervently on every sacred word. "Sometimes life flows easily, and sometimes you encounter rocks and rapids," he continued, "but if you hang in there and have faith, you will arrive at the ocean of your dreams." Again, the disciples swooned with ecstasy—more *oohs* and *aahs*—acting as if this was indeed the day they had been waiting for!

"Well, that's about it," Swami FedEx curtly concluded. "I have to go now and make some more deliveries." Reluctantly the devotees rose, bowed reverently, and sheepishly cleared the way for the anointed one. Amid profuse veneration, the driver made his way to the door.

Now here is the amazing postscript to the story: the program played the same trick on several FedEx drivers, each of whom found profound words the moment he sat on the cushion. The invitation to wax profound brought forth the inner wisdom in these unassuming fellows.

Deep within our heart, we all know the truth. The answers we seek, the power we strive for, the happiness and health that we want, and the acknowledgment we attempt to gain, abide inside us.

Given the opportunity (being placed on the cushion) or the challenge (being pushed against the wall), we know what we need to know, to do what we need to do. *Carpe diem!* Celebrate yourself and life today and every day!

God Calls It a Day

A long, long time ago, God was mopping his brow after finishing a very difficult task. "Whew," he said, "I just made twenty-four hours of alternating light and dark."

A nearby cherub asked, "What are you going to do now?"

God replied, "I think I'll call it a day."

Watch Out What You Ask For

A man and his wife, both of whom were sixty years of age, were walking on the beach in celebration of their fortieth wedding anniversary. They laughed when they spotted a bottle sticking out of the sand, but they picked it up and rubbed it (just for fun).

Sure enough, a genie appeared and said, "You have been a devoted couple for forty years, and I will grant each of you a wish—you may have *anything* you want."

Immediately the wife said, "All my life I have wanted to take a trip around the world." And POOF! The tickets for the trip were in her hands!

The husband slid up to the genie and whispered, "All my life, I have wanted a woman who was thirty years younger than I." And POOF! He was ninety years old!

Sixteen Wives

A little boy was attending his first wedding. After the ceremony, his cousin asked him, "How many women can a man marry?"

"Sixteen," the boy responded.

"How do you know that?" the cousin asked

"Easy," the little boy replied. "All you have to do is add it up just like the preacher said: four *better*, four *worse*, four *richer*, and four *poorer*."

SEEKING THE FOUNTAIN OF YOUTH

Happiness always comes from within. Happiness is not money, property, possessions, food, sex, or even the Fountain of Youth. You may look to pills, surgery, diets, exercise, etc. to stay forever young or whatever products that will promise youth to stay happy.

This reminds me of a story I read about a youthful-looking man who had been arrested for swindling people out of their money by selling them "age-reversing" Fountain of Youth pills. The judge who was hearing the case asked the city attorney if the man had a record of prior arrests. "Yes, your Honor," the attorney replied. "He was arrested in 2019, 2000, 1986, 1979, 1963, 1951, 1937, 1902, 1885, and 1877." The judge immediately dismissed the case.

Everything is funny, as long as it's happening to someone else.

~ WILL ROGERS

BE SPECIFIC ON WHAT YOU WANT

A couple met their demise together in a car crash and were met by St. Peter, who told them, "You have arrived on a very auspicious occasion." He said they could each go back to Earth for twenty-four hours and be anything they want.

The wife said, "I've always wanted to be a butterfly," and off she went.

The husband made his request, and off he went a little while later.

When the wife returned, she told St. Peter how splendid the experience of being a butterfly had been. She'd flitted and fluttered amid a panoply of flowers and loved every minute of her adventure. Then, she asked St. Peter where her husband was.

St. Peter explained that her husband had requested to be a stud, which he had always longed to be a stud.

"Oh?" said the wife. "Well, where is he now?"

"He should be returning shortly. He's currently on the freeway in Colorado attached to a car tire."

Light Leaking

A man climbed up to a mountaintop and stretched his arms to heaven and cried, "God, fill me full of light! I'm ready. I'm waiting!

The voice of God replied, "I'm always filling you with light—but you keep leaking."

Three Men and a Skateboard

Three men died and went to heaven. St. Peter asked the first man, "Were you faithful to your wife?" The man said that he had several affairs, so St. Peter gave him an economy car. The second man said he had only two affairs, so St. Peter gave him a medium-size car. The third man, who was faithful his entire marriage, was given a luxury car.

Sometime later, all three men got together. The man with the luxury car was crying. When one of the other men asked him why he was crying, he replied, "I just passed my wife, and she was on a skateboard."

From there to here, and here to there,
funny things are everywhere.

~ Dr. Seuss

I love people who make me laugh. I honestly think it's
the thing I like most, to laugh. It cures a multitude of ills.
It's probably the most important thing in a person.

~ Audrey Hepburn

Part Two

Cultivate Joy,
Optimism & Vitality

Chapter 10

Act, Speak & Write
in a Positive Light

A longing fulfilled is sweet to the soul.

~ PROVERBS 13:19

There are only two ways to live your life. One is as though nothing
is a miracle. The other is as though everything is a miracle.

~ ALBERT EINSTEIN

100 AFFIRMATIONS

The following is a sampling of one hundred affirmations, divided into four categories: Health, Prosperity, Spirituality, and Self-Esteem & Lifestyle. Use any or all of them as is—or change them to fit your own desires and goals, adding new ones to the list as you go.

Consider writing your favorites on small cards to place around your home or office so you can see and use them often. When you say, write, or think an affirmation, you are "acting as if" it is true. Choose affirmations you can repeat until you feel them as true. At that point, they become a part of your subconscious self-definition.

Health

1. I am grateful for nature's abundance of delicious, nutritious foods.

2. I am the picture of health; I radiate verve and vitality.

3. My body is healing and rejuvenating itself moment by moment.

4. I live in harmony with nature and provide my body with the best of everything.

5. I give thanks for increasing health, fitness, prosperity, and love.

6. My sleep is relaxing, rejuvenating, and refreshing.

7. My body is an expression of my love for life, a miracle of youthfulness.

8. Raw foods, such as fresh fruits and veggies, are some of my favorite foods, and I give them a place of honor in my daily diet.

9. My body is God's gift to me, and what I am becoming is my gift to God.

10. I take time each day to relax, turn within, breathe deeply, and let go of tension.

11. Exercise is a top priority in my life, and I find ways to be active daily.

12. I manage the stress in my life the same way I walk—with ease and grace.

13. My food choices reflect my love for myself and life.

14. I enjoy colorful, plant-based foods and choose to eat a variety each day.

15. I am losing extra weight and feeling great.

16. I take responsibility for my wellness lifestyle.

17. I have all the energy I need to accomplish my goals and fulfill my desires.

18. Today I renew my commitment to being healthy and resolve to make my word count.

19. I have an abundance of energy, and my body is free of aches and pains.

20. I eat foods that nourish my body and mind and boost my self-esteem.

21. I fall asleep at night effortlessly and wake up feeling refreshed.

22. I love my body and treat it like royalty.

23. My healthy, active lifestyle brings me great joy and appreciation for life.

24. Day by day, I am becoming healthier and more confident about all my choices.

25. I love to work out, and I do so each and every day.

26. Vibrant health is my natural state of being.

27. I breathe in health and vitality and exhale all tensions and worries.

Prosperity

1. I am worthy of receiving the unlimited offerings of the universe.

2. I always prosper in everything I do.

3. The more I give in love, the more I am given.

4. Everywhere I look I see opportunities to prosper.

5. An avalanche of abundance is flowing to me now.

6. I accept and expect prosperity in every area of my life.

7. I am attracting the people, circumstances, and resources to make my dreams come true.

8. The more I trust my intuition, the more prosperity comes my way.

9. I am amply rewarded for my creative ideas.

10. I rejoice in my continuing good fortune.

11. I am the creator of my life, and I choose to create a passionate adventure filled with success.

Spirituality

1. My will and Divine Will are one.

2. I release all my fear and worry and trust that all things are working together for my highest good.

3. I love to be outdoors to celebrate the spectacular beauty in nature.

4. A loving, powerful spirit moves through me, lighting my path.

5. I trust myself and my intuitive nature.

6. I give thanks and praise for all things and choose to be radiantly happy.

7. I welcome Spirit's guidance with an open, grateful mind and heart.

8. With each breath I take, I center my thoughts on being loving and peaceful.

9. My life is a harmonious expression of the insights and values of my higher self.

10. Each morning I give thanks for the gift of life and the beauty all around me.

11. In quiet and solitude, I listen to the whisperings of God and Divine inspiration in me.

12. Divine healing energy is flowing through me now, cleansing, purifying, and renewing every cell in my body.

13. I surrender to life and behold God's love and light in everyone and everything.

Self-Esteem & Lifestyle

1. I release my fears and insecurities and replace them with faith and confidence.

2. Everything about my life is sacred to me.

3. I am committed to living my highest potential in every area of my life.

4. I celebrate life today and every day.

5. All my goals and desires are coming to fruition in my life now.

6. I am the master of my life, and I have the power to create anything I desire.

7. I greet each day with a thankful and cheerful heart.

8. With a heart filled with faith and love, I appreciate and value myself more each day.

9. I communicate my feelings openly, lovingly, and honestly with my partner, family, friends, and coworkers.

10. I deserve to be happy, live fully, and celebrate life.

11. My home is my sanctuary and is filled with love, peace, and joy.

12. I receive great pleasure in pleasing my partner and do so often.

13. I am true to myself.

14. I am grateful for all life's lessons that bless me richly.

15. I live in a peaceful world, because I am a peaceful person.

16. I appreciate the people in my life and tell them, in special ways, what they mean to me.

17. I embrace each day with enthusiasm and find ways to uplift others.

18. I seek out new adventures and move out of my comfort zone.

19. I find ways to express my feelings of hurt in honest, loving ways.

20. All things are working together for good in my life, and I trust in the process.

21. I choose to surround myself with beauty and positive people.

22. I always treat others the way I would like to be treated—with kindness and respect.

23. I see all challenges as positive opportunities.

24. All that my heart desires is coming into my life now.

25. I live simply and pay attention to what's really essential.

26. I am grateful for all opportunities to grow and transform.

27. I am lovable, confident, and self-assured.

28. I draw to myself positive people who share my zest for life.

29. I take responsibility for my life, release blame, and let go of what no longer serves my highest good.

30. Today I find ways to simplify my life and all my affairs.

31. Today and every day, I let my inner child come out to play and celebrate life.

32. I am luminescent, and I choose to live each day with vigor, vim, and valor. (You can keep adding "V's"—veracity, vitality, vivacity, and verve!)

33. I release the past and embrace each moment with love.

34. I find ways to show my appreciation for myself and others.

35. Because I respect myself and others, I arrive on time and keep my word.

36. My body is strong, fit, sexy, and beautiful.

37. I let the tranquility that's in my heart infuse my intentions.

38. My persistence and determination work miracles.

39. I love myself unconditionally.

40. I am at peace with myself and the universe.

41. I make a positive difference in the world and have a joyous and positive impact on those around me.

42. I give thanks for every experience I have.

43. I am free from old pains. They have become a distant memory.

44. I embrace change, knowing that it transforms my life.

45. I give thanks for my new life and my new motivation to be the best I can be.

46. I bless and forgive everyone who has caused me pain; I let go of the past; I am free.

47. I choose to experience peace of mind.

48. Today I make a fresh start and begin to live on higher ground.

49. I have a clear vision of what I want to achieve, and I see it happening now. Thank you, God.

I am certain of nothing but of the holiness of the
heart's affections and the truth of imagination.

~ JOHN KEATS

I AM AFFIRMATIONS

This section includes some simple I AM Affirmations to use anytime you wish to feel your very best and to be more positive. Always be positive in your self-talk. The more you work on raising awareness of your positive self-talk, the less you will allow yourself to dwell on the negative. Stop listening to that garbage and start choosing positivity instead!

This is a very simple process. You can start your morning with affirmations that help you establish the positive mindset you want. If negativity pops up during the day, repeat some of your favorite I AM affirmations to quickly get back to your positive self-talk.

"I AM"—BIBLICALLY SPEAKING

The Hebrew word *ehyeh* means "I AM"; it is derived from the verb *hayah*, which means "to become, or to exist." This has come to be understood as "the one who is, and who was, and who is to come" (Rev. 4:8) or "the Eternal One."

Jesus used the phrase "I AM" in seven declarations about Himself. In all seven, He combines "I AM" with tremendous metaphors that express His saving relationship toward the world. All appear in the Gospel according to St. John. They are:

"I AM the Bread of Life" (John 6:35, 41, 48, 51).

"I AM the Light of the World" (John 8:12).

"I AM the Door of the Sheep" (John 10:7, 9).

"I AM the Good Shepherd" (John 10:11, 14).

"I AM the Resurrection and the Life" (John 11:25).

"I AM the Way, the Truth and the Life" (John 14:6).

"I AM the True Vine" (John 15:1, 5).

The following "I AM" affirmations are very powerful when spoken aloud or silently because they draw upon the power of the spirit within us to speak something in the present moment with a view to bringing it into manifestation in our present-day.

All affirmations should be positive, present tense, and personal for you. Let's say you are not feeling very peaceful. When you start repeatedly affirming, "I AM peaceful," you will begin to feel more peaceful. To incorporate deep breathing into this process, you may wish to say the words "I AM" slowly and deeply as you inhale. Then, as you slowly exhale, say the word "peaceful" or any other mental state you want.

This is a very positive exercise that will help you take charge of your thoughts and mood, and feel and stay positive, relaxed, faith-filled, and happy every day. I have been doing these "I AM" affirmations since I was a teenager and learned how and why to practice them daily from my grandmother.

Here are thirty-three suggested affirmations followed by space for seven more you might like to add. By the way, *I AM grateful and immensely chuffed that you are reading this book and practicing my favorite "I AM" affirmations.*

1. I AM peaceful.

2. I AM calm.

3. I AM resourceful.

4. I AM confident.

5. I AM beautiful.

6. I AM loving, lovable, and loved.

7. I AM faith-filled.

8. I AM victorious.

9. I AM prosperous.

10. I AM vivacious.

11. I AM energetic.

12. I AM wonderful.

13. I AM healed and healthy.

14. I AM relaxed.

15. I AM happy.

16. I AM joyful.

17. I AM optimistic.

18. I AM strong.

19. I AM God's child.

20. I AM Christ-centered.

21. I AM blessed.

22. I AM safe and secure.

23. I AM smart.

24. I AM loyal.

25. I AM wealthy.

26. I AM enough.

27. *I AM worthy.*

28. *I AM a survivor.*

29. *I AM powerful and empowered.*

30. *I AM unshakable.*

31. *I AM victorious.*

32. *I AM grateful.*

33. *I AM cradled in God's love, peace, and protection.*

Add in your own affirmations here:

34. I AM . . .

35. I AM . . .

36. I AM . . .

37. I AM . . .

38. I AM . . .

39. I AM . . .

40. I AM . . .

UPLIFTING POSITIVE WORDS = A POSITIVE LIFE

The words you choose when you speak or write can change the direction of your life from this moment forward. It's in your hands. Do you want to live a more positive, faithful, joyful, peaceful, balanced, and uplifted life or would you rather live as a victim of circumstances with a negative cloud hovering over you? If you choose the former, it starts with the words you select, and it would behoove you to only affirm with what you say and what you write the most positive words you can muster.

To support you in this process of speaking and writing in a more positive light, here are 260 words—some of my favorite positive words. As a logophile (lover of words), it delights me to share these with you.

See how many more can you think of and use today in your communications. Kids love to participate in this exercise, too. Can you come up with any other magnificently positive words not listed here? Communicate these life-enriching words with your family, friends, and business associates daily. If you make a three-day commitment to only think, act, speak, and write in a positive light, I guarantee that your life will miraculously change for the better. Are you up for the challenge?

I believe we can transform the quality of life on this planet by using more positive language and acting with kindness each day. Think kindness. Think upliftment. It starts with YOU! You must begin by showing kindness toward yourself and others and it will catch on like a ripple from a stone cast into a lake. As Gandhi said, "If we could change ourselves, the tendencies in the world would also change. As a man changes his own nature, so does the attitude of the world change towards him . . . We need not wait to see what others do."

Abundant, Accomplished, Achieving, Active, Admirable, Adorable, Adventurous, Admired, Affluent, Agreeable, Alert, Aligned, Alive, Amazing, Appealing, Appreciate, Artistic, Astounding, Astute, Attentive, Attractive, Auspicious, Authentic, Awake, Aware, Awesome

Beaming, Beautiful, Best, Blessed, Blissful, Bold, Bright, Brilliant, Brisk, Bucolic, Buoyant

Calm, Capable, Centered, Certain, Charming, Cheerful, Clear, Clever, Competent, Complete, Confident, Connected, Conscious, Considerate, Convenient, Courageous, Creative

Daring, Dazzling, Delicious, Delightful, Desirable, Determined, Diligent, Discerning, Discover, Dynamic

Eager, Easy, Efficient, Effortless, Elegant, Eloquent, Energetic, Endless, Enhancing, Engaging, Enormous, Enterprising, Enthusiastic, Enticing, Excellent, Exceptional, Exciting, Experienced, Exquisite

Fabulous, Fair, Farsighted, Fascinating, Fine, Flattering, Flourishing, Fortunate, Free, Friendly, Fulfilled, Fun

Generous, Genuine, Gifted, Glorious, Glowing, Good, Good-looking, Gorgeous, Graceful, Gracious, Grand, Great

Handsome, Happy, Hardy, Harmonious, Healed, Healthy, Helpful, Honest, Humorous

Ideal, Imaginative, Impressive, Industrious, Ingenious, Innovative, Inspired, Intelligent, Interested, Interesting, Intuitive, Inquisitive, Inventive, Invincible, Inviting, Irresistible

Joyous, Judicious

Keen, Kind, Knowing

Limitless, Lively, Loving, Lucky, Luminous

Magical, Magnificent, Marvelous, Masterful,
Mighty, Miraculous, Motivated

Natural, Neat, Nice, Nurturing, Noble

Optimistic, Outstanding

Passionate, Peaceful, Perfect, Persevering, Persistent, Playful,
Pleasing, Plentiful, Positive, Powerful, Precious, Prepared,
Productive, Profound, Prompt, Prosperous, Proud

Quaint, Qualified, Quality, Quick, Quintessential

Radiant, Reasonable, Refined, Refreshing, Relaxing,
Reliable, Remarkable, Resolute, Resourceful,
Respected, Responsible, Rewarding, Robust

Safe, Satisfied, Secure, Self-Reliant, Sensational, Sensual,
Sensible, Sensitive, Serene, Sharing, Skillful, Smart, Smashing,
Smooth, Sparkling, Spiritual, Splendid, Strong, Stunning,
Successful, Superb, Supercalifragilisticexpialidocious, Swift

Talented, Tenacious, Terrific, Thankful, Thrilling,
Thriving, Timely, Trusting, Truthful

Ultimate, Unique

Valiant, Valuable, Versatile, Verve, Vibrant, Victorious,
Vigor, Vigorous, Vim, Vivacious, Vivacity, Vivid

Warm, Wealthy, Well, Whole, Wise, Wonderful, Worthy

Young, Youthful

Zeal, Zest

The first wealth is health.

~ Ralph Waldo Emerson

Live in each season as it passes; breathe air, drink the drink,
taste the fruit, and resign yourself to the influences of each.
Let them be your only diet, drink, and botanical medicines.

~ Henry David Thoreau

 Today's Affirmation ———————————

My peaceful, happy thoughts reflect the light and love within me. I focus on what I desire and deserve, for I know that new thoughts create new conditions. I allow Love's thoughts to be my thoughts. I am renewed, regenerated, and restored for I am living a joyful, healthy life.

 12-Minute Action Step ———————————

If you were living the life of your dreams right now, what would it look like? If you knew you couldn't fail, how would you be living? In 12 minutes or less, write down your response as though this vision were your current reality. Read it often, and feel the joy you would experience in living this life. Return to this vision-reality often during this uplifted journey to fertilize the dream. Trust and believe. Think about what you want in your life today.

Chapter 11

Turning Your Dream into Reality

If A is a success in life, then A equals X plus Y plus Z. X is work, Y is play, and Z is keeping your mouth shut.

~ ALBERT EINSTEIN

The way for you to be happy and successful, to get more of the things you really want in life, is to get the combinations to the locks. Instead of spinning the dials of life hoping for a lucky break, as if you were playing a slot machine, you must instead study and emulate those who already have done what you want to do and achieved the results you want to achieve.

~ BRIAN TRACY

People often say we create our own reality. In fact, I've been suggesting it throughout this book. But what does that really mean? A few years ago, I had an amazing experience that showed me.

I was accustomed to going to the beach for an invigorating swim a few times each week, very early, and this was a splendid morning just before sunrise. After some stretching exercises and a short jog, I was ready for my swim. Because it was the end of summer, the water was still comfortably warm. But this morning there was something in the air that I couldn't quite identify. I felt it deep inside me—a shiver of anticipation, a faint knowing that today would be different, that this day would be one I would remember the rest of my life. I went out into the ocean, rode a few waves, and then swam past the swells.

I was aware of the peacefulness of the water. Sparkling and resplendent, it rejuvenated my body and soul with each stroke. A few minutes later, some old friends joined me, a group of pelicans who seemed to enjoy escorting me. These marvels of nature have always enthralled me. They were gliding flawlessly a few feet above my head, their wingspan so large that they almost eclipsed the light, when suddenly they flew away. Surprised, I waved good-bye as I turned over to begin the backstroke. It was then I saw something that made my heart plummet.

A large, dark, frightening fin was heading straight for me. Shark! I looked toward the beach. No one was there. I had always taken for granted that I would stay calm in a life-threatening situation. But not this time! As the fin continued in my direction, I simply froze and treaded water. I was so terrified; I couldn't swim away or even cry out. And then it happened—a sight that will forever warm my heart and soul. The fin danced out of the water. It was a dolphin, and it was followed by a school of about two dozen more!

Less than two weeks before, I had watched a television documentary on dolphins. During my meditation that evening, I had visualized myself swimming and playing with a school of dolphins. I accepted and affirmed that that was my desire and reality. I then thanked God for this wonderful experience.

There in the ocean that morning, the dolphins stayed with me for a full half hour, swimming, jumping out of the water, and jumping over me. I swam underwater with them, listening to their mellifluous sounds, touching their skin, feeling a connection and an exchange of love. For what seemed like hours, nothing else existed except my world of dolphins. I was oblivious to any thought of the past or future and lived right in the moment, rejoicing in the thrill of discovery.

Then, as quickly as they had arrived, the dolphins swam off, and I was left alone and immensely grateful. I swam back to shore, where by now a group of people had gathered, captivated by my dance with the dolphins. I answered many questions and tried to share what the experience had been like for me, but I found it very hard to put my feelings into words. Experiences that speak directly to the heart are often ineffable, difficult to express clearly through words.

The others drifted away, and I just sat there, enveloped in wonder at the experience of swimming with dolphins, and all I could do was cry—what had happened touched me so lovingly, so profoundly. What a beautiful lesson in living in the present and appreciating each moment. Because of that experience and so many others, I will never doubt the power of thought and belief to create any reality we choose.

PUTTING OUR THOUGHTS TO WORK

In the 1970s positive thinking became almost synonymous with success. In its early use in contexts such as Dale Carnegie's success courses, positive thinking meant using willpower and conscious, positive thoughts to achieve goals. Napoleon Hill's maxim for success, "What you can conceive and believe, you can achieve," was a popular positive-thinking slogan. Never underestimate the Divine potential of positive thinking. Rightly employed, this power of the mind is a catalyst that makes possible a wondrous transformation in our lives. It was Ralph Waldo Emerson who said, *"The good mind chooses what is positive, what is advancing—embraces the affirmative."*

Positive thinking includes belief in our own self-worth and in the value of everyone else and every circumstance. That positive belief leads to self-confidence, respect for others, and a lifestyle based on strong values. Sometimes we slip into the habit of negative thinking because we feel discouraged, depressed, lonely, isolated, or stressed. We all want fast and easy results. But life isn't like that. Life is meant to be a challenge, and one of its greatest lessons is that when our minds are full of fear, doubt, and clutter, good ideas can't get through. The best ideas and best decisions come when we're relaxed, open to impressions and responsive to them. In that state, we can find a way to link the present situation with wonderful opportunities to learn and grow.

Don't try to sit in a chair and think positively about something and expect it to happen. Keeping alive a goal or dream, or even hope, requires action. You have to make it happen—or at least help make it happen.

TAKE CHARGE OF YOUR MIND AND LIFE

You'll notice that successful people are very deliberate about choosing to be in charge of their lives. They (you?) don't get up in the morning and hope that they'll have a good day. They take full control of their lives, and, if they don't encounter the circumstances they want, they make them. Success and real fulfillment always begin with a dream. Successful people know nothing will happen unless they have the courage to take risks, remain vulnerable, make mistakes, and even fail. But life can't be lived on the sidelines if you want to be successful. There's enormous fun, as well as risk, in challenging yourself to do something you've always wanted to do.

Too often we live in our comfort zone instead of taking risks. How often did your mom tell you "Take a risk today, sweetie!" when she sent you off to school? Probably never. *Most of us are taught from a very early age to play small and play it safe rather than to play big and expand our horizons.* Our comfort zone will remain tiny all our lives unless we subject it to some growing pains.

What it really means to create your own reality is that our lives are a direct reflection of our thoughts, dreams, expectations, beliefs, hopes, feelings of self-worth, and desires. Put your thoughts and dreams and hopes toward what you want, lean into it, and you begin to take the steps necessary to reach your goals. It's not magic. Here's a quick example: One of my clients, Kathleen, doesn't like where she lives, but she can't afford to move. She's resides in an old, noisy apartment building, and her walls were in need a fresh coat of paint, the windows hadn't been washed in years, and she didn't have any plants or other living things besides herself and her cat.

> *Successful people know nothing will happen unless they have the courage to take risks, remain vulnerable, make mistakes, and even fail.*

It was no surprise to me that Kathleen was miserable, had a hard time sleeping, lacked energy, and felt depressed. She complained about her surroundings often in our counseling sessions but failed to do anything about it—that is until I presented her with a challenge and assignment. I explained to her that if she would simply paint some of the walls a soothing color such as soft green or pale blue or teal, bring in some fresh flowers and plants, get a simple water fountain and perhaps a sound device that plays the sounds of nature such as ocean waves, gentle rain, and singing birds, etc. to help block out the noisy neighbors, she would be much happier in her environment, sleep better, and have a more positive attitude. And then I said that if she would do this in the next week, I would gift her with a dinner party and make all the food for five of her favorite friends. Well, that put a smile on her face. In fact, she got so excited about these few changes—that cost less than $150—that she used a few days of vacation time at work to get the projects done within four days.

During the dinner party, everyone loved her personal and physical changes, and we all could feel her energy shift. She had gone from feeling sad, depressed, and enervated to being happy, hopeful, and energetic.

What can you change in your immediate surroundings today, this week, this month that will also put a smile on your face and in your heart and uplift you? Do it. Remember, we are not the victims of circumstance; we are the architect of our lives. Our conscious thoughts create an unconscious image of our lives, ourselves, and our feelings, and that unconscious image reproduces itself perfectly in our real-life circumstances.

When life gets complicated and we find ourselves with negative thoughts and feelings, it's tempting to think that it's the complications, conditions, or people that upset us. But that's not the way it really works. It's only *the way we think* about the things that happen to us that cause our upsets. We can choose not to become upset. We really can. And *as we change our thoughts and stop thinking of ourselves as victims, our lives shift and change in all kinds of positive ways.*

HOW TO BREAK THE VICIOUS CYCLE OF NEGATIVE THINKING

Let's look at an all-too-common example of how the principle of choice works: weight control. Let's just assume that you've always had difficulty controlling your weight. You've tried all kinds of diets and they've never worked, so you have negative feelings about diets. You've tried to limit the amount of food you eat without much success, so you don't have much faith in your self-control. You get on the scale every morning, and it reinforces your image of yourself as overweight. It really is a vicious cycle. To understand why you keep repeating the same patterns, you need to understand the way your mind works.

Brain researchers see the mind as composed of three primary parts: the conscious, the subconscious, and the superconscious. As your window to the world, the conscious mind runs your daily waking activities, such as making decisions, relating to others, and doing your work. The subconscious mind, at the same time, carries memories of all your experiences. It is a storage-and-retrieval center for all the information your conscious mind sends it based on your daily experiences—essentially a computer that is fed the data of your every thought, feeling, and experience. The superconscious mind is your connection to the Divine. I wrote about the superconscious in great detail in my two meditation chapters of my book *Wired for High-Level Wellness*.

Relating this to the example of weight control, if you get up every morning and worry about what clothes will fit, if you dread getting on your scale, if you dislike being seen in public, if you think about going on a diet but doubt that it will work (they don't—refer to my books *Invest in Yourself with Exercise* and *Wired for High-Level Wellness*), you are programming your subconscious computer with negative thoughts. Your subconscious mind creates reality according to its programming. If you think of yourself as being fat, as having little self-control, or as being unable to change, you will see those beliefs reflected in your life—and you won't lose a pound.

In Chapter 10, I offered you 100 health- and life-enriching affirmations. You can repeat these affirmations to yourself silently or out loud to help you turn around your thinking and programing from negative to positive.

The same is true for every other area of your life. Your subconscious beliefs and thoughts about yourself, your relationships with others, your money, your material possessions, your job, and so on, will be faithfully recreated in your life. You may be thinking, *No, that isn't true for me: I know that I really want to lose weight and tone my body (or make more money, or have a really good relationship), but I am not experiencing it in my life."* The answer lies in the vast difference between wanting something on the conscious level and wanting it on the subconscious level.

The conscious mind and the subconscious mind are often in conflict. Consciously you may want something, yet subconsciously you create mediocrity or failure. That's why positive thinking as commonly perceived doesn't work. As I lecture around the country and the world, I often hear statements such as, "I continually affirm, visualize, meditate, and believe in my highest good, but I rarely see results." It doesn't do much good to force yourself to think positive thoughts if your subconscious still harbors many negative beliefs. What you need to do is to reprogram your subconscious mind to break the vicious cycle of negative beliefs creating your negative reality. To do this, you must make some behavior changes on a conscious level that will contribute to new beliefs.

The birth of excellence begins with our awareness that our beliefs are a choice. We can choose beliefs that limit us, or we can choose beliefs that support us. The key is to choose beliefs that are conducive to success and to discard the ones that hold you back. Beliefs can turn on or shut off the flow of ideas. Our beliefs are what determine how much of our potential we'll be able to tap. Virgil, one of the greatest poets of ancient Rome, said, "*Possunt quia posse videntur,*" which basically means "They can because they think they can."

WHAT YOU THINK ABOUT YOU BRING ABOUT

In the world of metaphysics, there is an unwritten law of correspondence that says, "As within, so without." The way I explain this in my workshops is that we are always attracting to ourselves the equivalency of what we think, how we feel, and what we believe. Ralph Waldo Emerson said that we become what we think about all day long. In other words, your outer world tends to be a reflection of your inner (subconscious) world—like a mirror. What you see in the world around you will be consistent over time with the world inside you.

Studies reveal that successful, happy people think about successful, happy things most of the time. By the same token, unsuccessful, unhappy people concentrate their thoughts on people they dislike, situations they are angry about, and events that they do not wish to take place in their lives. These data point directly to the law of concentration, which says, "Whatever you dwell upon grows in your reality." These ideas come from all of the great masters in life—from Jesus, of course, and His disciples and also from other great minds such as Socrates, Aristotle, Pythagoras, Thoreau, Emerson, and Whitman. If you saw the movie or read the book called *The Secret,* you are aware of these "laws of the universe" that have come down through the ages and, when implemented in our lives, will transform us if we embrace them.

These two laws in combination explain much of success and most of failure. Whatever we think about most of the time, we bring about in our lives.

So, the starting point in making your dreams a reality is to discipline yourself to think and talk about only those things you want in your life, and to refuse to think and talk about anything other than what you want. These can be intangible as well as tangible things. Besides thinking and talking about the new job or material things you desire, talk and think about healthy things, such as being grateful. Try being loving instead of angry. Push aside all that negativity, those fears, doubts, and self-sabotaging, limiting thoughts and visions, and you will discover that all manner of remarkable things happen in your life that bring you closer to your dreams.

> *. . . discipline yourself to think and talk about only those things you want in your life, and to refuse to think and talk about anything other than what you want.*

It's equally important to feel the *feeling* of the dream fulfilled, of whatever it is you desire, whether it's being prosperous, fit, and healthy; being in a loving, supportive relationship; or being very successful at work. If you start acting a certain way, you eventually become it. The key to the process is to *capture the feeling*, because when you do that, you've captured the ability to internalize your idea, and then it's only a matter of time. Feeling refers to the intensity or amount of emotion that accompanies your mental pictures.

Emotion is central to all accomplishments. You might want to remember the following: T x F = R: *Thought times Feeling equals Realization.* The thought or picture multiplied by the feeling or emotion that accompanies it equals the speed at which it occurs in your reality. This is something I created over forty years ago to help my clients remember how important their thoughts and feelings are when they desire to create miracles in their lives.

My extensive research, as well as my own experience, has taught me to appreciate the importance of feelings. I like to describe emotion as an electromagnetic force field so strong that it sends up a vibration and pulls like vibrations to itself. It is a magnet for similar energy.

After interviewing many highly intelligent, successful people with diverse backgrounds and vast experience, I came to the conclusion that what we think about, and how we feel about the things we think about, are the determining factors in the way our life works out.

If we are thinking positive thoughts but not getting positive results, most of the time it's because the emotional channels have not been opened.

This can be done by practicing forgiveness toward ourselves and others, and by passionately releasing fear, anger, guilt, and any other feelings that block the presence of love inside us.

When we see our world only according to what surrounds us right now, we limit what we are going to have. As mentioned earlier, instead of thinking, "I'll believe it when I see it," try thinking, "I'll see it when I believe it."

For this to work, you must also get in the habit of saying what it is you desire. Be specific. Specifically, plant in your mind that which you choose to bring into your life. You see, the creative principle works according to the seeds you plant. If you plant scarcity, disease, and disaster, you get back scarcity, disease, and disaster. If you plant love, you get back love. Say what you want, be specific, and act *as if* what you want is already true. That's key.

Any feelings we want we can have, if we think intensely enough. Try it. It's remarkable, and it's true. We can even feel cool when it's hot or friendly when we'd rather be alone if we use our minds to paint the picture vividly enough. It's this powerful force of feeling, drawn into the subconscious mind, that acts as a generator to create what we desire.

POSITIVE ACTIONS BRING POSITIVE RESULTS

Here are some positive actions you can take to change your circumstances.

- If you feel that your beliefs about money are creating negative results in your life, examine the behaviors that support those negative beliefs. Maybe you are frugal in your grocery shopping, conscious of buying the cheapest brands and skipping the luxuries. Although frugality might be wise in light of your current financial situation, you should be aware that it also tends to reinforce your belief that you have very little money. One way to attack this belief is to substitute a new behavior for the old one. For example, the next time you're in a grocery store, allow yourself to indulge in a little luxury. While you're doing it, imagine that this capacity to indulge a little is your present reality, and feel it.

- If your problem is loneliness, make it a point to smile at one stranger every day, just as if you had plenty of friends and an abundance of love to share.

🖋 If you weigh more than you want to weigh, buy yourself something appealing that you would normally have denied yourself because of your present weight.

GROWING YOUR SELF-ESTEEM

It's important to understand that living your vision and creating what your heart desires is also related to how you feel about yourself. If you feel unworthy, it will be almost impossible for abundance to flow into your life. If you feel that you are important enough to ask and divine enough to receive, receiving will be your reward.

"Think of how a tree unfolds to all of its magnificent potential, always reaching for the sunshine and growing and flourishing," writes Wayne Dyer in *Change Your Thoughts—Change Your Life.* "Would you ever suggest to a tree, 'You should be ashamed of yourself for having that disgusting moss on your bark and for letting your limbs grow crooked?' Of course not. A tree allows the life force to work through it. You have the power within your thoughts to be as natural as the tree." He reminds us that all we need to do is to be ourselves.

WHAT YOU GIVE AWAY, YOU GET BACK MULTIPLIED

Another important aspect of changing your subconscious energy involves the law of circulation, which states that what you give away, you get back—multiplied. You must first give away the very thing you desire. If you desire increased prosperity in your life, for instance, don't be too penny-pinching because that would be manifesting a fear that there might not be enough. Share what you have with others and feel how the world begins to open to you as well.

Once you decide what you want, begin tithing. Tithing traditionally means to give a tenth of your income to your church, but tithing doesn't necessarily have to go to a church—and it doesn't have to be 10 percent. Tithe gifts can be in monetary form or a giving of yourself in time and/or deposits of love. I tithe money to those who feed my soul and nourish my spirituality and who are making a positive difference on this planet, whether they are individuals or organizations. I also give money and time to people less fortunate than I. Remember, though, it's futile to say, "Yes, when such-and-such money comes in, I will give a tenth of it as a tithe." You have to start helping those in need before that, acting in the spirit of "give that you may receive."

One day, after writing my prosperity affirmations and goals on cards, I went to the grocery store. While waiting in the checkout line, I suddenly called out to the harried mother in front of me, "I'll pay for those."

Needless to say, she was astonished! Quite honestly, so was I; the words seemed to have just popped out of my mouth. After some hesitancy on her part and some impressive cajolery on mine, she let me pay her bill. The pleasure I received made me feel rich inside. Later that same day, I ran into a person whom I had counseled several months before. At that time, she had been unable to pay, and I had written the sessions off as a good learning experience. This day, seemingly out of the blue, she wrote me a check for twice the amount she owed me, saying that my guidance had had a profound, positive effect on her life. I shouldn't have been surprised because I had "acted as if."

To act as if takes courage and trust. It's hard to start giving when you don't think you have enough, unless you act as if. Go out into the world as if you had the courage, and you'll find that the courage you wanted is already there. Do the thing, and the power is yours. Yes, it begins with a risk, but if you don't risk, you don't receive. That's how you generate power.

Your subconscious mind is extraordinarily powerful, but it is a servant, not a master. It coordinates every aspect of your thoughts, feelings, behaviors, words, actions, and emotions to fit a pattern consistent with your dominant mental pictures. It guides you to engage in the behaviors that will move you ever closer to achieving the goals you visualize and feel most of the time. If you visualize something that you fear, your subconscious mind will accept that as a command, too. It will then use its marvelous powers to bring your fears, instead of your dreams and aspirations, into reality.

Many people feel that their deepest beliefs and motivations are forever a mystery to them. They feel they don't understand the real reasons behind their actions, and as a result, they feel powerless to change their actions. They have it backward: we all have the ability to recognize our beliefs through our actions and to change them by changing our actions. Although beliefs may seem mysterious and complicated on a conscious level, on a subconscious level, they are usually simple. Our beliefs about ourselves are based entirely on our past experiences. All our experiences program our subconscious, and the result is what we are today.

That is not to say that all you will ever be is the sum of your experiences. Maybe you've noticed at some time or other that your life experiences are all very similar—it's just the people involved who keep changing. You can change that by choosing to feed different programming into your subconscious computer.

CHOOSE YOUR THOUGHTS AND WORDS WISELY

Two very effective ways to reprogram your subconscious mind are creative visualizations and affirmations. The idea is to alter your state of consciousness in such a way that you can temporarily set aside the conscious mind and concentrate specifically on the subconscious. According to brain researchers, suggestions given to your subconscious while in this altered state, whether they are images or affirmations, will be at least twenty times as effective as suggestions given in a normal state of consciousness. One of the best ways to alter or slow down your state of consciousness or brain wave activity is through relaxed deep breathing.

It's very helpful to feed your mind a clear mental picture of your desired goals for the coming day, the coming week, and the coming months just before going to sleep at night. I do this every night for about 10 minutes. As you drop off to sleep, your brain wave activity naturally slows down (as it naturally speeds up upon awakening), and your subconscious mind is most receptive to the input of new commands. Since your mental pictures are a command, take those last few minutes before you fall asleep to daydream and fantasize about exactly the person you want to be and the life you want to have. Your subconscious mind will then take the pictures down into its laboratory and work on them all night long. What often happens is that you wake up in the morning with ideas and insights that will help make those things you visualized a part of your life.

Most people have only vague, fuzzy pictures of what they want. They say they want to be rich or healthy or happy. But when you ask them exactly what that means to them, they don't really know. You must understand the importance of vividness in mental pictures. The more vividly you can see something that you want in your mind's eye, the more rapidly it will materialize in your reality.

Vividness requires precision and clarity of detail in your mental pictures. Spend some time examining your desired goals, drawing pictures of them either actually or mentally, or writing out clear descriptions of what your wishes would look like when they came true. Complex pictures will be accepted by your subconscious as a command and your subconscious mind will go immediately to work to coordinate all your other resources, internal and external, to bring those goals into your life.

Be precise. Be absolutely definite. Know what you want, visualize what you want, and say what you want. It will not do to say you want a lot of money or that you want a new car or a house. You must state exactly what it is that you want and hold that picture steadily before you, so strongly that you can feel the wish fulfilled.

If you want money (though if you are wise, you will not bother much about money—no one has ever taken a single coin into the next world), state definitely how much you want. It must be a definite sum. If prosperity is your goal, make part of your visualization definite plans for the good you will do with the prosperity you create. (Refer to Chapter 9: Opening Up to Abundance & Blessings in my book *Wired for High-Level Wellness* for all the key principles and suggestions to put you on the abundance train.)

Your visualizations can be turned into affirmations by making them real and vivid in your mind. Write down your major goals *in the present tense* on three-by-five index cards, one to a card, and review them on a regular basis. Read the goal—for example, "I have an hour each day for myself"—then close your eyes, breathe deeply, relax for a few seconds, and imagine what it would be like if you did indeed have that hour. Visualize some of the specific ways your life would change. Feel the feeling of calm and groundedness that comes with that extra time. Then open your eyes, smile, and go about your business, knowing in your mind's eye that you have already succeeded in achieving your goal.

Nearly three decades ago, one of my goals and dreams was to have a home-away-from-home, somewhere out in a natural setting where I could go to write and have some quiet and solitude. Although I wasn't sure where I wanted this home to be, I was very clear on some of my specific requirements: I wanted it to be a long way from a large city and crowds of people, and surrounded by trees and nature's sounds. The home itself needed to be made of wood and windows, have a spectacular view, and lend itself to my healthy lifestyle—sun, fresh air, organic garden, and space to work out. So, for a few months, I visualized this home. I wrote my vision down on three-by-five index cards and gave thanks that it was already a reality.

Fewer than six months later, I was invited to give a seven-day workshop in a town on the coast of Oregon. I had been there before, speaking at some Christian churches, a community center, and a local hospital. I had always thought it was a beautiful area but had never considered buying a home there. One evening I had a break during my workshop and was invited to visit some friends who lived on top of a forested hill overlooking the Pacific. During our conversation in their home, they mentioned that the house next door was for sale. I answered casually and didn't give the information any more thought until later: in the middle of the night, I was hit by a cosmic two-by-four and immediately realized I was supposed to buy that house next door to my friends. The realization seemed absurd because I hadn't even looked at the inside of the house. I simply knew it was meant to be mine and that it would be the perfect place for personal retreats and writing.

The next morning, I called my friends. They were delighted with my decision, even though they thought I was a little crazy! I called the realtor, and that's when I learned that the house was already in escrow, about to close. He would be happy to show me other homes, he said, but this one was no longer available. I told him, "You don't seem to understand. That's my home, and I'm not interested in looking at any others." I left my telephone number and asked him to call when the house was available. You can guess how the story turned out: it did become available, I made an offer, and it became my retreat home.

It certainly didn't come without roadblocks—the path of least resistance isn't always the best one. The whole process of creating my home presented me with one challenge after another. It taught me numerous lessons as well, such as the importance of belief and faith and not judging by appearances, such as being thankful for everything seen and unseen, and such as beholding the Divine in everyone and everything. By the way, my home-away-from-home was on top of a hill, surrounded by trees, overlooking the bay, had lots of light, and was filled with angels, just as I visualized it. I had never thought about that specific location, but I knew, when I had it, that it was the perfect place for me and was made possible because of my focused desire for it. After enjoying this living space for two decades, I then decided it was time to let it go so someone else could enjoy this beautiful home, and I have moved on to even greater adventures and goals, such as another home-away-from-home in England to be near many of my clients and family in that area.

TAKE A WORD INVENTORY

Like most of us, from time to time, I get into bad habits with words. Not too long ago, I was driving with David Craddock. The day was hot, and the traffic was heavy. A rude, reckless driver cut me off. I said in a loud voice, "I hate it when someone does that to me!" He looked very startled. He said, "Don't use the 'H' word. That's a terrible thing to put into your consciousness. Try instead, 'I prefer drivers not to cut me off in traffic,'" and then silently bless the driver."

I was in no mood to listen to a lecture. I felt like saying to him, "I hate it when somebody lectures me!" But I didn't do that because he was absolutely correct. Have you ever said, "That burns me up," "They're driving me crazy," "I am anxious to hear from you," or "This is backbreaking work"? These seemingly harmless expressions program garbage into your subconscious mind. For example, you don't want your body and mind to feel anxious. Change that phrase above to "I am eager to hear from you." Or "I look forward to hearing from you."

I hear people affirming they are "anxious" oftentimes throughout the day in the words they use, and I cringe when I hear them affirm this. The subconscious does not know that you don't really mean it. It plants those ideas in your experience storage center and plays them out into your life as if you really meant what you said. Just as an injurious diet weakens the body, leading inevitably to dis-ease, a regimen of negative thoughts and words debilitates the mind and soul, fostering unhappiness and an unfulfilled life.

Take an inventory of everything you say during the course of the day. Be aware of the words you use. Speak only those words that are positive, loving, and uplifting, and that represent what you want for yourself.

I've learned to pay attention to what I say (most of the time) and to interrupt negative expressions. When I find myself straying toward negativity, I usually say or think to myself "cancel" or "erase" and then change the words. I have also imagined in my mind's eye a large screen on which I write any negative expressions I've used and then draw an X through them. I have done this on paper, too, and then burned the paper. Use any method that is effective for you.

It can be a real challenge to find positive ways to say exactly what you mean. But it certainly can be done. For instance, notice how often you say, "I'm sorry" and instead try saying, "I apologize." Or perhaps instead of saying, "I'm afraid you have the wrong number" try, "You have the wrong number." After all, that is what you mean. For "I hate it when I my boss is in a bad mood," try "I prefer a cheerful workplace." As you find more ways to speak more accurately, you stop feeding your subconscious mind misinformation about yourself.

KEEPING YOUR WORD

You are as good as your word. In my opinion, when it comes to keeping your word, there is no such thing as a small situation. Perhaps it's no big deal to say we're going to call someone and then not do it, but it can be very important to the other person. It's very important to me that my friends and business associates be accountable—that their words count. When I learn that someone doesn't follow through on what he or she says they're going to do, and it's apparent that this is a pattern, I choose not to spend time with that person. To me, a verbal agreement is as serious and binding as a written one. In fact, I have verbal agreements, as opposed to written ones, with most of the companies for which I do consulting. People know my word is gold, and they can count on me.

I'm very inspired by people who make their word count. Every time my wonderful mom, June, made a promise, no matter how small or seemingly insignificant, she kept her word. If she made plans with someone and then was offered the opportunity to do something more exciting or interesting, she never hesitated one second before saying, "Thank you, I'd love to do it, but I already have a commitment." Mom's behavior invariably brought two reactions, both positive. The first friend was pleased because she and Mom did whatever they were going to do, and the second friend was impressed with her integrity. Mom was not only well liked, but she was also very happy and filled with joy. She was *as good as her word*. To me, there can be no higher praise than that.

Make your word count. It's a gift you give to your family, friends, business associates, community, and the world.

In a study conducted at Sussex University, subjects viewed a selection of television news broadcasts. The topics were positive, negative, or neutral. Not surprisingly, negative news broadcasts left the subjects in a bad mood and made most of them edgy. We always have a choice about what we look at and to what we give our attention. So reinforce positive thoughts, words, and actions by what you watch, and avoid putting your attention on negativity. Thoughts embroiled in negativity tarnish your perception of the beauties and miracles of life. Fill not only your conversation but also your consciousness with positive things. Surmount all life's challenges by following your heart and letting the Divine wisdom within you guide you to the realization of your dreams.

PATIENT PERSISTENCE IN THE GOOD

There's an unfathomable, yet recognizable, Divine order to this universe. It's ever-present and always working in alignment with what we need for our highest good and spiritual unfoldment and growth. I've learned not to analyze or question it anymore. It asks only for our trust, faith, and courage.

You are exactly where you need to be in life. At any moment you can choose to experience something else, simply by taking responsibility and consciously choosing to think differently. In the fantastic words of Nikos Kazantzakis who wrote *Zorba the Greek*, "You have your paintbrush and colors. Paint paradise, and in you go."

Assuming that one of your coveted goals is to create more prosperity in your life, the affirmation and action step to follow reflects this wish.

*When defeat comes, accept it as a signal that your
plans are not sound, rebuild those plans, and set
sail once more toward your coveted goal.*

~ Napoleon Hill

*Hope is one of the best ways to shed light on the process of
unfolding miracles—and it's part of the ongoing miracle itself.*

~ Thomas Kinkade

 ## Today's Affirmation

I am consciously aware of the spirit of Love, of God, within as my source, supply, and support. I deserve to prosper. The more I give of my money or myself, the more I prosper. I am connected to an unlimited source of abundance. My prosperity is coming to me now, and I give thanks.

 ## 12-Minute Action Step

Tithe your money today to a worthy person or organization. Do it with a loving heart. You might also prefer to put some money in an envelope and leave it at the door of someone you know who's going through a tough time. All you need to say is: "From someone who cares about you and appreciates you." Think prosperous thoughts today.

Chapter 12

Mindful &
Present Moment Living

*The ability to be in the present moment is a
major component of mental wellness.*

~ Abraham Maslow

*Every situation—no, every moment—is of infinite
worth; for it is the representative of a whole eternity.*

~ Johann Wolfgang von Goethe

iving *in* the moment is different from living *for* the moment. Children seem to be the masters of living in the moment, of being able to be totally engrossed in whatever they are doing. When they eat, they just eat; when they play, they just play; when they talk, they just talk. They throw themselves wholeheartedly into every activity.

I look back on my early childhood and remember not having any sense of time. My family frequently took long trips in the car. Usually within ten minutes of leaving, I would ask, "Are we there yet?" My only sense of time was now. It was sheer joy to have my family all together in the car taking trips to wonderful destinations. Seneca said, "True happiness is to . . . enjoy the present, without anxious dependence upon the future." As a child, I instinctively knew this, especially when I was with my family.

Carpe diem. That's Latin for "seize the day." Each day offers us an opportunity to look at the world anew and to celebrate being alive. You'll never have an opportunity to live this precious day again. Moment by moment, choose to be aware of everything around you. Notice the flowers, the air, your family pets, babies, the sunrise and sunset, the stars. Breathe in the radiance of these glorious miracles.

Have you ever noticed that young children are willing to try anything at a moment's notice? Even though they might have experienced the same thing before, they will express wide-eyed excitement and wonderment. Children don't use a yardstick to measure activities or compare the present with the past. They know they've played the game before or had someone read the same story just last night, yet the game or the story is still as fresh and as wonderful as it was the first time.

Think about your attitude when doing the dishes, vacuuming, or watering the plants. You probably find these activities boring. As I mentioned in Chapter 9, have you ever seen a child help with the dishes or vacuum or water the plants? A child acts as though it's just about the most exciting thing he or she has ever done. What a wonderful quality that is! It's only old thoughts and distorted attitudes that get in the way of celebrating each moment.

Often when I'm conducting a workshop or seminar in a beautiful, natural setting somewhere around the world, I ask the participants to go outside for 10 to 15 minutes, breathe deeply, and stroll the grounds, alone, in silence. I have them practice being totally absorbed in what they see, smell, taste, feel, and hear. To be with nature, letting its beauty into your awareness, is a wonderful experience. In taking this kind of walk, I have discovered that I feel a subtle, gentle communion with nature. The flowers, trees, birds, and even the insects seem to be in harmony with me.

When you give the present moment a chance to infuse your mind and heart, the glorious and serendipitous can blossom.

Most people work so hard at living that they forget how to life fully in the moment. When you give the present moment a chance to infuse your mind and heart, the glorious and serendipitous can blossom. Give the unexpected a chance to bloom through present-moment awareness combined with deep breathing.

Do your best each day to simplify your life and to value and experience the preciousness of nature and every moment. Rather than living with continual five- or ten-year plans, concentrate on living one day at a time, continuing to ask for guidance and direction each day. I ask my guardian angels daily to guide me and to bring more light and miracles my way. Don't look back in anger or regret, nor forward in fear or worry, but look around with conscious awareness and gratitude. George Gershwin, one of my favorite American composers and pianists, wrote, "My time is today."

To be fully present each moment, we must free ourselves from the past. Otherwise, the past will repeat itself and keep you trapped in it, as I write about in detail in my book *Be the Change*. When you're trapped in the past, you're not fully aware of the present; you can't see what's happening all around you.

No matter what issues you may be dealing with, the road to healing begins with a gentle step inward to seek the heart-light within. We must be gentle with ourselves and, with Divine help, be courageous. The shadow side of our nature is what we've hidden from ourselves out of fear. It is a repository filled with long-forgotten tears, secret anguish and pain, abdicated power, and thwarted dreams. It's the locked-away part of your soul. Your shadow is not itself dark, but it is hidden in a dark place where you have feared to go. You must take that step. If you feel it's too difficult to do on your own, seek help.

When you live in the present, breathe deeply, and keep awareness, you can live with heart, knowing that the love you are is all that is needed.

One of the splendors of being human is our capacity to learn from past mistakes. Don't let your fear hold you back. "I saw that all things I feared, and which feared me, had nothing good or bad in them save insofar as the mind was affected by them," wrote the Dutch philosopher Spinoza. *When you let go of fear, pain will unfold into joy, sadness will unfold to happiness, and hate will turn unto love.*

When you heal your past, your life will take on a new sense of wonder and celebration. You will become more aware of yourself and everything around you. When you live in the present, breathe deeply, and keep awareness, you can live with heart, knowing that the love you are is all that is needed. You will find yourself immersed in wisdom and peace and one with the Infinite, with God. Isn't that what living is all about? Don't wait any longer. Now is the time. Trust more and live with faith.

FAITHFULLY PRESENT IN THE NOW

In Chapter 9, I touched on faith, but because it's such an important part of being uplifted, I am adding in some more thoughts on it here. Comparatively few people today realize just how much faith-in-oneself (the part of oneself that is spiritual, perfect) has to do with achievement because the great majority of people never seem to conceive of faith as a being a genuine creative force. Yet the truth is that not only is faith a bona fide power, but it is the greatest one we will ever encounter.

In fact, I would go so far as to say that whatever you accomplish in your lifetime will be in direct proportion to the intensity and persistence of your faith. I think Martin Luther King, Jr., would probably agree. He wrote, "Faith is taking the first step even when you don't see the whole staircase." And Helen Keller gives us these sagacious words: "Faith is the strength by which a shattered world shall emerge into the light." These are both empowering quotations when you really think about what they were sharing with us.

DAVID AND GOLIATH

Consider the biblical story of David and Goliath (1 Samuel 17), which surely must rank as one of the greatest testaments ever written on the subject of faith. As you will recall, Goliath, the giant of Gath, came into the Israelite camp boasting pompously and taunting the Israelites to elect a man to do battle with him. The Israelites, naturally, were terrified, and, not surprisingly, none of them leaped forward to accept the challenge.

Sometime later, however, when Goliath returned to reiterate his challenge, David, an Israelite youth, overheard the giant's obnoxious boasting and he stepped forward to pick up the gauntlet. Finally, after much pleading before his elders for the dubious honor of facing Goliath in battle, the youth was accorded the great "privilege" of going forth to do battle.

The elders insisted, however, that David clothe himself in heavy protective armor. They also gave him a sword with which to smite his powerful adversary. But David said, "I am not used to these things, I cannot fight with these handicaps. These are not my weapons. I have other weapons with which to fight the giant." So, he stripped himself of all his armor and went into battle with no weapon other than a simple slingshot and a few pebbles he had gathered from the nearby brook.

When the giant leader of the Philistines, protected as he was with armor from head to toe, armed with mighty weapons, preceded by his shield-bearer, saw the unarmed, unprotected Israelite youth approaching, he was infuriated. He said to David, "Come to me, and I will give thee flesh unto the fowls of the air and to the beasts of the field."

Young David, however, never one to be intimidated, answered the giant saying, "Thou comest to me with a sword and a spear, and with a shield, but I come to thee in the name of the Lord of hosts, the God of the armies of Israel whom through has defied. This day will the Lord deliver thee into mine hands."

While the giant Goliath placed his faith in physical objects like armor, swords, and shields, David placed his solely in an unseen God. The result—the young Israelite shepherd defeated his far mightier foe! With nothing save a single stone from his sling, David struck Goliath, and the giant fell lifeless to the ground.

By accepting the principle "let go and let God," and believing that what-ever must happen to you to reach your goal will happen—like David—you, too, will successfully conquer the "giant" in your life (i.e., you will witness the physical manifestation of your image and in the proper time). You see, the trouble with those of us who fail to achieve what we desire is not that we lack the ability to do so, but that we lack the faith implicit in the "let go and let God" principle, which dictates whatever is necessary for us to reach our goal.

AN ENCHANTING ENCOUNTER ON HALLOWEEN

Before I end this chapter, I wanted to share with you a true story of how two little girls enriched my life and reminded me of the joy of living in the present moment. It was Halloween a few years ago. I was enjoying some quiet "me-time" in a café and being totally absorbed in the present moment and mindful of my surroundings in the Brentwood area of Los Angeles near my home at about two in the afternoon. The café was empty except for another table occupied by a mom and her twin girls who looked to be about five or six years old.

The girls were dressed in the same costumes, and they both looked like a princess, although I could not see the back of their attire. They were very animated and talkative, and I could tell that their mom seemed tired and overwhelmed. I, too, had wished that they could be more soft-spoken so I could enjoy my tea, soup, and salad more intently and not hear every word they were saying.

The mom's cell phone rang, and it was obvious from her excited response that it was important, yet it was hard for her to hear what her caller was saying. So she stood up, came to my table, and said that she needed to take this 10-minute call outdoors and could I please just keep an eye on her two girls. She said that they were used to her taking calls outside and would stay seated at the table. Their mom just wanted to let me know so I could keep an eye on them while she focused on her important call. "Sure, no problem," I said. "Take your time."

With one eye on the girls, I made my way over to the café's display of scrumptious homemade, natural desserts to see what I might want to purchase to take home with me. In my focus on the glorious display of tasty treats, I didn't see the brick step-up and the next thing I knew, I had tripped hard and was now lying on the café's floor. With a more bruised ego than a bruised body, I was glad that the only two other people who saw me fall were the twins.

Within about ten seconds of falling, they both ran over to me. One of them said, "Don't worry. We are angels and will take care of you. Show us your boo-boos."

Well, I was wearing a skirt and thought I'd go along with this precious scenario, as their gentle sweetness was so heartwarming to me. I showed them the minor scrapes on my lower legs. The other girl ran to her table to get some napkins and ran back and patted my leg and even kissed the bruises. I almost began to cry at their "lovingness." Nothing really hurt, and I wasn't bleeding, but I was so deeply touched by their genial gestures.

As I looked up, I saw that the mom was now inside the restaurant watching her girls take care of me. She gestured with her finger to her lips to not reveal that she was there. I could see that she was enjoying her daughters' actions toward me. After about three minutes, one of the girls told me, "Lady, take a deep breath and smile and your boo-boos will be all better. We are angels and we fixed you all up." The girls then helped me get up off the floor and then asked me why I wasn't wearing a Halloween costume. I told them that I was going home to get in my costume and that I would be dressing up as a butterfly. One of the twins said, "Angels are like butterflies. Do you want to go trick-or-treating with us tonight?"

Everything they did or said made me smile. I said I was not able to join them but that "I'd never forget how I had two beautiful angels take care of me today." Almost in unison, they said, "That's right, we are angels today and every day," and then they turned around, saw their mom walking back over to the table and they all sat back down.

As they were walking away, I noticed the wings on their costumes—they were dressed as adorable angels. They were, indeed, little angels who taught me on that very special day the importance of being kind to others (even strangers) and living in the present moment. I will never forget their kindness. I went to pay my bill, and I also paid for their lunch bill, without them knowing what I did. As I was leaving, I thanked them all for the special day they created for me, and I walked to my car with a big smile on my face that remained there for the rest of the day, night, and for weeks.

Write it on your heart that every day
is the best day of the year.

~ RALPH WALDO EMERSON

Optimism is the faith that leads to achievement.
Nothing can be done without hope and confidence.

~ HELEN KELLER

Today's Affirmation

I choose to live each moment to the fullest, one day at a time. I let go of the past and know that my future will be bright and happy because I live from love, trust, and faith. Divine order is taking place in my life right now.

 12-Minute Action Step

Find 12 minutes today to be by yourself. Whether in your home or office, or in your car or a place in nature, choose to be still, breathe deeply, keep your focus and attention on the present moment, and feel deep gratitude for your life. Think about dwelling in the present moment today. And while you are at it, think of all the things each day in which you always have faith such as the sun rising and setting each day, the change of seasons, the flowers growing in your garden, and the delicious taste of God's fresh fruits and vegetables.

Chapter 13

Food's Effect on Mood

The trick is to grow up without getting old.

~ Frank Lloyd Wright

The food you eat can be either the safest and most powerful form of medicine or the slowest form of poison.

~ Ann Wigmore

Almost everyone is familiar with the joy that comes from sharing a meal with family or friends. Eating is often a shared social experience, and pleasant memories and feelings are usually associated with these shared meals. Romantic relationships are often forged over home-cooked dinners or when dining out. We go out for meals to celebrate birthdays, graduations, anniversaries, and everything else, while we find comfort in the home-cooked styled meals we enjoyed as kids. Meals with family are often the only time family members come together during the week because of our increasingly demanding lives. Even the New Testament has more than several references to "breaking bread," something biblical figures did to promote social and spiritual bonds and to feel uplifted.

Although the positive emotions resulting from bonds created through food are obvious, what's less obvious to most is the fact that the negative emotions, which may arise afterward, can also be the direct results of that meal. It's becoming clearer to researchers every day that there is an undeniable gut-brain connection. The vagus nerve connects the two areas; while the gut sends signals about emotion to the brain, the brain, in turn, actually determines, and even alters, gut bacteria.

It seems that the writing is on the wall; of course, our food choices are affecting our moods. Unless we're choosing diets centered on wholesome plant-based foods, such as fresh fruits and vegetables, legumes, nuts and seeds, and homegrown sprouts, we may be setting ourselves up to feel irritable, depressed, anxious, angry, or even to develop something more serious like depression or exacerbate bipolar disorder. Studies have even revealed links between schizophrenia and diet. In this chapter, we'll evaluate some of the ways foods affect our moods and learn how we can make better dietary choices to optimize our well-being. And the next time you "break bread" with someone, you may decide that it's best to leave the literal bread out of the scenario and find a more "uplifting" alternative.

HOW GLUTEN AFFECTS MOOD AND OUR GUT ENVIRONMENT

You don't have to have celiac disease to have adverse reactions to gluten; it may just be more emotional than physical in nature for non-celiac sufferers. Gluten itself is problematic and is a topic we'll come back to. But first it's important to understand the role of glyphosate in the process of weakening our body's upper intestinal tracts. Our food system is, unfortunately, littered with chemicals, but this one really is especially egregious in terms of the destruction it causes to the ecosystem as well as our bodies.

So, what is it? Glyphosate is the herbicide used in Roundup, which is widely used on U.S. crops including wheat, rye, and barley. Meg Haworth, PhD, health and wellness author, and podcast host says that although you may not have a severe case, many Americans suffer from some level of leaky gut syndrome. "Most people have wildly unhealthy upper intestines," she claims, adding that "many of us have intestines which look like Swiss cheese." This leads to the chemicals leeching into the bloodstream and affecting the brain's regulation of serotonin and dopamine, the neurotransmitters required for a sense of well-being. When these are depleted, likely to result is some combination of irritability, depression, and anxiety. This is all in addition to the physical health implications that glyphosate has been determined to cause, most worryingly, non-Hodgkin's lymphoma.

But even if you eat a baguette in Austria, the one country where Roundup, as of the beginning of 2022, is currently banned, you may end up deciding to cancel your yodeling lessons due to a low mood. That's because you'll still be at risk to experience some form of depression, anxiety, irritability, or even a full-blown mental disorder because gluten itself doesn't need its accomplice, glyphosate, to wreak havoc. Gluten is responsible for causing "low moods" in studies of people without celiac disease. And it's even been linked to bipolar and depressive disorders as well as schizophrenia.

Although you may not be suffering from any of the latter, the fact that it can cause such mental instability is a stark fact that reveals gluten's terrifying power to alter body chemistry. So, it's no wonder that studies show that people not suffering from celiac disease, but who do have some gluten sensitivity, report improved moods after three days of gluten-restricted diets. This is compared to the study's participants who did continue to consume gluten. So skip the baguette, and the hills may still yet be alive with the sound of yodeling.

During your next visit to the grocery store, you may want to carefully consider what you're putting in your basket. Instead of the standard breads, pastas, baked goods, crackers, or even soup and beer, grab one of the gluten-free options, which are now so widely available. But even better might be to choose a plant-based food instead because, as I'll discuss later, fruits and vegetables supply not just nutrients for your body, but also for your brain, and could help boost your mood, even if you're already feeling pretty good!

> *To keep your body in great health throughout your life, choose from a variety of plant-based foods, including fresh fruits, vegetables, and legumes. Look at your diet as a bank account. Good food choices are sure-fire investments.*
>
> ~ WANDA HUBERMAN, EXECUTIVE DIRECTOR, NATIONAL HEALTH ASSOCIATION

PUT ON A HAPPY FACE WITHOUT ASPARTAME

If you've ever wondered why you may have shed a few pounds and were looking forward to an improved self-concept, new clothes, and thus a better overall outlook but were surprised when you instead found yourself sad, depressed, or irritable, it may be because of the diet alternatives you'd chosen. Aspartame, an artificial sweetener, is a ubiquitous sugar substitute and is loaded into all kinds of products, some of which may come as a surprise.

Although it most commonly shows up in diet sodas, frozen desserts, and juices, it may also be lurking in your nutrition bars, gum, and even flavored water. In fact, aspartame appears in about 6,000 products making it the most widely used sugar substitute. Two hundred times as sweet as sugar, aspartame is not surprisingly considered an "ideal" alternative for sweetening normally sugar-laden foods, the reason for its prevalence. And although choosing lower calorie products may be helping your waistline and making your dentist happy, it's likely it won't be making you happy. In fact, it may be making you quite unhappy.

Studies have found aspartame to cause dopamine- and serotonin-depleting effects in participants. This was evident when the participants described experiencing depression, anxiety, and irritability. In fact, one study was halted after some participants, in most cases who already had a history of depression, became too severely depressed for them to allow the study to continue. Although more testing is needed, there are fears that aspartame can lead to even more serious mental disorders as well as behavioral issues, especially in children. Some believe that the result of aspartame consumption is an even more depressed mood than you'd experience from a sugar crash. Don't despair though because you can still enjoy "sweetened" foods and beverages if you're forgoing sugar. Many people find stevia, a natural alternative to sugar, to be a satisfying sweetener. Just be sure to use it in moderation.

Personally, I think it's best to not use any sweeteners. It's better to reeducate your taste buds so they are not used to having sweet foods, and this even includes agave. While fraught with controversy because it's been touted as a low-glycemic sweetener—sending droves to the market to replace their sugar bowls—this ingredient contains excess fructose. And excess fructose (other than what's found in fresh fruits) increases the risk of metabolic syndrome, which primes you for brain shrinkage and mood instability. So my guidance to you is to stay away from add-on sweeteners, and when you are desiring something sweet, look, instead, to raw fresh fruit (apples, oranges, pears, berries, melons, kiwi, grapes, etc.) because they are chock-full of vitamins, minerals, flavonoids, enzymes, and natural water for healthful hydration.

UNFRIEND PROCESSED FOODS

For many, it's a shock to learn that the brain and gut are so intimately connected and affect each other so powerfully. But even if you are savvy about health and are already in on this fact, here's something that may yet still shock you: A whopping 90 percent of serotonin receptors are actually in the gut. This fact alone is enough to convince a skeptic of the link between the two regions of the body. There's even a new field called nutritional psychiatry, and many people training to become therapists are including certification in this area. This offers hope that future mental health care modalities of treatment will be more integrative. Although many Western medical doctors are still reluctant to acknowledge the food-mood connection, at least the field of psychology is advancing in the right direction.

One thing you will never catch these specialized practitioners promoting is fried and processed foods. Processed foods usually tend to contain one or more of the following: sugar, starch, food coloring, and/or hydrogenated fats. Somewhat ironically, the experience of eating processed foods triggers a dopamine-inducing effect, and it's why we so often forgo more nutritional foods; these foods trigger the reward center of the brain and cause cravings. But inflammation is the guest you may be inviting in, something bad for overall physical health. And it's also the cause of serotonin and dopamine leaving the party, causing the "hangover" to begin, and then you find yourself possibly with a low mood, irritable, anxious, or even, quite possibly, with full blown depression.

Unfortunately, these foods are appealing because they seem to offer solutions for our busy lives because they're often prepackaged and even microwaveable. Trying to balance work and home life is demanding and can lead to a lot of stress; therefore, grabbing some fast food or heating something up at home is an undeniably appealing way to manage time. But are we really doing ourselves any favors by making this choice? Unfortunately, this "life is moving too quickly for me to cook or indulge in self-care" mindset also causes so many of us to turn to antidepressants rather than modifying our behaviors and diets. The lesson here, once again, is that although it may momentarily be an attractive option, we're setting ourselves up for more stress, depression, and other negative feelings by causing inflammation in our bodies.

Investing in a little self-care by spending more time in the kitchen will pay off with more productivity. You'll quickly realize that your improved diet leads to more energy and a brighter outlook. This will be especially true if you involve other family members in the activity because studies show that cooking together is a bonding experience that can increase family harmony. And there are countless ways that this benefits kids, because not only will you develop bonds, possibly improving your relationships, but you'll also be teaching them about healthy eating, which can set them up for a lifetime of healthier choices. And don't forget about all the opportunities to be creative with cooking.

DAIRY

Once universally considered a diet staple and requisite part of a healthy and balanced diet, dairy has in recent years been implicated as a source of a whole host of health issues. You're probably familiar with some of them, but maybe you didn't know that it's also commonly associated with low moods and depression. Casein, a protein found in dairy, is the issue. The gut and brain respond to casein by creating antibodies that disrupt neurotransmitters and suppress the feel-good chemicals. A UCLA study indicates that dairy actually can affect the way the brain works. But it's not only that. Much of our milk contains hormones. You don't have to be a doctor to see how adding hormones to our bodies can send our them into chaos, leaving us in an emotional tailspin.

Still in the category of dairy, but possibly an exception to the above, is goat's milk. It contains more magnesium, a mood-boosting mineral, than cow's milk. And it's got probiotics, special fibers that create probiotics, which are necessary for good gut health. And studies in rats who consumed goat's milk have shown a reduction in oxidative stress, leading to decreased anxiety.

While I choose to not consume any dairy products at all, and I enjoy making or purchasing my own nondairy cheeses, sauces, and sour creams to use in my food preparations (see Chapter 14 for a nondairy sour cream recipe), if you do wish to eat dairy, I encourage you to learn more about dairy products made solely from goat's milk.

ALCOHOL CAN DAMPER MOOD

The party's over and you're left with a hangover. We all know about the price you pay for having too much of a good thing. But alcohol's effect on that next morning goes beyond the physical and, often, beyond just "the hangover day." Mood, as well as general health, is also quite often a victim of that hangover. This contributes to people often pouring another drink in an attempt to stave off the low mood, not realizing that they may be caught in a cycle, often a dangerous one.

Some Serious Alcoholic Side Effects

You don't need to abuse alcohol to experience some of the negative effects of overconsuming. Just one night of drinking can lead to several days of depression and anxiety because of the depletion of the feel-good guys we know so well now, serotonin and dopamine. Studies show that it can even cause anxiety and panic attacks in people who don't normally experience them. Many people drink with the intention of diminishing negative emotions and escaping from distress. This plan often backfires though since, the next day, you're likely to feel those difficult emotions even more intensely. Sure, you had some momentary relief perhaps. But the fallout the next day may reveal that it wasn't worth it. Moreover, alcohol consumption doesn't always necessarily lead to an "escape" and instead of feeling good in the moment, you may find those negative emotions exacerbated.

Serious alcohol abuse can result in even more frightening consequences. According to studies, alcoholism can lead to symptoms of psychosis and schizophrenia. This doesn't necessarily mean that a person is clinically psychotic or schizophrenic because they exhibit these symptoms; it means that their symptoms can mimic these serious disorders. The same is true of depression and anxiety. For a diagnosis, doctors need patients to be sober for several weeks to be able to determine whether the symptoms were alcohol related or whether they meet the standards for a clinical diagnosis of any of the above. And if the fact that alcohol abuse can generate such serious mental health issues isn't terrifying enough, get this: alcohol abuse can also cause psychosis and schizophrenia. That's quite a rap sheet.

The takeaway here is that alcohol is powerful. It alters brain chemistry and even disrupts hormone function. Of all of the substances we've discussed, alcohol most certainly is the most complicit in damaging your mood, not to mention your overall health.

(DIS)HONORABLE MENTIONS

So now that we know a bit more about how exactly those foods end up on our plates and destroy our moods, let's take a look at some of the poor-mood–inducing ingredients and which belong in the category of "mood killer."

- A UCLA study discloses that fructose damages brain cells and increases toxic molecules in the brain, which leads to all kinds of cognitive issues and is also a mood destroyer. This is not the fructose found in fresh, raw fruits, but from the additional fructose added to loads of packaged and processed foods.

- Industrial fats like hydrogenated vegetable oil and omega-6 fatty acids block the absorption of omega-3 fatty acids, which we want because they're important for helping maintain a positive mood. Flaxseeds, chia seeds, and walnuts are great sources of omega-3 fatty acids.

- Monosodium glutamate (MSG) is often vilified by nutritionists, as well it should be. It will leave you feeling moody and irritable as well as physically fatigued. MSG is an ingredient that turns up often where you don't expect it to, so be sure to read food labels.

- Saturated fats will mess with your blood sugar. As you may well be aware, when blood sugar is low due to hunger, we can get "hangry" as they say. You don't need to be hungry though to feel this way because saturated fats will tamper with blood sugar and may create that same "hangry" sensation.

- Refined carbohydrates, found in white bread, white flour, white rice, pasta, sodas, and more, have a high glycemic index. What does that mean? It means they spike blood sugar levels and insulin. Although that may make you feel momentarily energized, it ends up leaving you feeling not so great mood wise.

Chips, cereal, margarine, condiments, seasonings, baked goods, packaged meats, white bread, and anything containing sunflower, corn, soybean, and cottonseed oils are some of the foods with the above ingredients and therefore on the "naughty list."

HALL OF FAME

Eliminating or reducing the foods in the last section will certainly go a long way in improving your mood. But it's not just about eliminating food from the diet. What you replace those items with is just as important, especially because many foods can improve your mood and give you an extra boost, as long as you're also mostly avoiding the problematic foods we already discussed.

As I learned from my grandmother when I was in my teens and early twenties, and this wise nutrition lesson has only been strengthened through decades of research ever since, I believe that food is medicine. In fact, food is the most simple and effective form of drugs or prescriptions there is. When consuming the right nutrients, the natural, plant-based foods of the earth, the natural healing capabilities in our bodies kick into gear. Foods high in phytochemicals (phytonutrients), natural compounds found in a variety of fruits and vegetables, can even have the power to fight cancer and disease as well as uplift mood.

> . . . food is the most simple and effective form of drugs or prescriptions there is.

A clean diet can greatly improve mental health, and many people are beginning to realize that they can, by eating well and exercising, ditch their antidepressants. This is not to say that this is the solution for everyone on antidepressants, but it is a powerful statement about food's incredible power to determine how we feel.

As we already discussed, 90 percent of our serotonin receptors are in our guts. There are foods that create a healthy "biome," meaning that these serotonin receptors are quite possibly increased when certain foods act as **probiotics** for the gut. Other foods contain **flavonoids,** which increase blood flow to the brain, resulting in a better mood.

As referenced earlier, **omega-3 fatty acids** are linked to positive moods, and studies show that consumption in the form of fish oil is linked to lower levels of depression. (Make sure your fish oil is purified and free of mercury if you take it; Hallelujah Diet offers a clean fish oil capsule.)

Vitamin B6 is important to producing the neurotransmitters serotonin and dopamine. Other **B vitamins** also work to produce those, as well as norepinephrine and gamma aminobutyric acid (GABA).

Fiber as we all know is good for the gut, and by keeping the gut healthy, we're helping allow serotonin and dopamine to do their thing. Not only that, but fiber also helps to regulate blood sugar levels so as to prevent sugar spikes, which invariably undermine our mental stability.

The conclusion of a recent study published in *Neurology*, revealed that students (368 healthy university students aged 18 to 43 years) with a higher **carotenoid** (plant-based pigments known as much for their robust antioxidant power as their brilliant orange to reddish hues) intake may have a better quality of sleep and lower risk of depression.

Tryptophan is an amino acid and also a mood enhancer because of the affect it has on serotonin, while zinc and selenium may be as well, although more research is needed.

Many people are aware that the sun produces **vitamin D** and that a lack of sun exposure can lead to seasonal affective disorder (SAD), which causes depression. But the way around this, even in the wintertime, is to consume more vitamin D in your foods or in supplemental form.

Salvestrol is a powerful phytonutrient that has been found in studies, when consumed through dietary plants and supplementation, to effectively kill cancer cells while keeping healthy cells intact. The case studies of melanoma, bladder cancer, prostate cancer, lung cancer, and breast cancer used salvestrol supplementation as well as incorporated diet changes. Because of its antioxidant properties, it has also been found to help combat stress and anxiety and promote a calm mood. Keep in mind that salvestrol levels were found to be 30 percent higher in organic produce than nonorganic fruits and vegetables.

Finally, **folic acid, resveratrol, vitamin C, iron, iodine, magnesium, and antioxidants** are also touted to be mood boosters.

Although the list of minerals and vitamins and other assorted ingredients above is not exhaustive, it's pretty close. But you're probably not going to remember all of those details anyway. What you will remember though, hopefully, is the foods they're contained in. So, without further ado, here's a list of those containing the above and which you'll be sure to load up your cart with on your next grocery store visit, and the next one, and the next one, and the next one. Keep in mind that all produce is rich in fiber, which supports gut health and vitality.

High in vitamin B6: Bananas, carrots, spinach, leafy greens, sweet potatoes

High in B vitamins: Beans, lentils, spinach, collard greens, turnip greens, romaine lettuce, leafy greens, nutritional yeast, fortified cereal, sunflower seeds

High in flavonoids: Quinoa, berries, red cabbage, onions, kale, parsley, dark chocolate, citrus fruits, soybeans

High in resveratrol: Grapes, red grape juice, peanuts and peanut butter, dark chocolate, strawberries, blueberries, pistachios

High in folic acid: Bok choy, turnip greens, eggs, legumes, broccoli, bananas, citrus, nuts and seeds, asparagus, avocados, fortified grains

High in antioxidants: Berries, broccoli, apricots, raspberries, cherries, watermelon, cinnamon, thyme, peppermint, oregano and oregano oil, kidney beans, cranberries, artichokes, spinach, oranges

High in fiber and iron: Oats, quinoa, spinach, legumes, tofu, pumpkin seeds, dark chocolate

High in prebiotics (precursor to probiotics): Fermented foods, including sauerkraut, kimchi, miso soup, tempeh, yogurt, kombucha, and kefir

High in carotenoids: Carrots, orange/yellow/red bell peppers, apricots, collard greens, kale, acorn squash, sweet potatoes, spinach, pumpkin, tomatoes (especially canned tomatoes)

High in omega-3s fatty acids: Fatty fish, flaxseeds, chia seeds, walnuts, soybeans

High in vitamin D: Shiitake and portobello mushrooms, soy milk, fatty fish, egg yolks, fortified cereals, tofu, vitamin D supplements

High in magnesium: Chickpeas, dark chocolate, bananas, tofu, edamame, black beans, leafy greens, pumpkin and chia seeds, grains, avocados

High in tryptophan: Nuts and seeds, turkey and chicken, oats, banana, tofu, lentils, pumpkin seeds, sunflower seeds, chia seeds, spirulina, cheese, eggs

High in salvestrol: Strawberries, grapes, oranges, blueberries, black currants, tangerines, apples, cranberries, cauliflower, broccoli, bell peppers, cabbage, Brussels sprouts, olives, avocados, sage, rosemary, mint, parsley, basil, thyme

RAW FOODS ARE GREAT FOR UPLIFTING MOOD

Raw fruits and vegetables may be better for your mental health than cooked ones, according to a new study from the University of Otago in New Zealand. The study, published in *Frontiers in Psychology*, found that people who ate more uncooked produce had lower levels of symptoms related to depression and other mental illnesses, compared to those who ate more cooked, canned, or processed varieties. The study was only able to show an association between raw produce and better mental health, not a cause-and-effect relationship. But the researchers say the link could have to do with the fact that many fruits and vegetables have more nutrients in their natural state—and that those nutrients may have a positive impact on mood and brain chemistry.

For the study, researchers surveyed more than 400 young adults, ages 18 to 25, in the United States and New Zealand. People in this age group tend to consume a relatively low level of fruits and vegetables, the authors point out, and are also at high risk for mental health disorders. The participants were asked about their typical consumption of fruits and vegetables, including which specific varieties they ate and how the produce was prepared. They were also screened for symptoms of mental illnesses, like depression and anxiety. The study authors knew that plenty of other variables could influence both mental health and fruit and vegetable consumption. So they also made sure to consider participants' exercise habits, overall diet, existing health conditions, socioeconomic status, ethnicity, and gender.

Even after controlling for those lifestyle and demographic factors, the association between raw vegetables and positive mental health outcomes was significant. Raw fruit and vegetable consumption predicted lower levels of depression and improved levels of psychological well-being, the authors wrote, including positive mood, life satisfaction, and flourishing. By contrast, intake of fruit and vegetables that were processed (by cooking, canning, or other methods) was associated only with positive mood—not with any of the other mental health variables measured in the study.

Overall, the ten foods in the study that were most strongly associated with positive mental-health outcomes were carrots, bananas, apples, dark leafy greens (such as spinach), grapefruit, lettuce, citrus fruits, fresh berries, cucumber, and kiwifruit. In the raw vegetable category, celery, cabbage, red onion, tomato, and mushrooms were also associated with positive mood. The authors note that these veggies can be considered "salad fixings," and they cite previous research linking salad consumption with lower stress levels. In the processed produce category, pumpkin, mixed frozen vegetables, potatoes and sweet potatoes, broccoli, and eggplant were linked to positive mood, as well.

The researchers say their findings are important because most current health guidelines do not distinguish between raw and cooked or canned fruits and vegetables. "If our patterns are confirmed in intervention studies, it would suggest that health policies could focus on promoting the consumption of raw and unprocessed produce for optimal well-being," they wrote in their paper.

The study wasn't designed to answer the question of why raw foods might be better for mood and mental health, and the researchers can only speculate. But they say that nutritional differences between raw and cooked produce may play a role. "Raw fruits and vegetables may provide greater levels of micronutrients than processed fruits and vegetables, which could explain their stronger association with improved mental well-being," they wrote. For compounds like vitamin C and carotenoids that have been linked to mental health, "cooking and canning would most likely lead to a degradation in nutrients, thereby limiting their beneficial impact on mental health."

However, the study authors point out, this level of degradation varies from food to food—and from nutrient to nutrient. Some vitamins and minerals become diminished when cooked, while others may become more readily available, such as with tomatoes. More research is also needed to know whether differences between raw and cooked produce are actually enough to affect mood and mental health, the researchers wrote.

For peace of mind, delicious meals, and to support my mental health, my goal is to eat as many raw foods as possible every day, and on many days, I'll eat only delectable, beautiful, raw leafy green salads with lots of vegetables along with some fresh fruit, and I always feel better throughout the day—sleep better, have more energy and a sharper, more focused brain, and overall feel more uplifted.

HYDRATE WITH WATER

And, finally, let's remember the importance of water. It often turns out that when we're feeling cranky, it's actually a result of dehydration. Many people just simply don't drink enough. Just a 3 percent drop in your body's hydration level can have an effect on your mental health, leading to anxiety, depression, irritability, crankiness, and more.

The recommended water intake levels vary depending on your weight, daily exercise, and the climate in which you live, but roughly six to eight glasses of 8-ounce cups of purified, clean water are considered sufficient. Decaffeinated teas and fresh vegetable juices can contribute to your tally. For my preference in drinking and cooking water, please refer to my website for many articles I've written/posted on the Ionizer Plus Alkaline Water Electrolyzer, which I have been using in my kitchen for over twenty-five years to make fresh, purified water every day. I wouldn't be without this perfect pH health-boosting water in my healthy living program. On my website, you will find out how to get a discount on your purchase of one of these health-enriching devices.

FINAL THOUGHTS

Because you're reading this book, I know that you value your health, your personal relationships, personal growth, and self-reflection. You've worked hard to achieve more from life and are on a journey to discover more ways to enrich your life and the lives of those around you. You already bring so much to the table socially, professionally, and spiritually. What you're literally bringing to the table, though, is also affecting your mission, whether or not you realized it. The nutritional aspect of the spiritual and psychological growth we're seeking is undeniable. If you've been undermining yourself with your diet, there are many reasons to be optimistic though because you have to power to change your mood, and it's right at the end of your fork or spoon.

And let's not forget that these foods are not just healthy for the mind, but also for the body with a bonus side effect of improved circulation and thus brighter skin and hair as well as a slimmer physique. And that leads to one more way these foods might improve your mood, by improving the chances that you'll like what you see in the mirror.

Remember that the dietary modifications you make do not have to be all at once, and it's certainly not a paradigm requiring an all-or-nothing approach. Small changes can make a difference. Eliminating one or two of the "foods to avoid" while introducing some of the good foods on a more regular basis is a good way to start. This may require more time in the kitchen than your schedule seems to allow for, but as already discussed, when you start eating better, you actually have more energy and feel less sluggish, making it easier to find the time to cook.

But there are some shortcuts. I find smoothies to be a quick and delicious way to get a lot of fruits and veggies. (Refer to my book *Wired for High-Level Wellness* for some quick, nutritious, and delicious smoothie and other whole-food recipes.) Include almond milk as your liquid base combined with some tea or water or nondairy yogurt or, if you prefer, goat milk yogurt in that smoothie and you'll have a super-duper smoothie, a powerhouse of mood-enhancing ingredients. And don't forget that there's no prep work needed to break off a piece of dark chocolate, one of the most enjoyable ways to get some of the good stuff.

Many of the mood-deflating foods mentioned earlier, it's true, can be addicting. But even more addicting is feeling good. And once you do, you won't look back. You'll just be glowing from inside and out! Armed with all your new knowledge, you're on your way to feeling and looking better than ever.

HERBAL TEAS TO LIFT MOOD & LIGHTEN STRESS

Have You Met Melissa (Lemon Balm)?

Whether you know this uplifting herb as Melissa, lemon balm, sweet balm, or simply balm, you know this gentle yet effective remedy is a must for any natural medicine kit. One of my all-time favorites, the aromatic lemon balm has been providing soothing relief for centuries and is a popular home remedy with benefits for the entire family.

The Latin name for lemon balm is *Melissa officinalis*, and alas, there's no dramatic legend behind its namesake. The genus name *Melissa* is actually derived from the Greek for honeybee. Why? In the garden, the pleasant lemony scent and pretty flowering plant attract bees (back in the day, it was even reportedly rubbed on beehives to encourage bees to make high-quality honey).

Five Reasons to Love Lemon Balm

Centuries-old texts described lemon balm in such glowing terms as *elixir of life, heart's delight,* and *elixir of youth;* and as the herb *to sweeten the spirit* and *to make the heart merry.* European herbal guides cited it for memory, and Ayurvedic writings list lemon balm for digestion and mood support. What about today? Herbalists, love the lemony scented herb to:

- Promote positive mood and emotional well-being
- Calm nervous irritability, stress, and tension
- Relieve occasional indigestion (it's a member of the mint family)
- Support restful sleep for both adults and children

How to Use Lemon Balm

1. Add lemon balm to unpleasant tea blends to improve their flavor.
2. Make a tasty teatime blend by combining lemon balm, linden, and chamomile.
3. For occasional sleeplessness due to grief and heartbreak, blend lemon balm with rose and lavender.

Chamomile Tea

Another one of my favorites, chamomile, is more than just a calming beverage to consume before bedtime. Chamomile is an herb taken from the flowers of the Asteraceae plant family. People around the world have been using it as a natural remedy for several health conditions since ancient times. What makes it so special? Well, it contains a variety of bioactive phytochemicals, notably flavonoids that function as antioxidants. It also contains small amounts of minerals and vitamins, such as potassium, calcium, carotene, and folate, among other nutrients.

Several research studies suggest chamomile can benefit our bodies in a variety of ways, including a lower risk of death from heart disease, immune system support, and possible protection against some cancers. According to a research review, chamomile tea may even help women who suffer from premenstrual syndrome. Other researchers tout the tea's anti-inflammatory and anti-anxiety effect. And if that wasn't enough, other studies show chamomile might even slow age-related bone loss.

There are other benefits when using chamomile tea topically, too. I will sometimes brew up some chamomile tea in a saucepan, turn off the heat, and put my clean face over the steamed tea with a towel over my head to steam my skin. It's soothing and very hydrating. I also put used, damp chamomile tea bags over my closed eyes (clean and free from any makeup) and relax with the teabags on for 12 minutes, and voila, my eyes look refreshed.

St. John's Wort

If your goal is to brighten your mood, St. John's wort would be a good choice. It is a perennial herb that grows in the wild in its native European lands. However, due to its rising popularity in homeopathic medicine, many supplement manufacturers now cultivate St. John's wort all around the world. Depending on the country, St. John's wort may also be known as "goat weed" or "rosin rose."

St. John's wort flowers in the summer season, producing tiny yellow flowers that provide a significant effect on the chemical, hormonal, and physical behavior of the human body. St. John's wort is one of the few natural herbal remedies extensively studied by medicinal science.

As a result, many doctors may recommend that patients use St. John's wort to treat inflammation, nervous system disorders, and skin issues. Where it really shines is with depression.

Say Goodbye to Depression by Befriending St. John's Wort

St. John's wort has been described as "arnica for the nerves" because it eases stress, tension, and nervous irritability. It's also very popular for its antidepressant nature and has been used for a few decades to treat and relieve symptoms of depression. In fact, it's now a leading new-generation, natural, over-the-counter medication for the treatment of the disorder, and it's fast becoming the favorite natural remedy doctors and psychiatrists prescribe to their patients. My grandmother knew of the effectiveness of St. John's wort decades ago and recommended it to me when I was experiencing depression and anxiety as a teenager from being bullied at school and later after I had a serious car accident that led to severe depression.

The conventional treatment for depression is the administration of antidepressant medication, such as SSRIs. When a person experiences moderate and or severe depression, doctors and psychologists tend to prescribe SSRIs or antipsychotics. Fortunately, some physicians are changing their therapy treatments for a more natural approach to treating this mental health disorder. If you have bipolar or psychosis, it's critical you listen to your doctor or psychologist and follow your medication schedule, but you can take St John's wort under their direction as well.

St. John's wort contains a rare combination of polyphenol antioxidants that act on the nervous system and neurological pathways in the same manner as antidepressant compounds. They delay or inhibit certain neurotransmitters, including dopamine, norepinephrine, and serotonin.

So, perk up your spirits with St. John's wort! This popular "mood food" is one of the most requested herbs for supporting emotional well-being. I often combine it in a cup of tea with lemon balm and chamomile.

Other Nutritious Brews

When you're feeling down, stressed, or anxious, you can also brew yourself a cup of:

GREEN TEA: Drinking green tea may support a healthier mood, according to twenty-one reviewed studies on the topic. Scientists say that green tea's l-theanine, along with caffeine, may support lower stress levels, improved memory, and healthier brain function, too. Another body of research noticed that women were better able to relax when drinking green tea as well.

MATCHA TEA: Matcha tea, which is made from grinding whole green tea leaves, contains higher levels of l-theanine than regular green tea. This means it may have even more powerful mood-boosting effects. Scientists in one review of forty-nine studies found that the l-theanine and caffeine combination in matcha tea may help support relaxation, decrease tension, and promote feelings of calmness.

The l-theanine/caffeine combo also means you may experience a state of "relaxed alertness" where you're calm and ultra-focused at the same time.

TURMERIC TEA: Turmeric, which is part of the ginger family, has been used in traditional Chinese medicine (TCM) and Ayurveda for thousands of years. It contains over 200 phytochemical compounds, with the most well-studied being curcumin. Research shows this polyphenol may support healthy BDNF levels (brain-derived neurotrophic factor), which may improve your mood and help you better deal with stressful situations. In a meta-analysis of nine studies, scientists discovered curcumin may improve depression and anxiety symptoms, too.

To make your own turmeric tea, all you need is fresh or ground turmeric and hot water. Most mornings, I cut up three to six coin-thick slices of fresh turmeric root and also coins of ginger root and simmer them for 12 minutes for a delicious, resplendent golden-hued fresh tea.

Aromatherapeutic Teas for Better Moods

Along with teas and tisanes (dried herb infusions), studies are also starting to prove that aromatherapy may be beneficial for your mental health. Aromatherapy is the practice of using fragrant plant extracts and essential oils to promote improved health. Here are my favorite mood boosters:

MENTHOL: When researchers examined the menthol in peppermint and ylang-ylang extract, they learned that the peppermint helped enhance memory and alertness while the ylang-ylang increased calmness. So sipping on peppermint tea may help you breathe in these powerful aromas and relax.

LAVENDER extract helped improve both mood and anxiety in a small study of neurology patients in a long-term intensive care unit. Researchers found that the lavender contributed to better mood scores and lower psychological distress. I often drink lavender and rose teas combined with chamomile and/or lemon balm.

BERGAMOT EXTRACT, which emits a citrus smell, has also been shown to combat stress and anxiety when inhaled via aromatherapy. You'll often find bergamot in earl grey tea, or you can purchase it in tea bags. I have liquid hand soap, dish soap, and counter spray from a popular store all made with bergamot.

You can either sip teas with these extracts or add them to your essential oil diffuser while drinking the calming teas mentioned earlier. You'll double your mood-enhancing efforts and quickly slip into a state of stress-free bliss.

Final Thoughts on Drinking Tea for Mood Enhancement

If you're looking to boost your mood naturally, or need a quick pick-me-up, don't underestimate the power of tea leaves and aromatherapy to melt away your stress. Find comfort in the ritual of brewing the perfect cup of tea, inhaling the calming aromas, and taking a minute to meditate and find your center again. These natural remedies have been shown to support better moods. And they may be enough to lift your spirits in these uncertain times, like a rainbow after a terrible storm.

KEEP OLBAS NATURAL REMEDIES ON HAND

Originating in Basel, Switzerland, Olbas is a blend of natural essential oils specially formulated for all ages, from children to senior adults. Olbas delivers invigorating and soothing sensations to the nasal and bronchial areas, calms coughs, cools sore throats, relieves aches and pains, and much more. For over forty years, the entire line of essential Olbas natural remedies has been front and center in my home's natural medicine chest. Just breathing in the soothing sensations from the Olbas inhaler, oil, lozenges, herbal bath, salve, or tea always calms and relaxes me almost instantly. For more information or to order any of the very affordable Olbas products, please visit **Olbas.com**. Additionally, I write about these superlative products on my website, SusanSmithJones.com.

THE POWER OF MOLECULAR HYDROGEN INHALATION THERAPY

Before I end this chapter, I want to share with you about the mood-boosting, positive healing effects of molecular hydrogen inhalation therapy. If I need a mood-lifter, I will drink a tea where I've blended, perhaps, chamomile and lemon balm while I am breathing in the soothing, calming air from the hydrogen inhaler made by the Vital Reaction Company in Boulder, Colorado (refer to my website for detailed information, several articles, many studies, and how to get a substantial discount on your purchase of a hydrogen inhaler).

An inhaler produces regulated amounts of hydrogen gas mixed with oxygen, which saturates arterial blood, penetrates cell membranes, and easily crosses the blood-brain barrier to provide benefits at the subcellular level. In more than 1,000 scientific studies, the healing and health benefits of molecular hydrogen inhalation have been shown to include improved digestion, lowered blood pressure, pain relief, more youthful skin, increased energy, faster exercise recovery, brain health, allergy relief, easier weight loss, an uplifted mood, and much more.

I take Vital Reaction's portable unit with me when I travel, and at home, I will often use the 7% Hydrogen Inhaler for hours at a time while working at my desk, reading, or watching TV. It has made a profound difference in my health, energy, vitality, and mood enhancement.

Education is the best provision for old age.

~ ARISTOTLE

*He who is calm and of a happy nature will hardly
feel the pressure of age, but to him of the opposite
disposition, youth and age are equally burdensome.*

~ PLATO

Today's Affirmation

I choose to eat foods that make me feel good about myself. The foods I eat are fresh, natural, wholesome, and free of any preservatives, colorings, and refined sugar and sugar substitutes. As a result of my healthy diet, I am healthy, strong, and a shining example of God's light, enthusiasm, and radiance.

 ## 12-Minute Action Step

Look through your kitchen cupboards and refrigerator today and toss out what has expired or is not something you'd want to eat anymore because it doesn't support your goal of vibrant health. Next, start a new grocery list with only wholesome foods and make sure to add on this list some foods you've never eaten before or that you haven't enjoyed in a long time. For example, when was the last time you had a kiwi or an artichoke or endive? Be courageous and adventurous today with your grocery list.

Chapter 14

Establish Healthy Habits with Exercise & Superfoods

*I still get wildly enthusiastic about little things . . . I play with
leaves. I skip down the street, and run against the wind.*

~ Leo Buscaglia

*Far away there in the sunshine are my highest aspirations.
I may not reach them, but I can look at them to see their
beauty, believe in them, and try to follow where they lead.*

~ Louisa May Alcott

Modern living has channeled the average American into an increasingly
sedentary existence. We human beings, however, were designed and
built for movement, and our bodies have not adapted well to this reduced
level of activity. As we've learned, what we put into our bodies is of utmost
importance, but how we use and move them is just as integral.

For many adults with sedentary occupations, physical activity provides
an outlet for job-related tensions or mental fatigue. In addition to reducing
tension in the body, exercise can boost spirits and help us feel good about
ourselves. Exercise has also been found to aid in weight control or reduction,
to improve posture, and to increase energy. Further, my experience indicates
that many cases, in fact about half, of lower back pain can be traced to poor
muscle tone and inflexibility. Proper exercise can often prevent or correct
lower back pain. Research also indicates that much of the degeneration of
bodily function and structure associated with premature aging seems to be
reduced by a program of vigorous, regular exercise.

Regular exercise is necessary to develop and maintain not only an optimal level of health but also a youthful appearance, mental clarity, and high energy. Regular exercise increases muscle strength and endurance. It enhances the function of the lungs, heart, and blood vessels; it increases the flexibility of the joints; and improves coordination and efficiency of movement.

But before you can experience any of the benefits of vigorous exercise, you must take responsibility for your own fitness program and for choosing those activities that promote fitness. My aim in this chapter is to cite research that will convince you of the advantages of following a well-rounded fitness program. I will concentrate on how exercise contributes to your self-image, happiness, peace of mind, and an upliftment of your life. I have gone into this topic in much greater detail in my free Exercise Webinar and in my book *Invest in Yourself with Exercise*. There you'll find loads more information that will empower you to make exercise a regular part of your health program.

"A sound mind in a sound body" emanates from a traditional Latin motto. Researchers are finding, however, that there's much more to the adage than might first appear. It seems that our sense of happiness and well-being depends on how much exercise we get. Malcolm Carruthers, head of a British medical team, believes that "most people could ban the blues with a simple, vigorous ten-minute exercise session three times a week." He came to this conclusion after spending four years studying the effect of norepinephrine on 200 people. Norepinephrine is a depression-destroying hormone, "The chemical key to happiness," according to Carruthers. Ten minutes of exercise doubles the level of norepinephrine in the body.

Enkephalin is another spirit-lifting chemical produced in the brain during vigorous aerobic exercise. Enkephalins are the source of the feeling known as runner's high. Enkephalin is a type of endorphin—a morphine-like chemical that serves as a natural opiate, increasing pain tolerance and producing euphoric feelings. A study at Massachusetts General Hospital found a rise of more than 145 percent in endorphins during one hour of vigorous exercise. So, you might want to heed the words of Paul Dudley White, MD, who once said: "Walk your dog every day, whether you have a dog or not."

Exercise can work in conjunction with psychotherapy to alleviate depression, according to work done at the Menninger Clinic in Topeka, Kansas. "It's not a panacea, but it is a useful adjunct for treating depression," says the clinic's Robert Conroy. One of Conroy's hypotheses is that exercise boosts self-image by changing an individual's worldview from that of passive bystander to active participant. People who exercise believe they have control over their health and the quality of their lives.

Exercise works better than tranquilizers do to eliminate symptoms of tension and anxiety. Herbert de Vries, exercise physiology lab director at the University of Southern California, conducted a classic study of tense and anxious people. As one part of the experiment, he administered 400-milligram doses of meprobamate, the main ingredient in many tranquilizers. In the second part, he had the same group of people take a walk vigorous enough to raise their heart rates over a hundred beats per minute. De Vries measured tension levels by monitoring the amount of electrical activity in the subjects' muscles. "Measuring electrical activity in muscles is the most objective way to measure a person's nervousness," he says. He found that after exercise, electrical activity was 20 percent less than the subjects' normal rate. After being dosed with meprobamate, the subjects showed little change in the electrical activity in their muscles. "Movement is strong medicine," de Vries concluded.

By releasing tension, exercise alleviates those tension-related bodily malfunctions such as ulcers, migraine headaches, asthma, skin eruptions, high blood pressure, and heart disease. Exercise also leads to a good night's sleep, a key to mental well-being.

Aerobic activity is the kind of exercise that produces truly beneficial psychological and biochemical changes. Vigorous, rhythmical activities such as jogging, brisk walking, running, swimming, aerobic dancing, rowing, cross-country skiing, hiking, cycling, and stair-climbing appear to send messages to the brain as well as the endocrine system to shape up and feel good. Also, keep this in mind: Exercise outdoors in nature, such as hiking, walking at your local park, biking, or jogging at the beach whenever you have a choice of indoor or outdoor workouts. Hiking is my favorite way to exercise. You not only strengthen your body; you are strengthening your mind and soul as well.

Exercise is a rewarding and enjoyable means of taking control of your psychological and physical well-being. A well-designed physical fitness program can add years of fulfillment, vibrant health, and peace of mind to your life. (And that knowledge alone has a potent positive effect on mental well-being.)

WHOLE-BODY VIBRATION EXERCISE

Before I end this section on exercise, I want to share with you one of my favorite ways to get exercise in my home. It's with whole-body vibration exercise. If you visit my website, SusanSmithJones.com, you can read my detailed article, which includes a clinical study I did, about how this easy exercise can help to support brain health, improve mood, strengthen bones, boost circulation, support balance, and so much more. With great versatility, you can simply stand on the machine and let your body vibrate as you get healthier with each session, or you can carry out what I do, which is to couple the vibration exercise with using resistant bands, dumbbells, and more. I even do squats, planks, and ab work on my device.

The vibration device I use is by RockSolidWholesale.com—model RS2200. If you use the promo code LiveFit, you'll receive free shipping in addition to a free resistance band package, as well as a substantial 90 percent discount on this machine. To order, visit their website or contact their team of experts at: 888-476-9995. Celebrate the miracle of your body with exercise.

Continuous effort—not strength or intelligence—
is the key to unlocking our potential.

~ WINSTON CHURCHILL

Shake yourself awake. Develop a hobby. Let the winds of
enthusiasm sweep through you. Live today with gusto.

~ DALE CARNEGIE

Today's Affirmation

I love to exercise, and I do so regularly. Exercise brings me more energy, mental clarity, self-confidence, and peace of mind. Taking care of my body is my way of saying thank you to God for my health and my life.

 *12-Minute Action Step*

Find a way to exercise today for at least 12 minutes. You could even step in place while watching TV. Be active today. Think about how much you want to get into peak shape.

USING FOODS AS MEDICINE

Each patient carries his own doctor inside him.

~ ALBERT SCHWEITZER

When you put your force, energy, and love behind something, the results will be astounding and rewarding.

~ DAVID CRADDOCK

If we were to trace the roots of modern medicine, they would lead back to the rich soil of the earth's fields and forests. On every continent, stretching back centuries, native cultures turned to indigenous plants to develop healing practices. More than 4,500 years ago, Chinese and Indian healers began to organize bodies of knowledge about the medicinal properties of herbs. In the first century AD, the Greek physician Dioscorides compiled a guide to 500 healing herbs, which endured as the standard text of medical arts through the Middle Ages. The European desire for curative herbs and spices of the Far East motivated Columbus to set sail in the fifteenth century so that he could find a shortcut to these lands. When he encountered the New

World, he stumbled upon the herbal riches of North America and the vast knowledge of healing practices passed down from the Mayan, Aztec, and other native civilizations.

Humans relied almost entirely upon plants to treat illnesses, both minor and serious, up until only about the early 1900s. It wasn't until scientists discovered how to make purified and concentrated derivatives of plants that modern pharmaceuticals rose to prominence. Today, in the American healthcare system, whole plants are rarely used therapeutically, but 80 of 150 of the most popular pharmaceutical products sold today contain active ingredients derived from herbal sources, including morphine (derived from the opium poppy), cough-relieving ephedrine (from *Ephedra sinica*), and the heart failure drug ad digoxin (derived from the common foxglove).

Yet despite modern Western medicine's debt to nature's pharmacy, traditional herbal medicine and Western (allopathic) practice took divergent paths in the twentieth century. Synthesized drugs began to take priority over the original botanical sources. American medical universities excluded herbal healing modalities from their curricula because such practices were regarded as based in superstition rather than in science. In India, under British rule, the herbal traditions of Ayurvedic medicine were pushed aside in favor of Western methods.

. . . specific herbs and foods can indeed have a positive impact on essential physiological functions and help protect us from disease.

Today, the paths of herbal and allopathic medicine are crossing once again. The dangerous side effects of some pharmaceuticals, as evidenced in the recall of drugs such as thalidomide and Fen-Phen, have alerted the medical establishment to the pitfalls of chemically synthesized substances. Further, some conventional medicines such as antibiotics are growing less effective as antibiotic-resistant bacteria are on the rise. In addition, a new understanding of the role of diet, stress, and lifestyle in the development of diseases has prompted a renewed appreciation for natural interventions. Perhaps, most important, a growing body of scientific literature is revealing that much of the wisdom of the ancients was scientifically sound; specific herbs and foods can indeed have a positive impact on essential physiological functions and help protect us from disease.

In seeking remedies from the farm, not the pharmacy, we reconnect with the natural environment and with the traditions of our ancestors. My own grandmother, Fritzie, taught me how to take care of my body from head to toe, inside and out, using only natural remedies. She taught me how to use foods, herbs, spices, as well as other lifestyle choices to support healthy digestion, elimination, and sleep; restore weakened immunity; calm stress; soothe colds and flu; keep my heart healthy and bones strong; and promote detoxification and rejuvenation. Because of her wisdom, I don't need to use medication. The Native American Indians would agree with my grandmother. They said, "When you need an answer, listen to Nature."

Across America, we are seeing a rebirth of natural healing. The wisdom of our grandparents and the history mentioned above regarding natural remedies can play an important role in our health care today. Each generation grows from experience, and, over time, we have seen that the overuse of antibiotics has created deadly antibiotic-resistant bacteria. Throughout the world there is a growing concern that many illness-producing microorganisms such as bacteria, viruses, fungi, and parasites are becoming resistant to the drugs used to fight them. *Prevention of illness is the key, but when one does get sick, understanding how to use natural remedies that have been proven throughout the centuries to heal our bodies, without producing harmful side effects, can be very helpful.*

In my travels and studies over four decades, I learned nature's plants can be used as medicine and have used hundreds of natural remedies. I have witnessed tremendous results in myself, my family and friends, and my clients. While you always want to consult your physician, especially if you are taking any type of allopathic medicine, the following is just a brief sampling of some natural remedies that really work. For more information, please refer to my website, SusanSmithJones.com, and my book *Wired for High-Level Wellness*.

Before I present twelve of my favorite age-defying super foods, I want to first define what a superfood—or, as I coined over thirty years ago, a *nature-food*—is to me. All foods are not equal. Some are full of calories and void of nutrition, while others are low on calories and so packed with nutrition that they earn the title of "superfood." There's a difference between food volume versus nutritional potency—you don't need a lot of food to get a lot of nutrition. For example, blueberries are considered a superfood because they contain significant amounts of antioxidants, anthocyanins, vitamin C, manganese, and dietary fiber with relatively few calories. Superfoods are the best whole foods out there, but not one is a magic bullet; make sure you include many different superfoods to help maintain optimal health.

EAT YOUR WAY TO VIBRANT HEALTH

Let's now get off to a great start with any one of these twelve age-defying plant-based foods that also happen to be, at the same time, heart-strengthening, cancer-busting, energy-boosting, and body-slimming superfoods. They are all easy to find in your supermarket or natural foods store.

Parsnips

Parsnips could be nicknamed the "beauty food" because of the way their nutritional components help strengthen hair and nails and improve skin quality. People who suffer from acne or skin disorders will appreciate the skin-flattering benefits of their unique balance of potassium, phosphorus, and vitamin C.

Avocados

Avocados have more protein than any other fruit. Sometimes known as "nature's butter," they have only about a quarter of the fat calories contained in the same weight of dairy butter. Ounce for ounce, they also provide more heart-healthy monounsaturated fat, vitamin E, folate, potassium, and fiber than other fruits. You can mash avocado on gluten-free whole-grain toast, into baked potatoes, and even use it as a hydrating mask. They also exceed other fruits as a source of the powerful antioxidant lutein, which appears to protect arteries from hardening and the eyes from cataracts and macular degeneration.

Barley Grass

One of the earliest grown sweetgrasses in the world, with its history tracing back before 5,000 BC, barley grass is young, soft green shoots that crop up on the barley plant. It has a number of health benefits associated with it, which may include relief from ulcerative colitis and boosting the immune system. It also maintains healthy skin and has rejuvenating effects on the entire body. An abundance of superoxide dismutase in barley grass makes it a wonder tonic!

Barley is a nutrient-rich superfood loaded with vitamins such as vitamin A; B vitamins like thiamine, riboflavin, niacin, B6, and folate (B9); as well as vitamin C, vitamin E, and vitamin K. It contains electrolytes, including magnesium, phosphorus, and potassium along with other essential minerals such as zinc, iron, and calcium. Barley grass is also a rich provider of powerful antioxidants, essential amino acids, and beneficial enzymes. It also supplies valuable fiber and is free from any cholesterol.

For years, each day I have taken 1 tablespoon or more of raw barley grass powder called BarleyMax (made from fresh barley juice) that I get from Hallelujah Diet (MyHDiet.com). It comes in original, mint, and berry. You can add it to smoothies, stir it in water, or simply put a teaspoon of the powder into your mouth, as I do, and let it slowly dissolve. (I also take daily and highly recommend their raw beet powder, BeetMax.)

Bananas

Monkeys may be wiser than we think—their favorite food is among the most nutritious of tropical fruits. Fiber from green, unripe bananas reduces bad cholesterol and increases good cholesterol by as much as 30 percent, while a ripe banana is one of the best ways to soothe an upset stomach. Bananas are a wonderful source of energy, can relieve heartburn, and will also help decrease the risk of stroke. And with the possible exception of strawberries, no other fresh fruit is higher in minerals.

Broccoli

Broccoli has almost twice as much protein as steak—11.2 grams per 100 calories compared with only 5.4 grams. (Most of the calories in meat come from fat, but the calories in green veggies come from protein.) Broccoli is one of nature's most potent superfoods. It has been proved effective against cancer, heart disease, and a host of other serious conditions. Its powerful sulforaphane content delivers a double punch to cancer-causing chemicals—destroying any carcinogenic compounds that you have ingested, then creating enzymes that eat up any carcinogens left over from that reaction—and it also contains indole-3-carbinol, which helps the body to metabolize estrogen, potentially warding off breast cancer.

Parsley

This common herb is a powerhouse of the nutrients that rejuvenate and detoxify. Include it when you make fresh juice. Nibble a few leaves when you want your breath to be sweeter. Chop it into salads, soups, sandwiches, and pasta dishes. Parsley is also a stress-buster, and studies have shown it to be effective in reducing depression, lowering cholesterol and strengthening kidneys. Many herbalists recommend parsley to relieve the symptoms of rheumatism and premenstrual syndrome (PMS).

Cinnamon

This ancient spice (obtained from the bark of Asian evergreens) and highly versatile flavoring helps to relieve bloating and stabilize blood sugar. Cinnamon contains methylhydroxychalcone polymer (MHCP), which speeds up the processing of sugar in your body. So, putting cinnamon sticks in your tea or water, or sprinkling just a tiny amount on desserts, fruits, cereal, and into smoothies will make your insulin release much more efficient, which may slow aging and help ward off diabetes and obesity.

Oats

Inexpensive, readily available, and incredibly easy to incorporate into your life, oats contain twice as much protein as brown rice and are an excellent source of complex carbohydrates to maintain your energy levels through the day. They improve your resistance to stress, help to regulate the thyroid, soothe the nervous and digestive systems, reduce cigarette cravings, and stabilize blood sugar levels.

Garlic

Herbalists have used garlic to treat all sorts of diseases for thousands of years. As well as being scrumptious, it's a rich source of the sulfur compounds that keep your body chemistry in balance—fighting infections, slowing down the production of cholesterol, and lowering blood pressure. There is even evidence that garlic helps to fight cancer and improves the action of the liver and the gallbladder. Add garlic to your cooking and salad dressings, or roast unpeeled cloves for 40 to 45 minutes, then peel and mash them into purées and sauces.

Tomatoes

This beautiful low-calorie fruit is jam-packed with nutrients and phyto-chemicals, which boost the body's immune defenses. Whether in soups, sauces, or salads, tomatoes are rich in vitamins C and B and also contain lycopene, which appears to act as a protective factor against cancer (and may also benefit the heart). Cooked tomatoes contain more lycopene than raw, and most of the nutritional value is contained in the skin, so, ounce for ounce, cherry tomatoes are more nutritious than large ones.

Almonds

Two ounces of almonds give you more than 50 percent of your daily mag-nesium requirement—a mineral that's important for heart health. Eating almonds every day for at least a month has been shown to reduce choles-terol and lower other risk factors for heart disease. A study also suggests that they may reduce the risk of colon cancer. Sprinkle them in salads or grind into pastry.

Cashews

I thought I'd end with one of my favorite nuts—the cashew and give it a place of honor in this chapter and include a couple recipes.

The cashew is one of the elitist nuts, just like the almond, and its artis-tic shape is so beautiful to me. They are not only incredible in taste but have myriad factors that make them so enjoyable and functional in many households.

Cashews are kidney-shaped seeds sourced from the cashew tree. These cashews are native to Brazil and were introduced by colonists to Africa and India. It is available around the year in a variety of forms—from raw, roasted, and salted to covered in chocolate, caramel, and other toppings. The multifunctional cashew has a great shelf life if you can store them prop-erly. I always keep my cashews (and other nuts and seeds) in the refrigerator to afford them a longer shelf life. And if I find organic cashews on sale for a great price, I will stock up and get extra and store what I won't use over a month in the freezer.

Cashews are incredibly nutritious, but they are also high in calories, so you do not want to eat them on a daily basis or eat lots of them at once. In other words, don't sit and eat them while you're on autopilot watching TV or you will probably gain weight. Now if gaining weight is your objective, then add them into your daily diet. When I'm working with clients who actually need to put on some extra weight, I encourage them to add cashews to their smoothies, on top of salads, and mixed into grains.

Cashews are good sources of essential fatty acids; vitamins E and K; folate; minerals like calcium, copper, potassium, magnesium, and zinc; antioxidants, fiber; proteins; and carbs.

Studies have shown that cashews may help control diabetes, boost immunity, strengthen bones, reduce blood pressure, prevent cardiovascular infections, boost brain cells, enhance male fertility, improve eyesight, and beautify hair.

I limit my intake of raw or roasted cashews to no more than about six a day unless I've done a really strenuous, hardcore workout that day in which case I might go for twelve cashews. In a sauce or cream, I realize that it's harder to tell how many cashews you are getting. Enjoy cashews in moderation and then splurge, as I do, with more cashews or sauces on special occasions. While just one Brazil nut will give you the amount of selenium your body needs for the day, six cashews will offer you the benefits mentioned above. A little goes a long way with this God-given, detectable gem of a nut.

EASY CASHEW CREAM: A PLANT-BASED SECRET SAUCE

When looking for plant-based alternatives to staple ingredients, it helps to find something as versatile as the original. And that's exactly what you get with cashew cream. Among the countless dairy substitutes, cashew cream is one of the best at delivering a truly cream-like texture, and when used properly, may even convince your guests that the dish they're eating contains real dairy.

This versatile ingredient can be used in countless applications, bringing the culinary qualities of heavy cream without the dairy. I have been using this recipe for decades and learned how to make it from my grandmother when I was a teenager. Using my Vitamix makes this recipe a breeze to produce.

⅔ cup water	1 small shallot, peeled
2 cups raw or roasted cashews*	1 teaspoon sea salt, optional
1 lemon, peeled	½ teaspoon ground black pepper
2 small garlic clove, peeled	

* Raw cashews will make a more neutral-flavored cream that's great for sweet recipes, while roasted cashews bring a stronger, nuttier flavor that better compliments savory dishes.

1. Place all ingredients into the Vitamix or other blender in the order listed and secure the lid.

2. Start the blender on its lowest speed, then quickly increase to its highest speed.

3. Blend for 30 seconds, using the tamper to press ingredients toward the blades.

4. Scoop out the cashew cream into a bowl or storage container.

Variation: Double the amount of water in this recipe to create a tangy sour cream sauce, a great condiment for vegetable tacos or as a garnish for soup. I sometimes add in a ¼ teaspoon of lemon zest, too, to give it even more pizzazz.

Note: Many recipes you'll find online call for soaking the cashews overnight to soften them (and I sometimes do this to increase the nutritional value of the nuts; please refer to my book *Kitchen Gardening: Rejuvenate with Home-grown Sprouts* for more info on this), but the blending power of a Vitamix makes that step unnecessary.

Storage: Store the cashew cream in the refrigerator, and use it as needed in other recipes. It will stay good in an airtight container for about four to five days.

TIPS

Thin the cashew cream with water for instant cashew milk as a base for smoothies or to use on your morning cereals or oatmeal.

Mix in chopped chives, basil, thyme, parsley, or other fresh herbs for a dairy-free bagel schmear.

Mix it with nutritional yeast, red bell pepper, garlic powder, onion powder, red pepper flakes, and few other ingredients to make a scrumptious dairy-free queso dip.

Blend it with your favorite frozen fruit in a Vitamix to make a quick, dairy-free frozen dessert. I often use frozen chunks of mango, blueberries, bananas, raspberries, strawberries, or papayas.

Blend in a tomato or two along with a stalk of celery and use it as a salad dressing.

APPLES AND APPLE CIDER VINEGAR

Apples are one of the most popular fruits and also one of the most nutritious—and backed by lots of scientific research. They are packed with fiber, vitamin C, potassium, vitamin K, vitamin A, vitamins E, B1, B2, and B6 plus manganese and cooper. They are also loaded with polyphenols, which are responsible for many of the health benefits. But remember that to get the most out of apples, leave the skin on because it contains half of the fiber and many of the polyphenols.

Additionally, apples have been linked to a lower risk of heart disease, easier weight loss, lower risk of diabetes, and have positive prebiotic effects that lead to good gut bacteria. Apples also support healthy digestion, blood pressure, and cholesterol; help fight asthma, support bone health, and protect the brain—with benefits for age-related mental decline. I'm sure you will agree that all of these benefits, and more that I didn't list here, will *uplift* your health and vitality and keep you happier and less depressed.

Specifically, apple cider vinegar, if taken before meals, helps the proteins in our food to be broken down into amino acids, which further leads to the creation of tryptophan. Tryptophan plays a critical role in the releasing of the neurotransmitter serotonin, our "feel-good" neurotransmitter. Serotonin helps elevate our mood and feel calm, helping us fight depression. It makes us feel happy and relaxed.

As I have already disclosed in this book, my goal is to treat depression and mental decline naturally, and two of the best ways to do this is through daily exercise and diet. The healthier and nutritious our diet will be, the quicker we will be able to recover from depression. For that, we need to focus our attention on food items that assist in the secretion of serotonin in the brain. The more serotonin is secreted during depression in our brain, the happier we will be and the more uplifted we will feel. Apple cider vinegar does exactly that. I first learned about this superfood when I was a teenager from my grandmother and have been enjoying its benefits ever since.

Drinks like apple cider vinegar are natural mood boosters which help to increase blood sugar levels by assisting in the digestion process as they break down the enzymes in the stomach and the intestines. This makes you feel more energized as opposed to the tired feeling one has during depression and a negative mood. Put simply, apple cider vinegar gives you the extra boost you need to get through the day.

Being so enthusiastic about the health benefits of apple cider vinegar (ACV), I devoted an entire chapter in my book *A Hug in a Mug: Using Herbal Teas, Culinary Spices & Fresh Juices as Medicine* with some of the history of AVC, how it supports high-level wellness, and how and when to use it in your daily healthy living program, as I do. You will be surprised in what you read on how many ailments and health issues ACV benefits.

Make a choice to join the National Health Association (NHA). Their mission statement is ***"Health results from healthful living."*** The value you'll get with the best life-changing health information will be immeasurable. From their quarterly stellar magazine *Health Science* to their conferences, videos, and so much more, you will be totally uplifted.

My holistic health articles have appeared in *Health Science* for decades, and I have also been a featured speaker at many of their conferences around the United States. Visit their website for more info or to become a member at **HealthScience.com**, or you can call their office to join: **330-953-1002**.

*When you discover a way to profoundly change your
life, you never look back. Invite Susan Smith Jones to
guide you to vibrant health and youthful vitality.*

~ Neal Barnard, MD

*As you apply Susan's suggestions in your kitchen and life, you'll be
embarking on a great adventure in both self-care and compassion.*

~ Victoria Moran

 ## Today's Affirmation

I select from a rainbow of natural foods. Whether breakfast, lunch, dinner, or a snack, I enjoy eating foods grown close to nature. I am grateful
for the abundance of energy and vitality I feel as a result. I love my body
and take care of it each day with healthy foods and positive, uplifting
thoughts.

 ## 12-Minute Action Step

Select a natural, colorful fruit or veggie to eat today that is out of the
ordinary for you and consume it in its raw state. Maybe try a new kind
of apple you've never eaten before or a different color of radish or beet.
Eat slowly and savor every bite. Imagine the energy of the food infusing
your body with vitality. Also, whip up some cashew cream sauce today
and come up with a creative way to include this delicious sauce to jazz
up one of your regular recipes.

Chapter 15

Celebrate Your Relationships

Kindness in women, not their beauteous looks, shall win my love.

~ WILLIAM SHAKESPEARE

The beginning of love is to let those we love be perfectly themselves, and not to twist them to fit our own image. Otherwise, we love only the reflection of ourselves we find in them.

~ THOMAS MERTON

One of the great joys in life comes from the relationships we form with others. At the same time, relationships can also present some of our greatest challenges. In other words, through our relationships, we can almost instantly feel uplifted or lowered.

Benjamin Franklin once said, "Well done is better than well said," and I was so blessed to have an amazing mom, June, who taught me by her shining example about love, kindness, joy, forgiveness, enthusiasm, vitality, and always the importance of living by the Golden Rule. She always had remarkable and enlightening ways of teaching me life lessons that were easy to understand and also implement in my life. In fact, a quote she used to remind me about was by Albert Einstein who said, "If you can't explain it to a six-year-old, you don't understand it yourself," which is the motto I've incorporated to this day when giving motivational talks, teaching classes, or doing media interviews. Einstein also tells us that "Weak people revenge. Strong people forgive. Intelligent people ignore." June's brilliant guidance and loving presence still resonates deeply in my heart to this present day.

To experience harmony in our relationships, we must learn to see and love the Divine in others and understand that lasting relationships result from *being* the right person, not *finding* the right person. A basic spiritual principle is that there is only oneness: We are all one with everyone and everything we encounter. Instead of trying to change or fix someone whom we see as the source of problems or difficulties, we can remind ourselves who that person really is. Instead of focusing on outer appearance and behavior—quirks, idiosyncrasies, clothes, hairstyles—we can look at one another with the thought, "That is a soul, a child of God. That human being is an expression of the Infinite." By doing so, we acquire greater understanding and new perspective: that person has feelings, just as I do. She has thoughts and opinions, aspirations and dreams that are just as important to her as mine are to me. The life force of God in that person is manifesting in her personality and in the services she performs, in the way she treats others and in her whole way of being. Because I know who I am, a divine child of God, I can focus on the divinity in others.

> *A basic spiritual principle is that there is only oneness: We are all one with everyone and everything we encounter.*

As you absorb this higher image of who you are, many wonderful benefits follow. You no longer relate to yourself as a creature whose satisfaction comes solely from physical pleasures. You stop relating to others in terms of their physical appearance. Because you know that your worth derives from the eternal self within you, and because you know that this same spirit lives in the hearts of all, you relate to everyone with respect, kindness, and love, no matter the circumstance.

This change of attitude is one of the most joyful benefits of spiritual experience, yet it brings enormous responsibilities. To see ourselves in all others, we must become detached from our own ego. Otherwise, we will get emotionally entangled in other people's problems and lose sight of our oneness with Spirit. You must practice detachment if you want to create loving, harmonious relationships. Being spiritually detached means being a very loving person. It also means being able to stand back and let go of your own needs and preferences. Without this detachment, you cannot help but manipulate other people, which will only create conflict in your relationships.

Peace comes from practicing detachment continuously—at home, at work, with friends and relatives, and especially with difficult people. A spiritually detached person will not let a relationship degenerate to provocation and response. The test is simple: even if you are upset or angry with me, can I remain calm, loving, and kind with you and help you overcome your anger? If you persist in being upset with me, can I still act lovingly toward you?

A dislike for people is really a reflection on us rather than on those we do not like. We tend to see others not as they really are, but as we are. Our relationships are always mirrors, reflecting some aspect of ourselves. Pay close attention when a particular pattern is mirrored back from three or more different people. To an angry person, everyone seems angry and full of hostility. To a suspicious person, everybody seems suspect. To a loving, tenderhearted, and uplifted person, everybody is worthy of love; every occasion is an opportunity to see the best in the other person.

> To a loving, tenderhearted, and uplifted person, everybody is worthy of love; every occasion is an opportunity to see the best in the other person.

I'm not saying that if you are loving and detached, you'll never experience difficulty in relationships. People will still get angry or fail to treat you nicely. And with people who treat us unkindly and disrespectfully, we must look harder to see the Divine in them. There may be relationships that are unhealthy and abusive. In those instances, you usually need to remove yourself from the environment while both of you get help. Still, you can love that other person (although you don't have to love his or her behavior) and put him or her in the hands of Love. As I write about in Chapter 5, forgiveness is also part of this process.

With practice and commitment to your own divinity, you will see that people will begin to come around. Being around someone who's loving, gentle, tender, and peaceful softens others' hearts. And when we bring to a relationship our awareness of our own divinity and keep our hearts open, it is amazing how people's attitudes toward us change.

If we want to get along with others, we should not treat people as objects, but as human beings who are children of Light and deserving of our love and peace. In one of his talks, I once heard Buckminster Fuller say, "We are not nouns, we are verbs." People who have rigid images of others think of themselves and their fellow human beings as nouns, or as things. Those who keep the awareness of their oneness close at hand and strive to understand and appreciate others more behave more like verbs—enthusiastic, open, active, creative, and able to change themselves and to make changes in the world. They keep one goal in mind: *to identify and remove all the blockages to the awareness of Spirit's presence in everything and everyone, including themselves.*

TEACH CHILDREN TO BELIEVE IN THEMSELVES

Everyone wants to feel loved, appreciated, nurtured, and supported. This is particularly true for children and teenagers. Our role as parents is to support, guide, and nurture them and to provide an environment in which our children experience high self-esteem and are free to discover their God-given talents. Too often we may be tempted to manipulate or coerce them into doing what we think they ought to be doing. We need to trust that the Infinite is revealing its highest vision to our children. We must help our children believe in themselves and live their vision. Remember, our children are not here to fulfill our unrealized dreams, nor do they exist to help us resolve all of our unfinished business. They are God's children, and Spirit already has a wonderful journey prepared for them. Our role is to love them unconditionally, to support and guide them, and to help them realize how capable they are. To do this, we must feel lovable, capable, and worthy ourselves.

Children reflect the consciousness of their parents. When your children are causing problems, look at what needs adjusting in your own life. Case in point: Last month, I went to the movies with a friend and his teenage daughter. When my friend purchased the tickets, although he should have paid the adult price for all of us (his daughter was fifteen and she looked about eleven), he said, "Two adults and one child." Just a few days prior, he had been talking with his daughter about the importance of always telling the truth. Which message do you think spoke more loudly to his daughter?

In my counseling practice, people often come to me wanting advice on how to discipline their problem children. Before I address that question, I first look at the parents, how they feel about themselves and what values and attitudes they are conveying to their children. Until we deal with our own consciousness and take care of unfinished business, all of our attempts to "fix" a problem child are only going to compound the situation. In every situation, whether it's a children or adult relationship, I always ask myself, "What is this situation telling me about myself? What is this challenge revealing to me? How can I be more loving to the other person?" I know that if I can raise my consciousness to the level of the heart-light within me, especially in the most difficult and trying of times, then I will be able to see more clearly, to respond instead of react, and to resolve differences instead of increasing conflict.

It's been my experience in my counseling work with all kinds of relationships that problems usually escalate when the spiritual element is not present in a relationship. When we feel separate from our spiritual selves, we become more fearful and try to control everything. We listen to the voice of the ego, and what we hear is how to live more fearfully. Letting go of negative thoughts and removing fear improves dealings with individuals in every area of life. If a relationship is truly a giving one, for example, a couple will decide together to be gentle and kind to everyone they see.

BECOME YOUR OWN BEST FRIEND

Demonstrating peace, kindness, love, and gentleness in daily life means having a loving connection not just to another person, but to ourselves as well, which means surrendering ourselves to God and seeing God in all our relationships. One of the greatest gifts you can give is to help others experience themselves as beautiful, lovable, capable, and deserving.

One of the greatest gifts you can give is to help others experience themselves as beautiful, lovable, capable, and deserving.

Something happened yesterday that reminded me I have a way to go in my effort to establish loving relationships with everyone. I was talking to a close friend on the telephone. He is usually very tender-hearted and kind with me, and that shows in his voice and his way of being. But yesterday morning was different; he sounded distant, cold, and harsh. He was frustrated with work, he was fighting off a cold, and he wanted to clarify a plan we were making for a special celebration. Instead of responding to him with love and tenderness, I reacted by saying, "Well, there's no need to be so mean and harsh; maybe we should talk about this another time when you're in a better mood." As you can imagine, that only upset him more and distanced him further. He became more hostile, and I felt ready to give up. Trying to see the divinity in this man was the furthest thing from my mind. We got off the telephone saying we were both okay, even though neither of us meant it.

I thought all day about that phone conversation. I realized that I was too attached to the way I expected my friend to be. I was unwilling to acknowledge that anyone can have a bad day. I didn't have to take his attitude as a personal attack. I could, instead, choose to offer my understanding and patience. After an entire day went by, I finally got brave enough to call and apologize for my behavior. I told him I would work on being more understanding and loving and wouldn't take his distancing mood changes personally. At the same time, he acknowledged that he didn't need to take out his frustrations with work on me and, because he cared for me so much and knows how much I value others being tenderhearted and loving, he would work on his behavior and attitude. All in all, through communication and a willingness to move forward, we were able to resolve the conflict and come closer together in spirit.

A FEW MORE THOUGHTS ON RELATIONSHIPS AND LOVE

Here are some thoughts I offered during a radio interview recently when the host asked me point blank, "What is love?" and "How can we harness our loving nature with so much uncertainty and chaos enveloping our lives?" And this is what I proffered.

Can we choose to be loving all the time? Yes, it's a tall order, isn't it? Many people are not able to choose love at will. It's just something that happens sometimes; it just shows up. Maybe you can recall times when it felt so good. You could feel the love coming through you. It might have been brought on by someone who really expressed their love for you, and you felt that energy and it took you right into it as well. Maybe your grandchild came running up to greet you after you hadn't seen her for a time and she threw her arms around you and hugged you, so happy to see you—a greeting like that takes you to your heart quickly.

So there were experiences in your life when you felt love moving through you. But many people don't know how to duplicate it, how to maintain it, and how to have that feeling of energy pouring through them with some consistency. That's what we're here on the earth to learn. That's part of our spiritual evolution, our mission—to learn and understand how we can feel that feeling moving through us with consistency.

The word "love" can have certain meaning for different people. Some people love food; others love their hobby—to golf, ride horses, to paint, etc. Many people apply the word "love" to a variety of powerful emotions that are associated with romantic love—even though some of these emotions can hardly be considered love at all. Some of these emotions have to do with self-worth, with security, and with sexual desire or possessing and controlling another person. These things are not love.

> Love is a spiritual energy. It is the movement of Spirit, the very energy of God moving through you that is unifying with all life.

Love is a spiritual energy. It is the movement of Spirit, the very energy of God moving through you that is unifying with all life. You can feel no sense of separation when the Spirit of God is moving through you as love. You just feel a connectedness, a oneness. And you see with a higher perception that looks beyond the flaws to the heart, the core, the essence of all life. So there's a whole new advanced type of perception in seeing and being.

When it comes to love, we have to push through our fears, our vulnerabilities, our discomforts, and our old patterns, as I write about in the pages of this book.

IT IS ALWAYS US

This discussion reminds me of a funny joke about a middle-aged couple who was having problems in their marriage and went to see a therapist. They hadn't been happy for a number of years. The therapist talked to the couple for a while and asked questions, and then finally identified one of the major problems: The husband had an inability to show love and affection. The wife expressed that she never really felt any love from him in recent years.

So the therapist said to the husband, "You need to work on being better able to express love to your wife." The husband replied, "What do you mean? We live in a nice home; she has all the clothes she wants." "Wait a minute," interrupted the therapist. "What your wife needs is love and affection."

The husband said, "I bought her a new car just ten months ago, and she just made a trip back to see her mom, and I didn't even blink an eye. And she's taking a night class, and I'm okay with that, too." Finally, the therapist stood up, walked over to the wife, and took her hand in his. Then he put his other arm around her and gave her a big hug. He said, "You see, this is what your wife needs at least once every day." The husband replied, "But I don't have time to bring her in here for that every day!"

You see how lost we can become in when we stay in our heads. We don't think it's about us. And it always is. Take that 12-inch journey and move from your head to your heart and let the Spirit of God flow through you and direct you in everything you think, feel, say, and do.

I like to think that God's harp strings connect all hearts. When we choose to distance ourselves from others, some of those harp strings break, and the music we hear is no longer harmonious. When we choose to see the Divine in everyone and to respond lovingly no matter how someone else treats us, we create beautiful music.

When we choose to see the Divine in everyone and to respond lovingly no matter how someone else treats us, we create beautiful music.

On a personal note, when I was uncertain, perplexed, or nonplussed about what to do or what action to take, my mom always said to me: "Ask yourself one question: What is in your heart?" Often, it's simply about asking the right questions and then listening for the answer. She also taught me this very valuable, life-enriching lesson about inviting faith to orchestrate my day and this is how I strive to live daily: *When I believe in a relationship, a plan, or a task, I give myself wholeheartedly to it. When I am God-centered, however, I do my best. I bring love and compassion to every interaction and inspiration to every activity.*

I'd like to end with one of my favorite quotes from Gerald (Jerry) Jampolsky's book *Out of the Darkness, Into the Light:* "Our purpose in relationships is just to see the spirit of love in each other, the light of love in everyone."

In one of my many visits with my dear friend, Jerry, years ago while we were at a dinner party at John Denver's home in Aspen, Colorado, when we were both invited speakers at John's first annual "Choices for the Future" Symposium in 1986, Jerry shared with me a list of practical and effective goals for creating more harmonious relationships that I wrote down during our visit and never forgot—endeavoring to incorporate them in all of my relationships:

1. No game playing

2. No pretense

3. No defenses

4. Respect for myself

5. Respect for others

6. Respect for life itself

7. A constant awareness that I am a child of God, and so is everyone else.

Some think love can be measured by the butterflies in their tummy. Others think love can be measured in bunches of flowers, or by using the word "forever." But love can only truly be measured by actions. It can be a small thing, such as peeling an orange for a person you love because you know they don't like doing it.

~ Marian Keyes

Truth is, I'll never know all there is to know about you just as you will never know all there is to know about me. Humans are by nature too complicated to be understood fully. So, we can choose either to approach our fellow human beings with suspicion or to approach them with an open mind, a dash of optimism, and a great deal of candor.

~ Tom Hanks

Today's Affirmation

I know that the essence of my being is love, and I choose to extend this love to everyone in my life. Regardless of outer circumstances, I remain peaceful and tenderhearted. I love myself and others unconditionally and know that we are all children of God. In our oneness, I see divinity in everything and everyone.

12-Minute Action Step

Uplift yourself and others today by writing or calling three people and letting them know how important and special they are to you. It will color their day positively and will make you feel uplifted and happy, too.

Chapter 16

21 Days to Build Positive, Life~Affirming Habits

No man can sincerely help another
without also helping himself.

~ RALPH WALDO EMERSON

This is the one true joy in life: to being used for a
purpose recognized by yourself as a mighty one.

~ GEORGE BERNARD SHAW

One of the greatest truths of life is that it flows from the inside out. We're affected by what happens inside—our feelings and our thoughts—which, in turn, affect our emotions, the words we speak, and the actions we choose to take. What you feel or experience at any point in time is up to you. Change your thoughts, and you change your life. If you want to scale the mountain of life with gusto and reach the acme of human potential on the highest peak, then take charge of your thoughts and become the CEO of your life.

Easier said than done, right? While I touched on this subject of 21-day agreements earlier in the book, this chapter goes into more detail on how to change bad habits, foster health- and life-enhancing habits, and to make "favorable" 21-day agreements to enrich your life and follow through on what you say you want to do or accomplish. And to help you stay committed to your 21-day agreements, print out the 21-day agreement page that you can fill out, which can be found on my website, SusanSmithJones.com.

MIND POWER & EXERCISE MOTIVATION

A great place to start on all matters motivation and commitment is with the important role of your mind in creating positive change. Your mind is a powerful tool for bringing about beneficial change and success, but it isn't always your friend. Sometimes it's a less-than-willing partner; at points, it may actually undermine your good intentions. As an example, let's look at how your thoughts can make or break a new exercise program.

Everyone knows that exercise is of paramount importance in creating vibrant health. Perhaps you've taken up walking or jogging and promised yourself that you're going to hit the trail at least every other day. At first, you have a lot of motivation and meet your goals. But as the days spin by, your resolve starts to flag a bit. It seems that something always comes up that appears to be more important than exercise. Perhaps you need to be in the office early and can't take time for a morning run, or you might have to take one of your children somewhere and it prevents you from taking your afternoon walk. Maybe you stay out late one night, and an extra hour of sleep seems more inviting than a few laps in the pool.

I have found that the "buddy system" always works wonders to help keep you on track with your goals. Find someone to exercise with you or even participate in a 21-day program with you. You might have different agreements, but you can still support each other—even if you don't live together or, perhaps, even live in another state or country than your "buddy partner." Just agree to check in with each other daily on your progress.

Whatever circumstances you create (they rarely just *arise*), and no matter how legitimate they seem at the time, be aware that your mind is more than happy to help you create excuses so that you can slip back into familiar patterns. According to behavioral psychologists, *it takes 21 days of consistently repeating an activity before your mind accepts it as a habit.* Whatever you do for 21 days makes or breaks a habit. And it really works!

Three Surefire Steps to Stay Motivated to Exercise

1. Choose an exercise program that includes activities you honestly like to do. Ideally, you'll pick a variety—such as jogging, walking, hiking, bicycling, swimming, and weightlifting—that collectively work different

muscle groups and offer diversity. Most important, select activities you won't dread doing a minimum of three times a week.

2. Create an exercise plan that seems easy to accomplish. You might, for instance, want to make an agreement with yourself that you'll spend 30 minutes jogging or walking (depending upon the way you feel) every day. Or you might agree to spend 15 minutes stretching or doing yoga each morning. Don't create a plan so difficult that it sets you up to fail, such as running or biking long distances every day. *Your mind and body are designed to rebel against drastic changes, and their protests will see to it that you don't succeed.*

3. Resolve to stay with your agreement every day for 21 days. If you skip a day in your program for some reason, you must begin the cycle over again. The reasoning behind this is simple: Because it takes 21 days to form a new habit, it will probably take that long for your mind and body to stop resisting the new pattern. Three weeks isn't a very long time, so if you find your mind coming up with excuses, as it will, you can regain control by reminding yourself that you only have to do it for 21 days.

If at the end of that time you still don't enjoy the activity or feel you aren't receiving any benefit, you always can reevaluate. What you'll almost surely find is that by the end of the trial period, you'll no longer mind doing the exercise. It will have become a normal part of your life. At this point, you'll be ready to incorporate a slightly more demanding fitness program, which I describe in detail in my books *Choose to Thrive*, *Wired for High-Level Wellness*, and *Invest in Yourself with Exercise*. I discuss how to stay motivated and empowered to achieve any goal in your life in record-breaking time.

This 21-day process can be used in any area you choose, including changing your eating habits, drinking more water, getting more sleep, breathing more deeply, simplifying your home or office space (such as spending 15 to 20 minutes daily cleaning out and organizing drawers, closets, and cupboards), expanding your vocabulary, or establishing a meditation or prayer program. Using it to help you relinquish negative health- and life-destroying habits is also very effective. For example, make a 21-day agreement to give up processed foods, alcohol, cigarettes, swearing, candy, soda, or a diet laddened with trans and saturated fats. By the way, as a way to further empower you to stay positive and head in the direction of your goals, dreams, and commitments, visit my website SusanSmithJones.com often for the new daily quotes and affirmations.

DISCIPLINE AND COMMITMENT

Consider the importance of discipline and commitment. Discipline is a choice. If you're to achieve your highest potential, you must practice self-discipline in every aspect of your life. Success and fulfillment are available to you only if you learn to control your body, mind, and emotions.

Discipline, to me, means *the ability to carry out a resolution long after the mood has left you.* It also means doing what you say you're going to do—with courage, eagerness, and enthusiasm. If your attitude is positive, you'll get positive results. *There's no way to achieve 100 percent success without putting in 100 percent effort.*

A disciplined mind creates a disciplined body, and from that comes an exhilarated mind.

With such resolution comes freedom and peace of mind. A disciplined person isn't at the mercy of external circumstances. Whereas someone without this quality is usually lazy, undirected, unhappy, or depressed, someone with it is in control of what she thinks, feels, says, and does. A disciplined mind creates a disciplined body, and from that comes an exhilarated mind. It's a powerful cycle and one that will change your live for the better.

This characteristic ignites your inherent inner power and helps create miracles in your life. Breakthroughs occur when people are willing to live out their vision and commitment and to honor their decisions. When you're committed, you allow nothing to deter you from reaching your goals. Discipline keeps you going even when you are not feeling motivated. You don't make excuses, and you follow through and do what you say that you're going to do.

IMPLEMENTING A FAVORABLE
21-DAY AGREEMENT OR COMMITMENT

Encouraging you to focus on your goals, stay motivated, keep your word, and ignite your inner power so you can release bad habits and embrace new, positive habits is what this chapter is all about. Make extra copies of the 21-day document on my website (type "21-Day Agreement" in the search bar). You can also print out a calendar from your computer and post it someplace you can see it daily. Use it often as you make and follow through on your agreements with yourself.

I have used and taught this efficacious technique for over forty years. Each month, I make an agreement to embrace or release a habit. Thus, I make at least 12 positive changes in my life each year. Sometimes I'll combine two things for the month such as drinking more water and exercising more. I usually start the process at the beginning of the month because then it coincides with the days on the calendar. The last week of each month, after the 21-day program is over and I've accomplished my goal(s), I am generally more relaxed and flexible with my daily habits.

After filling in the first sentence with your agreement, use the 21 lines to record a daily, "diary-like" progress report. For example, if you agree to walk every morning for 30 minutes, you write down what you did each day, along with a short commentary, such as the following:

Day 1: Walked 30 minutes; legs felt strong and I'm motivated.

Day 2: Still feel motivated, but harder to get up today.

Day 3: I no longer like Susan. Her idea stinks. My thighs and butt are so sore today that I can hardly sit down . . .

Day 21: I feel so empowered because I kept my word and exercised for 21 days in a row. I started because I demanded it of my body. Now my healthy lifestyle is my top priority, and I know I can do anything that I set my mind to do. Susan was right!

If you make one 21-day agreement each month (start with this simple one-agreement plan if you are new to this process), you will make 12 beneficial changes in your life each year. Whether you give up something unhealthful, such as any foods made with white sugar or white flour, or you add in something salubrious, such as eating more leafy greens or exercising daily, at the end of 21 consecutive days (if you skip a day, you must start back over again from day 1), you either will have established a new habit or will no longer crave what you gave up. For easy access right now, download the 21-Day Agreement form at SusanSmithJones.com.

The reason I exercise is for the quality of life I enjoy.
~ KENNETH COOPER

A vigorous five-mile walk will do more good for
an unhappy but otherwise healthy adult than all
the medicine and psychology in the world.
~ PAUL DUDLEY WHITE

 ## Today's Affirmation

Today I choose to commit to a 21-day agreement in an area of my fitness routine that needs some upgrading. It's day one for me, and I eagerly and enthusiastically write down my commitment for 21 consecutive days and follow through with what I have agreed to do. I keep my word and enjoy taking loving care of my God-given body.

 ## 12-Minute Action Step

Find a place in your home today, and every day, where you can do push-aways off a counter or a wall, if you are a beginner. The lower you get your body, the harder it will be. In no time at all of daily practice, you will see yourself getting stronger and firmer in your chest, shoulders, and arms. Start off with 12 deep and slow repetitions and build up the number as you get stronger. In 21 consecutive days, you will see a marked improvement in your strength, and it will make you feel uplifted and empowered. And the stronger you get, the lower you can go until you'll be able to do pushups on the floor.

Chapter 17

Cultivate Your
Very Best Life

*Though we travel the world over to find the beautiful,
we must carry it with us or we find it not.*

~ RALPH WALDO EMERSON

*The purpose of life, after all, is to live it, to taste
experience to the utmost, to reach out eagerly and
without fear for newer and richer experience.*

~ ELEANOR ROOSEVELT

Since our changing, complex civilization entered the twenty-first century, the need for a harmonious approach to living is emerging as an absolute necessity. We must view the world from the top of the mountain rather than from deep in the valley. "Think Globally, Act Locally," as they say. We can all make a difference on this planet by how we choose to live our lives. As Carl Jung wrote, "It all depends on how we look at things, and not on how they are in themselves."

My mom used to tell me that I must stand out in my life in a big way and don't play it safe or live without courage. She would say, "You don't want to be an extra in the movie of your life." What she was saying is that by how I live my life—from what I think, how I feel, what I say, and the actions I take—I can make a positive difference in the quality of life on this spaceship Earth and, in a small way, bring more harmony to this planet, or I can do the opposite. What I express will ripple out and add to the consciousness of this living planet. So, the choices I make day in, day out need to be harmonizing, uplifting, and positive.

Here's another way to think of this: We must dwell on the harmony that underlies the universe. With clarity and inner guidance, we can begin to see correlations between events and circumstances; we can see that everything works by the law of cause and effect. To expect otherwise is to have a fractured perspective and mental confusion. As my grandmother, Fritzie, would always remind me, "The Spirit of all life seeks expression through those individuals who, through Divine love, open their hearts to one another and reflect the light so all may live together in peace."

This we know: All things are connected
Like the blood which unites one family.
All things are connected.
Whatever befalls the Earth
Befalls the sons of the Earth.
Man did not weave the web of life.
He is merely a strand in it.
Whatever he does to the web,
He does to himself.

~ Chief Seattle, upon surrendering his tribal lands, 1856

For peace to exist, you must first love yourself and then love each other. In Romans 12:10, we read: "Love each other with genuine affection, and take delight in honoring each other." By simply taking loving care of ourselves, we can enrich and uplift the quality of life on this planet. You make a difference.

Our bodies are made up of trillions of cells; all these cells constitute our beings. To maintain perfect health, each of these cells must operate at peak performance. If we have sick or weak cells, then our healthy cells must work harder so that the body as a whole can be healthy. Our planet is like a body, and we are all its individual cells. We are not separate from our fellow humans. There is no room for negative thinking, withholding forgiveness, bitterness toward others, or selfishness. What happens in one area ultimately affects the whole of the world. It is our responsibility to this body that we call our planet to be a healthy, happy, peaceful cell that radiates only goodness, positivity, oneness, and love.

Although the physical body and the body of humanity work along the same principles of harmony and cooperation, there is one difference. The cells of the body don't choose how they function. Their inherent working and functioning come from an inner wisdom. But people do choose how they live and cooperate with one another. Harmony is not thrust upon us. We have a choice. And when we choose not to work together harmoniously, when we elect to stay separate and uncooperative, we experience collective illness—just as the body experiences disease when its components don't work well together. When we do work well together in cooperation, with compassion and peaceful hearts, we experience collective well-being—life as it is meant to be. This is the key to creating a world of peace: harmonious cooperation.

Albert Einstein is considered one of the most brilliant minds of the twentieth century. Not only was he a scientist, but he was also a deep-thinking metaphysician who recognized the unity and oneness behind all life. He conveys that thought in this passage I found on GoodReads.com:

> A human being is a part of the whole called by us "Universe," a part limited in time and space. He experiences himself, his thoughts and feelings, as something separated from the rest, a kind of optical delusion of his consciousness. This delusion is a kind of prison for us, restricting us to our personal desire and to affection for a few persons nearest to us. Our task must be to free ourselves from this prison by widening our circle of compassion to embrace all living creatures and the whole of nature in its beauty.

The separation and division that have so long colored our lives on this planet must be examined and corrected. To create peace on Earth, we must stop dividing the world, the nations, the races, the religions, the sexes, the ages, and the resources, and know that it's time to come together and live in harmony and love. It was Jesus who said, "Love one another" (John 13:34–35).

In his book *The Hundredth Monkey*, Ken Keyes Jr. tells of a phenomenon that scientists observed when they studied the eating habits of macaque monkeys. One monkey discovered that by washing sweet potatoes before eating them, they tasted better. She taught her mother and friends until one day there were ninety-nine monkeys who knew how to wash their sweet potatoes. The next day, when the hundredth monkey learned how to wash sweet potatoes, an amazing thing happened. The rest of the colony miraculously knew how to wash sweet potatoes, too. Not only that, but monkeys on other islands all started washing their potatoes. Keyes applies this "hundredth monkey" phenomenon to humanity. When more of us individually choose to make a difference with our lives, when we realize we do make a difference and start *acting* with that knowledge, more and more of us will hop on the bandwagon, until we reach the "millionth person" and peace spreads across the globe!

Let's take a closer look at the incredible wholeness and oneness of our bodies. On a television program not long ago, I saw something that dissolved the outer limits of my perception of wholeness and the body. In this study on television, a woman gave a blood sample from which the white cells were isolated and then attached, with an electrode, to an electroencephalograph (EEG). The woman was then put in a room next door, not in any way connected to her extracted cells. She was asked questions, some of which evoked an emotional response. Her cells in the room next door registered the response. Next, she was asked to go to a high-crime, dangerous area of downtown San Diego at night to see if her extracted cells could pick up her emotions from a distance of several miles. At one point, she was approached and harassed by a pimp. Immediately, her cells back in the laboratory registered her fear.

Don't ever underestimate the power of thought and the wholeness of your body, mind, and spirit. Recognize that throughout all life, there is oneness. We all share the commonality of Spirit. Even scientists and theologians are now coming together to recognize and affirm the one force working behind everything.

Albert Szent-Györgyi, Nobel Prize–winning biochemist, writes about *syntropy*, a drive toward greater order as a fundamental principle of nature. This is an inherent drive within the life force to perfect itself and to reach higher and higher levels of organization, order, and dynamic harmony, and to move toward a synthesis of wholeness and self-perfection.

English physicist David Bohm, who was a colleague of Einstein, believed that the information of the entire universe is contained in each of its parts. Within all the separate things and events is a wholeness that is available to each part.

The way I like to approach oneness and wholeness is from a spiritual point of view. Your life is God's life. Your being and God's being are one. God is not only outside you but also within you. God is Omnipotent—all-powerful; God is Omniscient—knowing all things; God is Omnipresent—present in all places at the same time (He's not omnipast!). Isn't that fantastic? It's cause for celebration!

As I said at the beginning of this chapter, we live in a busy, constantly changing, complex world. Yet beyond all the external movement, there resides a divine, unchanging, ever-present spirit that is the source of all happiness, prosperity, joy, and inner peace. We must open our hearts and receive this spirit of life. We must align ourselves with the purposes of heaven and act in accord. When we do this, we will have all the natural forces working with us, supporting us, helping us. As Ernest Holmes said:

> It is in our own heart, our own mind, our own consciousness, our own being, where we live twenty-four hours a day, awake or asleep, that that eternal share of the Infinite comes to us, because every man is some part of the essence of God, not as a fragment, but as a totality.

As a constant reminder that we are one with God and with each other, I practice the beautiful Indian salutation *Namaste*. Translated, it means, "I honor (or salute) the divinity you are (in you)." In the East many people greet their friends and others with folded hands and the word *Namaste*. When I meet someone, I usually do this silently and without folding my hands. I inwardly acknowledge, "I honor the divinity you are." In this way, I bless myself by being reminded of the truth, and I bless others by seeing their real spiritual essence and the spiritual connection between us.

This salutation sounds a note of reverence and spiritual awareness. Practiced with faith and dynamic intent, it helps to build the kind of inner attitude that manifests itself in harmonious human relations. *Namaste* is also a way to demonstrate the ability to function simultaneously at two levels—that of the personality and that of the soul. Finally, it's a gentle reminder that *behind all the changes and complexities of our world, there is that omnipotent, omniscient, and omnipresent loving light that also resides at the center of our hearts. When you rest in that knowledge, you float in an ocean of peace.*

On a personal note, this is how I strive to live daily. Each day is another opportunity to strengthen our relationship with God and to see the Divine in everyone and everything. *My wish is to make each day a love note and a prayer to God.* I don't want my love and zeal for God to get mundane. I want it to be special. To serve God, to love God and to enjoy God, for me, is the sweetest freedom in the world and what makes life wonderful. I want to lose and energize myself in something bigger than myself, as expressed so aptly by Norman Vincent Peale: "The more you lose yourself in something bigger than yourself, the more energy you will have."

> Each day is another opportunity to strengthen our relationship with God and to see the Divine in everyone and everything.

BETTY'S AMAZING STORY OF COURAGE, TRUST, ONENESS & MIRACLES

This is a true story about a lovely lady who lived in Pacific Palisades in Southern California whose narrative could be made into Hallmark movie. Here's how I first met this remarkable, tenderhearted woman.

Many years ago, I was walking and exercising on the splendid bluff in Santa Monica overlooking the Santa Monica Bay where I frequently visit since it's close to where I live. This one particular morning when I was walking, I passed by a lady who appeared to be in her early sixties who was sitting on a bench facing the ocean. She was on her cell phone and profusely crying. My heart went out to her as I could see how distressed she was. I kept walking and asked God what should I do.

When I walked back about ten minutes later going in the opposite direction, she was still on the bench, but no longer crying; Betty was reading her Bible and sitting quietly by herself. I made a decision to sit down next to her and see if I could be of any support. When I introduced myself, with a surprised look on her face, she said she already knew who I was because she attended one of my talks in Santa Monica a month before and sat in the back row because she had arrived late. So I never saw her, really, before this morning on the bench. We talked for about two hours, and this is what I learned.

Betty's best friend, Sally, who had lived next door to her for three decades, was hospitalized a week before, nothing serious and expected to live. But that morning when I saw her so distraught, she had just gotten a call from Sally's husband saying that Sally had passed away peacefully in her sleep at the hospital. This was not the news she had expected to hear, and Betty knew that Sally's husband would need her to be strong for him. That's why she stayed longer on the bench to read the Bible and try to compose herself before driving over to Sally's home to help comfort the family.

Before Betty left, we exchanged telephone numbers and said we'd get together at a local café in about a week or so for a visit. Over lunch, I was riveted when hearing Betty's lifelong story and many adventures. She had been adopted when she was just a baby by a loving couple in Southern California. As an only child, she grew up being fond of nature and hiking, and she loved gardening (so we had loads in common). In fact, Betty has been the founder and head of her local Garden Club for years. She married her high school sweetheart and told me there was no greater human being on the planet than her loving husband, and he passed away three years before I met Betty.

One of Betty's big dreams throughout her entire life since she was about ten years old (and loved watching Queen Elizabeth on the TV) was to visit England, where she had never been before, and tour as many public flower gardens as possible, whether through the National Trust or otherwise. Sadly, she and Sally had planned a trip together to fly to England one month after Sally's demise.

Betty was chuffed when she heard that I have been to England many times where I have a few businesses and many friends and family. In fact, just one month before I met Betty, I had returned from my trip to the UK where I stayed in a lovely bed-and-breakfast (although I now have a cottage in the area) and even toured many of the local gardens, being an avid gardener myself. She took copious notes on everything I mentioned because she was determined to go on this trip by herself since the airline ticket had already been purchased. She knew that Sally would be with her in spirit during this trip.

I suggested that she stay in the same bed-and-breakfast as I did because not only was it charming and cozy with beautiful rooms and decor throughout, but the wonderful gentleman, Ben, who lived next door was an avid book collector of all the classics and a keen gardener with a private English garden unlike anything I had ever seen in person before in someone's front and backyards on about three acres of land. Truth be told, I spent most of my free time visiting Ben and his family, and their gardens, and enjoying great conversations about literature, flowers, gardening, playing backgammon, and sipping lots of afternoon tea with them. Betty said she could hardly wait to stay at this same inn and also visit with Ben and his family, too.

In case you are also an enthusiast of the British culture, the inn next to Ben's estate was in the Staffordshire Moorlands, which borders the Derbyshire hills. This is beautiful countryside, like you see in the movies, with natural hills and valleys, wonderful hiking trails everywhere, farmhouses and farmland with horses, cows, and sheep. The pastoral beauty really needs to be seen and experienced firsthand to be fully appreciated. There are lush gardens everywhere and many of the roads that lead to and from quaint towns and villages are lined with wild hydrangeas, and the villages all have hanging flower baskets in front of the shops and restaurants. Needless to say, it's very different from where I live in the Brentwood area of Los Angeles.

If you ever saw one of my favorite movies, *Pride & Prejudice,* with Keira Knightley as Elizabeth Bennet and Matthew MacFadyen as Mr. Darcy, the estate where Mr. Darcy lived in this movie was filmed at the Chatsworth House, which is in Derbyshire, not far from Ben's home and the inn. If interested, when you go to England, you can take a tour of the Chatsworth House and gardens, which will inspire you to spruce up your garden when you get home, even if you just have pots of flowers on your porch or a few hanging plants inside your home.

Now before I share with you the end of this beautiful story, there's something else that might also amaze you. Betty told me that before her parents passed away, they told Betty that she had a fraternal twin brother, whom she had never met but had always longed to know; they thought her brother was adopted by another family who had moved to England. She even mentioned to me that she would do some investigative work before her trip and also while in England to see if there was any possibility or opportunity to locate her brother.

We ended our lunch with big hugs, and I told her I would call Ben and make the introduction to Ben about Betty's arrival date and tell my friends at inn to save the best room for Betty, which I did. Of course, I told her that

I wanted a full report about her trip when she returned, and Betty said she would make lunch for us in her home for our long, leisurely afternoon visit, which couldn't come soon enough for me!

Betty's trip was monumental, to say the least. She toured many gardens, loved staying at the inn, and even extended her trip for six weeks extra over the scheduled two weeks that were initially planned. Why? The moment she met Ben, she felt an instant connection to him, like he was family. He felt the same way about her, too, and together they did their detective work, along with DNA testing, and discovered that they were, indeed, fraternal twins. Ben was Betty's brother. The wonderful joy they both felt to have finally met each other was ineffable and life-changing for both of them. Ben invited Betty to come and live on his estate since there was plenty of room and his wife, children, and grandchildren also were all over the moon about meeting their delightful new relative, Betty, and having her live with them.

Within three months of returning home, Betty sold her home and all her furnishings in Pacific Palisades and, lock, stock, and barrel, completely moved to England to start a new chapter of her life—loving every second of time with her new family, and she considered it a true miracle. Now that's a great ending to the story that started out with sadness and crying, don't you think?

You've heard the expression that timing is everything. Some may think of this initial encounter with Betty as a mere coincidence, but as mentioned in the Introduction, I think that a coincidence (aka "Godwink") is when God brings the perfect timing and elements together for a miracle to occur and then remains anonymous. If I had walked on the bluff earlier or later, or decided not to sit down with Betty, I would have missed meeting her. If I had not stayed in that particular bed-and-breakfast in England, I would have not been able to tell her about where to stay or my visits with Ben and his family. If Betty decided to cancel her trip to England after Sally's demise, this story would have had a different ending, or if Sally's passing occurred later in the day, I would not have met Betty. But, instead, all the elements came together for the perfect outcome and a reunion with a family.

Even during struggles and challenges, we must be brave, trust that there is a higher plan for us, and know that everything will unfold in the right timing to bring us more peace and joy in our lives.

I would like to end this chapter with a passage about peace from my book *Be the Change.*

There can be no greater goal in life than peace. What asset could be of more value to use than unshakable calmness and tranquility? What better evidence of spiritual strength could we have than a peaceful mind and heart?

Peace of mind comes from accepting what you can't control and taking responsibility for what you can. It grows out of faith in your higher power and your spiritual nature. It comes when you let go of guilt, fear, and doubt. It is the result of forgiving yourself and others for all human imperfection. When you forget the delusion that something, someday, will make you happy, you can concentrate on finding peace and contentment in the present moment. Inner peace is always in the here and now, waiting quietly for you to discover it.

Cultivate your oneness, wholeness, and very best life, and as you do, you will be uplifting yourself and others.

Tact is after all is a kind of mind-reading.
~ Sarah Orne Jewett

The opposite of love is not hate, it's indifference.
The opposite of faith is not heresy, it's indifference.
The opposite of life is not death, it's indifference.
~ Elie Wiesel

 *Today's Affirmation*

I am lovingly connected to all beings and to all creation. I see God in everyone I meet and feel His presence in my heart and in my life. I rejoice in His oneness, knowing that I have the spirit of life supporting me and loving me as I journey to the top of the mountain. I am one with God.

 *12-Minute Action Step*

Silently greet everyone today as though they are filled with radiant light and love. Treat them as though they are your best friend. If you are spending this day alone, call someone and silently bless them during the conversation. In addition, honor and bless *you* today and respect the miracle of your body, your life, and the essence of who you are. Think wholeness and oneness today.

Second Intermission

Humor Time

The secret to humor is surprise.

~ ARISTOTLE

It's your outlook on life that counts. If you take yourself lightly and don't take yourself too seriously, pretty soon you can find the humor in our everyday lives. And sometimes it can be a lifesaver.

~ BETTY WHITE

TITHE: THE LIFE OF TWO BILLS

Over the decades, I have given the Sunday services and workshops at a few hundred churches in North America and worldwide, and it was a common practice to do an offering. Before these offerings, I would often share this funny story, which always got a laugh from the audience and encouraged them to be generous.

An armored truck was on its way to the bank after picking up all the deposits for the day from various stores. In the back of the truck, a bag of money fell over and a $100 and a $1 bill fell out. And the $100 started talking about the exciting life it had.

It said, "I've been all over Rodeo Drive in Beverly Hills . . . been to Gucci's, Channel, Polo Store, Winston jewelers . . . what a fantastic life." And then the $100 asked the $1, What's your life been like?"

The $1 replied, "It's been pretty predictable. I've been to church and back, to church and back."

FRECKLES

An elderly woman and her little grandson, whose face was sprinkled with bright freckles, spent the day at the zoo. Lots of children were waiting in line to get their cheeks painted by a local artist who was decorating them with tiger paws.

"You've got so many freckles, there's no place to paint!" a girl in the line said to the little fellow.

Embarrassed, the boy dropped his head.

His grandmother knelt down next to him and said, "I love your freckles. When I was a little girl, I always wanted freckles." She traced her finger across the child's cheek. "Freckles are beautiful."

The boy looked up. "Really?"

"Of course," said the grandmother. "Why just name me one thing that's prettier than freckles."

The little boy thought for a moment, peered intensely into his grandmother's face, and softly whispered, "Wrinkles."

PSYCHIATRIC HOTLINE

Hello, welcome to the Psychiatric Hotline.

If you are obsessive-compulsive, please press one repeatedly.

If you are codependent, please ask someone to press 2.

If you have multiple personalities, please press 3, 4, 5, and 6.

If you are schizophrenic, listen carefully, and a little voice will tell you which number to press.

If you are paranoid, we know who you are and what you want. Just stay on the line so we can trace the call.

THE INSULT

Upon arriving home, a husband was met at the door by his sobbing wife. Tearfully, she explained, "The pharmacist insulted me terribly this morning on the phone."

Immediately the husband drove downtown to confront the pharmacist and demanded an apology. Before he could say more than a word or two, the pharmacist said, "Now just a minute! Listen to my side of it.

"This morning the alarm failed to go off, so I was late getting up. I went without breakfast and hurried out to the car, only to realize that I had locked the house and my car keys were inside. I had to break a window to get my keys. Then, driving a little too fast, I got a speeding ticket.

"Later, when I was about three blocks from the store, I had a flat tire. When I finally got to the store, there were a bunch of people waiting for me to open up. I opened the store and started waiting on these people. All the while the darn phone was ringing off the hook! I had to break open a roll of nickels against the cash register drawer to make change, and they spilled all over the floor. I got down on my hands and knees top pick up the nickels. The phone was still ringing. When I came up, I cracked my head on the open cash drawer. That made me stagger back against a showcase with a bunch of perfume bottles on it, and half of them hit the floor and broke.

"Meanwhile, the phone is still ringing with no let up. When I finally got to answer it, it was your wife. She wanted to know how to use a rectal thermometer. And believe me mister, As God is my witness . . . all I did was tell her!"

THREE HYMNS

One Sunday a pastor told his congregation that the church needed some extra money and asked the people to prayerfully consider giving a little extra in the offering plate. He said that whoever gave the most would be able to pick out three hymns. After the offering plates were passed, the pastor glanced down and noticed that someone had placed a $1,000 bill in the offering.

He was so excited that he immediately shared his joy with his congregation and said he'd like to personally thank the person who placed the money in the plate. A very quiet, elderly, saintly lady all the way in the back shyly raised her had. The pastor asked her to come to the front.

Slowly she made her way to the pastor. He told her how wonderful it was that she gave so much and in thanksgiving asked her to select three hymns. Her eyes brightened as she looked over the congregation. Then, pointing to the three most handsome men in the building, she said, "I'll take Him and Him and Him!"

Spelling Test to Get into Heaven

Lynn died and went to heaven and was met by St. Peter, who told her that before she could go through the pearly gates and enter heaven, she would have to pass a spelling test.

"Okay," said Lynn. "Give me the test. I'm ready and eager to begin my new life."

When St. Peter asked her to spell the word "light," Lynn enthusiastically said, "L-I-G-H-T," and in she went.

Lynn was in heaven for less than a month and having a great time, when St. Peter asked her to watch the gate while he ran a few errands. So Lynn found herself at the gate, giving a spelling test to all the new arrivals. Suddenly, her husband approached, so excited to see her.

"What happened to you?" she asked.

Her husband explained that he had been returning home from an evening out with a new lady friend and was hit by a truck.

Lynn nodded and then told him, "Before you can go through the pearly gates and enter heaven, you have to pass a spelling test."

"I'm ready, dear," her husband eagerly replied. "What's the word?"

"Czechoslovakia!"

A Misunderstanding

A new monk had just arrived at the monastery and was introduced to the older monk. The older monk asked him, for his first assignment, to translate their Bible to make a newer edition.

Pleased but overwhelmed by his project, the new monk said to the older monk, "It's been translated several times. How do you know if your current edition is accurate?"

"Well," said the older monk, "that's a good question. Why don't I go to the archives and try to find the original?"

The older monk was gone for several days, and the new monk was getting worried. He went down to the archives and was surprised to find the older monk sitting on the floor, crying.

"What's wrong?" asked the new monk.

And the older monk responded, "The word was *celebrate*!"

In Great Health

The healthy, robust, vibrant seventy-five-year-old man went to see his doctor for his annual physical. The doctor, in seeing how healthy he was, just had to ask him how his father had died.

The man replied, "What do you mean, my father is still living; he's a hundred years old and in great health."

Then, the doctor just had to ask how his grandfather had died.

And once again, the man replied, "My grandfather is still living, too. He's a hundred and twenty-five and also in great health. In fact, next week he's getting married."

To that the doctor quipped, "Why would he want to do something like that?"

And the man blurted, "Who says he wants to?"

Nuns on the Highway

An officer stopped a van filled with nuns. Before he could say anything, the nun driving said, "Why are you stopping us, officer? I'm sure I was driving safely. What is wrong?"

The officer replied, "You're driving twenty miles per hour on the freeway, and that can be dangerous."

"But, officer," protested the nun, "I always drive the *exact* speed limit and the sign back there said twenty!"

"Sister, that's the number of the highway," the officer explained. "You're on Highway *20* and the speed limit is *65* miles per hour."

All the nuns gasped.

"Why is everyone looking so pale? I'm not going to cite you. This is just a warning."

"Well, officer," said the nun in the driver's seat. "It's because we just got off Highway 110!"

(We can choose to slow down life's hectic pace and live calmly.)

LA Girls

Some of the girls in LA have some really crazy hairstyles—all spiked up and sticking out—lots of mousse. Why, the other day at one of my workshops, this girl walked out when it was over; she had so much mousse in her hair that an elk followed her home.

A Priest and a Cab Driver

A priest and a cab driver arrived at the pearly gates at the same time. After interviewing both, St. Peter opened the gates and let the cab driver into heaven, but he told the priest to have a seat and await further consideration.

Outraged, the priest complained, "How can you let that man into heaven before me? I was a priest for fifty years, and I gave thousands of sermons! All he did was drive a car around the city!"

"That's right," St. Peter answered. "And when you preached, people slept. But when this man drove, people prayed."

(I'm hoping that what I share with you in this book won't put you to sleep!)

My mission in life is not merely to survive, but to thrive; and to do so with some passion, some compassion, some humor, and some style.

~ Maya Angelou

Honest good humor is the oil and wine of a merry meeting, and there is no jovial companionship equal to that where the jokes are rather small and laughter abundant.

~ Washington Irving

Part Three

❧

Flying High in Life

Chapter 18

12~Minute Action Steps to More Joy, Faith, Peace, Love, Kindness & Vitality

Self-trust is the first secret of success.

~ Ralph Waldo Emerson

No one can make you feel inferior without your consent.

~ Eleanor Roosevelt

Throughout this book I have offered myriad 12-Minute Action Steps you can take to enrich your life physically, mentally, emotionally, and spiritually. The sky is the limit with what you can to in 12 minutes or fewer. Why 12 minutes?

Well, first of all it's an amount of time that's doable for most people. In other words, I'm not suggesting you take an action step for a weekend or day, or three hours or even 30 minutes. Most busy people can find a way to carve out a block of 1 to 12 minutes to take an action step to enrich their lives or the life of someone else. Moreover, the number 12 is one of my three favorite numbers in addition to the numbers 21 and 3. The numbers 12 or 21 themselves reduce down through the composite of their component numbers as an addition to 3 (1 + 2 = 3). Also, the number 12 has so much significance in sacred writings and elsewhere, as you'll read about next.

BIBLICAL, SPIRITUAL & SACRED SIGNIFICANCE

Numbers are essential parts of our existence. The number 12, in particular, has a spiritual significance that most people may not be aware of, so if you keep coming across this mystifying, powerful number, know that there's a sacred meaning behind it. (Maybe the NFL quarterback players Aaron Rodgers and Tom Brady, whose jersey numbers have always been 12, know about its significance.)

The number 12 features prominently in the Bible. In the Old Testament, the Book of Genesis states that there were 12 sons of Jacob and that those 12 sons formed the 12 tribes of Israel. The New Testament tells us that Jesus had 12 apostles. According to the Book of Revelation, the Kingdom of God has 12 gates guarded by 12 angels. Furthermore, the number 12 is displayed in many other contexts, such as the 12 months of the year that comprise our calendar and the 12 constellations of the zodiac that reflect our universe.

You may be surprised to learn that the number 12 in the Bible is mentioned a total of 187 times. It has a noticeable authority that transcends most other angel numbers. For example, in the Holy Gospels, we learn about the 12 apostles and the authority that they wielded with Jesus as their leader. They were known as the 12 disciples in the beginning, but they later became known as the 12 apostles. In addition, when Jesus fed the five thousand, the disciples gathered 12 baskets of leftover food (Matthew 14:20).

Whenever the number 12 is used in biblical numerology, it signifies a particular setting in its complete nature—the 12 tribes of Israel, the 12 stars, the 12 apostles, the 12 princes, and so on.

The number 12 is also associated with an anointed service. In the Bible, 12 men were anointed by a prophet of God to carry out a unique task. These were Aaron along with his four sons (Nadab, Abihu, Eleazar, and Ithamar) who were anointed into the priesthood in Exodus 29:7–9), Saul, David, David's son Absalom, King Jehu, Kings Joash and Jehoahaz of Judah, and King Solomon.

IN THE HEBREW CULTURE

Certain numbers in Hebrew culture have a particularly profound meaning. It is within that Hebrew culture that the significance of the number

12 focuses on God's Divine Kingdom and His Holy Temple, and it is from these focal points of understanding that the further interpretations of the number 12 follow.

The twelfth character of the Hebrew alphabet, "Lamed" (pronounced *lah-med*), literally means perfection or Solomon-like wisdom. Its presence is found in multiple places within the Brit Chadashah (New Covenant) and the Tanakh (Old Covenant).

Based on how often this number is used in both the Old and New Testaments, it's fair to say that you're blessed and highly favored if you encounter or come across this number often, which you will on many pages of this book. What a blessing as many believers may never even have the opportunity to experience the number 12 with all its attendant powers.

IN DAILY LIFE

Did you know that the number 12 has a particularly strong influence over your life? If you keep coming across the number 12 on a regular basis, don't ignore the meaning behind it—it's a sign that your angels are trying to relay an important message to you.

The number 12 comes to inspire progress and to open up new beginnings. It's also a sign of independence, inspiration, and growth. So, by now you can see clearly why I've selected the number 12 for the minutes that are designated to undertake the action steps.

ANGELIC INFLUENCE

Always remember that the number 12 is composed of two angel numbers: 1 and 2. Angel number 1 means that you'll achieve your goals only if you maintain a positive attitude. On the other hand, angel number 2 means that your angels are right by your side to help in your pursuit of perfection.

WHAT DOES THE BIBLE NUMBER 12 ADVISE US TO DO?

Focus on your soul mission. The number 12 is closely related to your inner strength and wisdom, and it advises you to use your sensitivity and wisdom to get to your desired destination. Your angels understand that you have negative traits, just like everyone else. However, your angels advise you through the number 12 to overcome your imperfections and focus on your positive side.

FAMILY RELATIONS

The number 12 also focuses on your family relations. It advises you to make the atmosphere for peace, faith, and love. Every good thing you do on Earth earns you a reward in heaven. Therefore, let this revelation inspire you to be the best version of yourself and in this *uplifted* book, I offer lots of suggestions to be the best version of yourself along with action steps you can take to enrich your life in 12 minutes or fewer.

THE BOTTOM LINE

All in all, the number 12 has a great significance in the Bible and our daily lives in general. As mentioned, Jacob perfected his presence in Israel when he sired 12 sons, and the new city referred to in the Book of Revelation has 12 angels, 12 gates, 12 sons who formed 12 tribes, and so on.

So, the next time you see the number 12, be reminded of your life purpose and the deep meaning it holds. Take a few moments to focus on this number when you see it, to feel your connection with God as the Divine presence in your life and your angels, and to reflect on what you can think, say, or do immediately to enhance the quality of your life or the life of someone else.

 12-Minute Action Steps ————————————

Here are 103 more suggestions for 12-Minute Action Steps with an additional nine blank lines to write in your own inclination. Remember, 12 minutes isn't much time, and the cumulative effects of 12-Minute Action Steps will make a positive, uplifting difference in your life on so many levels. For up to 12 minutes or fewer, you may want to . . .

1. Sit down for a cup of delicious tea or freshly made juice.

2. Write down at least three things for which you are grateful.

3. Clean out a drawer or cupboard of your home. In fact, have regular clearouts. Clutter can add to feelings of tension and a clean, clear home allows a clearer, more peaceful, uplifted mind.

4. Write someone a note about why you appreciate him or her.

5. Cut some fresh flowers from the garden to put in a vase in your home.

6. Sit quietly and do some deep breathing.

7. Think about all the people who have blessed your life.

8. Enjoy a piece of fresh fruit like an apple, orange, or pear.

9. Visualize with your mind's eye one of your heartfelt goals as already achieved.

10. Do some exercise such as stepping in place or lifting some weights for 12 reps.

11. Put some beautiful, fresh sheets on your bed.

12. Listen to some of your favorite music that uplifts you.

13. Make a delicious salad with lots of raw cut-up veggies in it.

14. Watch a funny video online with dogs and cats in it.

15. Sit quietly and think about someone special in your life and send them love.

16. Tell someone you love them.

17. Put a vase of flowers together for someone special or someone who needs this upliftment.

18. Shovel some snow off a neighbor's walkway.

19. Plant some flowers in front of one of your favorite shops that might be struggling.

20. Offer to drive an elderly neighbor to a doctor's appointment or to the grocery store.

21. Make your bed first thing in the morning and make it as perfect as you can. It will set your day up to continue "getting it done." It's one of the first lessons our military learn.

22. After your bed is made, sit quietly to meditate. Learn the different kinds of meditation in my book *Wired for High-Level Wellness.*

23. If you're feeling tired in the afternoon, take a 12-minute power nap! It takes the "grumpies" away.

24. If you have intentionally or unintentionally hurt someone, apologize immediately! It only takes seconds to do this. Ask for forgiveness and make yourself aware of how and what you say.

25. On an empty stomach, drink a tall glass of purified water with some fresh lemon in it. Every cell in your body will smile with this hydration.

26. When you receive a gift of food in a container that you need to wash and return, put something lovely inside the dish when you return it with a thoughtful note of thanks.

27. Never miss a chance to recycle. Our planet depends on each one of us. Keep a container in your kitchen just for this.

28. If you've done something that is really unexpected and funny, share it with your friends and family. You'll both laugh! Laughing is one of the healthiest things for our mind and body.

29. Do your own mani-pedi and facials. It feels good to look good! I like to put hydrating beauty masks on my face for about 10 to 12 minutes and then wash it off.

30. Pray often. God is the best listener and guide.

31. Read your Bible. It is so uplifting. All the wisdom you could ever conceive is there.

32. Watch the birds outside.

33. Write a love note to your partner or someone else in your family.

34. Offer morning and evening prayers to God.

35. Before you go to sleep, review the day to identify where and how you can improve.

36. Write down one or more uplifting thoughts you can memorize or read throughout the day. Put them in locations where you can be reminded of the positive messages often.

37. Telephone a needy friend and offer a kind word.

38. Put one of your favorite photos in a frame to place somewhere special in your home.

39. Pay a few bills while listening to your favorite music.

40. Light a candle in your home. It symbolizes that your guardian angels are watching over you.

41. Put a hydrating mask on your hair, which only take a couple minutes, and then keep it on for 12 minutes (sometimes I leave mine on overnight) before washing it out.

42. Clean your kitchen sink and countertops. My mom always used to remind me of this: *When your kitchen is clean, your home is clean.* I always feel better when my kitchen is clean and organized.

43. Go through what's in your refrigerator and freezer and toss out anything too old or expired. And while you're at it, make sure the refrigerator shelves are also clean.

44. Never miss a chance to shut up (zip your lips) when you don't know what you're talking about.

45. Work on a jigsaw puzzle.

46. Expand your vocabulary by working on a crossword puzzle.

47. Take some of the raw veggies from your clean refrigerator and cut them up to enjoy throughout the day or two with some healthy dip.

48. Put together some fresh salad dressing to use on your salads.

49. Drink a large glass of purified water with some fresh lemon in it.

50. Go for a walk on your block or on a treadmill.

51. Sit quietly and take five long, deep breaths and focus on your lungs and diaphragm as you do this. This is a quick and easy way to instantly feel calm and uplifted.

52. Enjoy the nature in your yard or a local park or anywhere outdoors. Too much concrete is never a good thing. Spending time in nature can make you feel younger and happier.

53. Listen to the birds singing and enjoy the peace and tranquility.

54. Watch a beautiful sunrise or sunset and see how many colors you can identify.

55. Mist your houseplants with some fresh water and watch them smile and perk up right before your eyes.

56. Get a coloring book and start creating your masterpiece. There are so many coloring books available for kids and adults, so select one that resonates in your heart with a theme that uplifts you. And, remember, you don't always need to stay within the lines when coloring.

57. Look up a new word in the dictionary and use it as many times as you can in speaking and writing throughout the day.

58. If you catch yourself cursing, cancel it immediately and replace the word with a more positive word. Refer to Chapter 10 for 260 positive words.

59. Play with your pet. Get down on the floor, if possible, and enjoy your cat, dog, or other animal. If you can't get on the floor, bring your furry friend onto your lap and share your love with them.

60. Walk barefoot on natural ground such as the grass in your yard, the sand at the beach, or the ocean water. This is called Earthing or grounding, and it's very beneficial for the body. Please refer to my book *Wired for High-Level Wellness* for the detailed health benefits of Earthing such as reducing inflammation, pain, and depression and improving energy, vitality, and mood.

61. Be mindful right where you are. Be fully present in the moment and acutely aware of your five senses: touch, taste, sight, hearing, and smell. This leaves less time for your mind to worry and think about "what ifs."

62. Do a ten-finger breathing exercise within 12 minutes. As though you are tracing your hand on a piece of paper, use a finger from your other hand (instead of a writing or coloring utensil) to trace all your fingers, including your thumb—inhaling and exhaling slowly and deeply with each finger. In other words, one inhale and exhale for each finger, slowly and deliberately while you take long, slow deep breaths. Then switch hands and repeat the tracing. If it hasn't been 12 minutes and you're already finished, continue for another round and go slower this time. This will calm your mind and uplift your thoughts and heart.

63. Write down at least 12 things you like about yourself. The more we like ourselves, the greater our peace of mind and upliftment. With more

self-love, we experience less insecurity, and, as a result, our inner peace is heightened.

64. Laugh a lot. The world is instantly a better place when you can see the funny side of life. Laughter is a great antidote for stress and releases hormones that help us relax. Don't take yourself too seriously. Find something that can make you laugh.

65. Go for regular health checks. Take a few minutes to call your doctor to schedule an appointment to see her or him in person or to have a virtual appointment. Be kind to yourself and make the most of what you have.

66. If you don't have young children of your own to delight you, watch some videos of young children, babies, or toddlers and think about all the ways you would enjoy being more childlike. Which of their characteristics can you duplicate in your life?

67. Take stock. Every now and then, it's a good idea to take a few minutes to check whether you're happy with the quality of your life. Do you like your job? Your relationship? Are you on the right track? Make adjustments, if necessary, to restore inner joy and calm.

68. Write out or upgrade you goals for your fitness for the next week, month, and quarter. Goals help keep us going in the right direction and give us a sense of purpose. Create short-term and long-term goals for your health and for other areas of your life.

69. Take up to 12 minutes for a worry-free time. We have somewhere between 25,000 and 75,000 thoughts per day, of which 80 percent are random "nonsense." During this worry-free time, think deeply of a time that you felt really peaceful and content and linger over those thoughts.

70. Enjoy a few minutes to frolic. My dictionary describes this word as: "To behave playfully and uninhibitedly; romp." What can you do in a few minutes of frolicking? Maybe dance in your underwear, go outside and run through the sprinklers on a hot day, giggle at the thought of someone seeing you dance or sing without inhibition, dance with your partner in a shopping mall whether or not you hear music, carry the invisible dog leash with you when there's no dog at the end of the leash, or put on two different color shoes when you go out on errands. The sky's the limit with how you can frolic today.

71. If something is bothering you, let it go. Affirm to yourself, *I choose to let this go.* Yes, there are some things you just cannot change, no matter how hard you try. Know when to cut your losses and detach. (Just like Elsa does in *Frozen!*)

72. Be kind today every chance you have. It's free and will uplift your life. When we show kindness, it gives us an inner boost, too. My mom always taught me to live by the Golden Rule.

73. Find out when and where you can donate blood with the Red Cross and make the appointment. They are always in need for fresh blood from donors. I learned from my mom about the importance of doing this, and being O negative, the universal donor, I strive to donate on a regular basis. It always makes me feel good to donate.

74. Get to bed 12 minutes earlier at night. When we're tired and grumpy, nothing goes so smoothly. Get eight hours of sleep per night and regenerate your body and uplift your mind.

75. Visualize one of your health and fitness goals. Maybe your goal is to lose weight or to build up your strength and vitality. For 12 minutes, see in your mind's eye your goal and dreams already accomplished and assume the joyous feeling of the wish fulfilled.

76. Take a few minutes to pray and meditate on peace. Find your favorite passages in the Bible on peace and commit them to memory. If you feel stressed out, meditate on these passages; say them to yourself silently or out loud, and this will keep you uplifted, calm, and positive.

77. Take a three-minute break if you've been sitting for one hour. These breaks could be filled with movement such as walking, stepping in place, arms out and twisting from side to side, or reaching up to the ceiling and back down to the floor a few times.

78. Create a "to-do" list at the end of your workday for the following day to help with your organization. You can always tweak it as necessary when you wake up and start your day.

79. When you wake up in the morning, even before you get out of get out of bed, see with your mind's eye your day going swimmingly. See yourself accomplishing all of your tasks with joy, élan, verve, vim, and aplomb.

80. Do a brain release. It's not uncommon to have lots of things swirling around in your head regarding what you need to get done on a particular day. Do a brain release by getting them out of your head on to piece of paper, or if you're electronically inclined, on your computer or phone. Knowing what you need to do is the first step to working smarter, not harder.

81. Have breakfast in bed instead of the kitchen table. Maybe someone else can make it for you and bring it in to you.

82. Talk to a stranger. Smile, or better yet, strike up a conversation with someone in line at the grocery store or coffee shop. This just might bring happiness and upliftment to you both.

83. Send a snail mail notecard to someone who needs some cheering up and upliftment.

84. Send a donation to your favorite charity, religious organization, or friend in need.

85. Power down your gadgets. They could be making you sick. Stress, depression, and vision impairment are just a few of the negative consequences of spending too much time on your phones, tablets, and computer. Power down. Unplug. Maybe after work, on weekends or whenever you can, disconnect from email, text messaging, and social media. Instead, increase your connectivity to the people around you.

86. Have more cuddle time with your partner. It will make both of you feel more uplifted and happier.

87. Get a new houseplant. Surrounding yourself with nature will elevate your mood. Plants will also improve indoor air quality. The more time you spend around leafy, green things, the better you are going to feel and the more uplifted your mind will be.

88. Always give thanks. Grateful people are more likely to be happy, uplifted, and optimistic. Don't save it all for the fourth Thursday in November, if you live in America—Thanksgiving Day. Get into the habit of showing gratitude for the circumstances and people around you.

89. Do some spring cleaning any time of the year. As mentioned, the extra clutter we accumulate over the years can be counterproductive, leaving us feeling disorganized and claustrophobic. Our goal is to open space

in our homes for the winds of heaven to move through easily and effortlessly. In either one room or maybe in a few rooms of your home, find some things you don't need or want, or that no longer spark joy, as organizing consultant and author Marie Kondo would say, and put them into a give-away bag to take to your car so you can donate them to your favorite charity.

90. Pay it forward. Find a way to offer a random act of kindness, which will definitely make you feel uplifted. For a good deed, you could pay for the next order in a drive-through restaurant. Tape a scratch-off lottery ticket to a random car's windshield, put coins in parking meters that have run out, or buy some long-stem flowers from your local flower store and put a few under the windshield wipers of parked cars and also keep some for yourself.

91. Put a vase of fragrant roses on your bedside table. These days, it seems to be harder to find fragrant roses if you don't have them in your yard. The fragrance of roses is very uplifting and will help you drift off to sleep with a smile on your face. And if you can't find the fragrant roses, get some rose essential oil and put a few drops on your pillowcases and the inside of your wrists.

92. Lavender essential oil is very relaxing. A few drops on your pillowcase before bedtime will support you in sleeping more like a baby. Putting this lavender oil in a diffuser next to your bed will also help you champion more restful sleep. Better yet, combine the lavender and rose oils together in a few drops on your pillowcase or diffuser, and you will reap the healing benefits.

93. When you are doing your walk around the neighborhood, if you see rose or other lovely flowers in someone's yard, stop and smell the roses. Good fragrances such as floral scents can actually uplift you and make you happier. Or if it's the dead of winter, I sometimes wear my lavender or rose colognes when walking to help me imagine the flowers all around me.

94. Take a hot shower or bath before going to bed to relax your muscles and help you sleep better. It's a simple way to increase the melatonin in your body, a hormone that supports restful, easy sleep. And before you get into bed, put on a spritz of your favorite cologne or perfume. I rarely miss a night doing this simple bedtime ritual.

95. Read some passages out of one of your favorite nonfiction books or a novel. Escape into a fantasy realm for a little while, which can boost your happiness. Let your imagination run away with it.

96. You've heard of the "runner's high," but did you know that you can achieve the same high by singing your heart out. Singing alone or in a choir boosts the endorphins and dopamine in your body—the same as you get when jogging a few miles. In fact, I've been known to sing when I do my power walks. The singer's high proffers a variety of added benefits from stress reduction and pain alleviation to an overall feeling of upliftment and contentment.

97. Organize your bedroom. Good sleep is essential for feeling uplifted. You will breathe easier at night if your bedroom is clutter-free. A bedroom should be like a sanctuary. Remember, whether your bedroom or other rooms of your home, a tidy living space bolsters happiness, promotes productivity, decreases depression, and enhances peace of mind. Also, consider wearing blue pajamas to bed. Just as the blue sky and color of water can elevate your mood, wearing the color blue can also boost confidence, reduce stress, and bolster happiness. So, whether going to bed or being out and about during the day, wearing the color blue is always a great choice.

98. Any free time you have available, spend it out in nature because nature recharges and invigorates us. Maybe you are driving home from work or after running errands and you pass by a local park with trees and other plants. Take a few minutes to stop, smell the roses, take off your shoes, walk on the grass, or simply sit on a park bench and take in all the beauty around you. Not only does Mother Nature bring us joy, but she also gives us energy. Maybe that's why my favorite way to exercise is by hiking in my local mountains in Santa Monica or walking at the beach. Spending time with Mother Nature is my favorite thing to do.

99. Smile. This only takes a second or two. And smile like you mean it. Studies show that the act of turning up the corners of your mouth will make you feel better. That's because a smile—even a forced one—decreases stress.

100. Get some natural sunshine on your skin. Sunshine gives us a natural boost of serotonin, the hormone that makes us happy. If you're working

indoors all day and the sun is out, take a 12-minute break and stroll outside for a healthy dose of UV rays. Studies reveal that sunshine, in healthy doses, can also boost fertility and help prevent diabetes, multiple sclerosis, seasonal affective disorder, depression, and more.

101. When driving in your car, put on cotton gloves to protect the skin on your hands from getting too much sun. I've done this simple practice when driving for decades, and I am pleased to say that my hands look much younger than my age.

102. Every time you walk by a mirror and see your reflection, whether it's from your torso up, just your face, or your entire body, be sure say something positive to yourself in the mirror about yourself. Maybe you say, "You are beautiful, and I love you." Or "I am so proud of you and the courage you have to live your dreams." Or "Smile more, you magnificent person, so the world will feel my enthusiasm and joy for life." Or "Hello gorgeous, I celebrate you and I celebrate life."

103. Do the Finger Relaxation Meditation. I use this meditation daily when I need to relax, chill out, reduce stress and anxiety, when I am meditating, or even when I'm in the middle of a major traffic jam in Los Angeles. I use my 10 fingers (thumbs included) for this simple exercise.

With eyes closed or open (if I am driving or stuck in traffic, my eyes are wide open), I slowly and deeply breathe in and breathe out and with each of the 10 inhalations and exhalations (an inhale and exhale is one repetition), I ever so slightly press in a finger so I know where I am in the series of ten (like Catholics use beads when saying the rosary, but we are using our fingers). For example, I might start with my thumb and move it about one quarter inch (ever so slightly) telling me that I'm on the first repetition of 10, and I'll breathe in very, very slowly, hold my breath a few seconds, and then slowly exhale. That is one repetition. I'll do this 10 times (for a set of 10 repetitions), using my 10 fingers to remind me if where I am in the series.

If I am not driving and I can really focus on this, with each inhalation, I will say silently to myself the word "Peace" and then hold my breath briefly after which I very slowly exhale to the words, "Be Still." (These sacred and powerful words are from the Bible, Psalm 46:10.)

If you breathe in really slowly and deeply, you might find you're totally relaxed with one series of 10 repetitions. I find I can go three times with this series within 10 minutes, but if I only have three minutes, I can still relax and do this for at least one round of 10 reps and reap the benefits.

Add in your own 12-Minute Action Steps to enrich your life in this space here:

104.

105.

106.

107.

108.

109.

110.

111.

112.

If I had flowers for every time I thought of you,
I could walk through my garden forever.

~ ALFRED LORD TENNYSON

Trust yourself. Create the kind of self that you will be happy to
live with all your life. Make the most of yourself by fanning the
tiny, inner sparks of possibility into flames of achievement.

~ GOLDA MEIR

Chapter 19

Celebrate Yourself & Life Workbook

The whole of science is nothing more than
a refinement of everyday thinking.

~ ALBERT EINSTEIN

Take a deep breath and trust that life, despite its
ups and downs, is essentially wonderful.

~ THOMAS KINKADE

KNOW THYSELF & SOAR WITH THE EAGLES

The following questions and suggestions are designed to support you in learning more about yourself and in creating your own personal pathway to joy, faith, peace, kindness, and vitality. Rather than providing space for you to write in the book—just in case you want to loan this book to a friend or family member, I encourage you to use a tablet of paper or, better yet, get a lovely book with blank pages to write directly in the book with your favorite color pen.

In the search to "know thyself," there aren't any right or wrong answers. As you deepen your self-discovery, this Workbook chapter will allow you to refer back to earlier ideas and add new ones. It will be there to help and encourage you to make positive changes in your attitudes, thoughts, beliefs, actions, and lifestyle. The Self-Discovery Questions and Action Choices are grouped to emphasize specific themes in the book. Don't skip over this part! As Socrates said, *"An unexamined life is not worth living."*

And, by the way, many of these questions are great ones to ask someone you're dating and might think they will make a great lifetime partner. Hearing how they respond or answer these questions will help you get to know this person better and to ascertain if you two are compatible.

HOW WILL I CELEBRATE MYSELF?

Self-Discovery Questions

1. What does it mean to me to be healthy? How would I feel if I were in perfect health?

2. Have I received value from being unwell in the past? Would someone pay more attention to me, for example?

3. In the past, whom have I blamed, or what situations have I blamed, for my failures?

4. How do people treat me? Assuming that I've taught them how to treat me by the way I treat myself, what changes can I make in myself and my behavior that will support my newfound magnificence?

5. Have I ever felt limited in what I could be or do because of what others have said about me? As I let go of limiting opinions and beliefs and tune in to my own inner signals, what new possibilities become exciting and available to me?

Action Choices

1. Following is a list of at least five things I love about myself:

2. These are a few things I can do to increase my self-confidence and self-image:

3. Because I must take myself with me everywhere I go, I now choose to start loving myself unconditionally and consistently. Following is a description of myself as the radiant being I am:

4. Here are some of the reasons why I deserve to be optimally healthy and fully functioning:

5. I choose to find myself more attractive than ever before. I am wonderful. I now take a few minutes to paint a word picture of myself as the exquisite person I am, emphasizing my many positive qualities.

HOW WILL I EMBRACE MY AUTHENTIC SELF?

Self-Discovery Questions

1. What do I feel angry about?

2. What do I feel upset about?

3. What do I feel depressed or hopeless about?

4. What things have caused me anxiety in the past?

5. What am I feeling happy and joyful about?

6. What specific time can I set aside each day to be by myself and relax?

7. What people in my life can I ask for help in eliminating negative thoughts and words?

Action Choices

1. I will sit quietly with my eyes closed for the next few minutes, envisioning myself as a peaceful, relaxed, confident, and happy person. What follows is a description of how that looked and felt:

2. Before I go to sleep at night, I will sit quietly and forgive myself and anyone else I feel has hurt me in any way. These are the people who need immediate attention:

3. I will choose one person with whom I have not been feeling in harmony, close my eyes, and picture us facing each other in a circle of white or pink light. I will lovingly share my feelings with that person and resolve any conflict, and then finish by seeing our hearts connect in unconditional love. I will describe my ideal relationship with this person.

4. If I need to forgive a person who has passed away, I will sit down and write that individual a letter offering forgiveness and love. These are the feelings I will express:

5. If I know someone who is experiencing lots of stress, anxiety, depression, hopelessness, or helplessness, I will contact that person as soon as possible and encourage him or her to talk while I listen without judging, criticizing, or offering advice. This is someone I know who needs a friend simply to listen and care.

6. From this day forward, I will give this many hugs a day:

7. I know now that the better I handle stress, the healthier and happier I'll be. Here are some ways I've handled stress in the past:

8. This is how I choose to deal with stress from now on, in ways that support my immune system and well-being:

HOW WILL I LIVE MY HIGHEST VISION?

Self-Discovery Questions

1. Am I living my ideal life now? If not, why not?

2. What are my goals in the following areas?

   🔥 Relationships   🔥 Interests and Hobbies

   🔥 Career   🔥 Health

   🔥 Finances   🔥 Self-Esteem

   🔥 Fitness   🔥 Spirituality

3. If I knew I couldn't fail, what would I do in my life?

Action Choices

1. 1. Following is my ideal vision of myself, living my ideal life. This is how my life would be, how the world around me would be, and how I would feel:

2. These are changes I can make immediately that will move me closer to my vision:

3. These are the words and phrases that I now choose to eliminate from my vocabulary:

4. To create relationships the way I want them to be, I will not try to change anyone else but will change my own thoughts and attitudes in the following ways:

HOW WILL I CHOOSE TO BE HEALTHY?

Self-Discovery Questions

1. What foods do I need to eliminate from my diet because they don't support my health?

2. In what ways have I been treating myself without love through my eating behavior?

3. How can I change the way I prepare food to increase my health and well-being?

4. What beliefs do I hold about food that sabotage my healthiness?

Action Choices

1. Dr. Maxwell Maltz's 1960 book *Psycho-Cybernetics* informed the world that whatever we can do for 21 days becomes a habit. For 21 days I will eliminate the following from my diet and add the following to my diet:

2. Starting today with the first thing on the list, I will use these books, magazines, or audio programs to assist me in my health program:

3. Listed here are some supplements that I now choose to include in my nutritional program to enhance my health:

4. Following are at least five affirmations that support my being vibrantly healthy:

5. Each day I will spend at least three minutes visualizing myself as a healthy, radiant being who treats herself or himself respectfully and lovingly. This is precisely how I will appear in my vision:

The lowest ebb is the turn of the tide.

~ Henry Wadsworth Longfellow

HOW WILL I GET FIT FOR LIFE?

Self-Discovery Questions

1. How do I feel about exercise?

2. Which fitness activities do I, or can I, engage in that I enjoy?

3. What beliefs do I have about my body that have been working against me?

4. What excuses seem to come up frequently that interfere with my exercising?

Action Choices

1. Here are my exercise and fitness goals for the following month, three months, six months, and year:

2. The areas of my body that need special attention, and the exercises that will address them, are:

3. My body, whatever its level of fitness, is splendiferous. Here are a few of the miraculous things it can do, for which I am grateful:

4. The supremely fit self I visualize while I am working out looks like this:

HOW WILL I LET MY HEART-LIGHT SHINE?

Self-Discovery Questions

1. In what areas of my life am I too serious?

2. Would I describe myself as a happy, positive person? Am I the type of person I would like to have for a friend?

3. How do I feel when I am around children?

4. What qualities do I see in children that I'd like to integrate more fully into my own life?

5. In what areas of my life am I too rigid and orderly—too "adult"?

6. How often do I give myself permission to act silly and crazy?

7. Do I spend my present moments feeling guilty about the past or worrying about the future, or do I truly embrace the here and now?

Action Choices

1. If I were to let the child in me out to explore, play, and be spontaneous and creative, my life would change in the following ways:

2. To get more in touch with my inner child, I am going to spend some time observing children at play, as well as participating with them. I can do this in the following ways:

3. These are some fun things I can do for those I care about (for example, write a special note, send flowers, or record a song):

4. Here are some things I tried in the past six months that I had never tried before:

5. Here are some new ventures I choose to undertake in the coming six months:

6. Here are some changes I can make to lighten up and become a little less serious:

7. I will choose one of the following people I have wanted to meet or know better and make plans to get together next week:

8. Now that I spend time visualizing my ideal life every day, I will take the next few moments to imagine one of my goals as already achieved. This is how I feel:

HOW WILL I EMBRACE THE SACRED WITHIN AND AROUND ME?

Self-Discovery Questions

1. What do I want most out of my life?

2. What is my personal definition of success?

3. What does peace mean to me, and when do I feel most happy and at peace?

4. How do I feel about being alone?

5. What are things I do to avoid being alone and having quietude?

6. How old do I feel?

7. What past changes in my attitude have enriched my life?

8. f I knew I had just one year to live, what changes would I make now? What has kept me from making them already?

Action Choices

1. These are some ways I will spend the time during each day that I have set aside just for me:

2. Following are ways I choose to simplify my life:

3. In the past, my negative emotions have sometimes immobilized me. This is ending because I will now take action and show my mettle in the following ways:

4. If this were the last year of my life, the following things would be most important to me:

5. These are some changes I can make in my life to experience more peace:

6. Here is a list of affirmations that support my power to share peacefulness and enrich life on this planet:

There is a time for everything, and a season
for every activity under heaven.

~ Ecclesiastics 3:1

These are only hints and guesses,
Hints followed by guesses, and the rest
Is prayer, observance, discipline, thought, and action.

~ T. S. Eliot

Chapter 20

Uplift & Empower Your Life with Books

Out of clutter, find simplicity. From discord, find harmony. In the middle of difficulty, lies opportunity

~ ALBERT EINSTEIN

Is not birth, beauty, good shape, discourse, Manhood, learning, gentleness, virtue, youth, liberality, and such like, the spice and salt that season a man?

~ WILLIAM SHAKESPEARE

Since I was a little girl, I've been passionate about reading books (and now writing books, too). I strive to read two to three books each week and always carry one with me wherever I go. You will never find me without a book to read anytime, anywhere.

When was the last time you read a good book just for the fun of it, besides this book you are reading now? If it's been a while, you are definitely missing out. Literature and books afford countless rewards to you—the reader. Some of the countless benefits include stress reduction, vocabulary expansion, improved focus and concentration, enhanced writing skills, serenity and calmness, knowledge, mental stimulation, memory improvement, and free entertainment. In fact, research shows that just 30 minutes of reading a day (including this book!) can allow you to physically reset, lowering your blood pressure, heart rate, and stress level. In other words, books are more than words on a page. You, the reader, bring the words to life. Apply what you read and look for ways to experience more peace, faith, confidence, and vigor in your life than ever before.

Books tell us the stories of places we haven't been to before, people we don't know, and worlds we can only imagine. You never feel lonely or alone when you have a good book to read. Anytime of the day or night, books can keep you company and delight you to the depths of your being. Reading awakens dormant imagination and stimulates the mind in ways watching TV or going to the movies can never do.

If you would like an uplifting book experience that will enrich every area of your life, including your health and healing, level of prosperity, self-esteem and confidence, family and relationships and strength in faith, you've come to the right place, this book, and also check out BooksToUplift.com.

In light of my proclivity and voracious desire to read, and because this is a book about upliftment, here are some special thoughts for you about reading and books that I'm hoping will sprout ideas in your mind, sprout positive feelings in your heart, and sprout passion in the very core of you to celebrate, with me, the grandeur of great books. I read once that Sir Winston Churchill read a book every night, even during the Blitz. He said it made him think better. I would agree with that sentiment. I also agree with the first quote to follow this section by Churchill, who happens to share my birthday.

So herewith, I joyfully share these quotes with you in the hope that they will inspire you to pick up more real books, like this one you are holding now, feel and smell the pages (unless you are reading on a device), and read it carefully to see what resonates in your heart or motivates you to enrich and uplift your life.

If you cannot read all your books . . . fondle them—peer into them, let them fall open where they will, read from the first sentence that arrests the eye, set them back on the shelves with your own hands, arrange them on your own plan so that you at least know where they are. Let them be your friends; let them, at any rate, be your acquaintances.

~ Winston Churchill

Books are such a great way to spend time with your children, open lines of communication with your children, and just build that strong foundation.

~ Victoria Osteen

Until I feared I would lose it, I never loved to read. One does not love breathing.

~ Harper Lee

Many people, myself among them, feel better at the mere sight of a book.

~ Jane Smiley

Books are the plane, and the train, and the road. They are the destination, and the journey. They are home.

~ Anna Quindlen

Reading is escape, and the opposite of escape; it's a way to make contact with reality after a day of making things up, and it's a way of making contact with someone else's imagination after a day that's all too real.

~ Nora Ephron

She read books as one would breathe air, to fill up and live.

~ Annie Dillard

A word after a word after a word is power.

~ Margaret Atwood

Books were my pass to personal freedom.

~ Oprah Winfrey

*Either write something worth reading or
do something worth writing.*

~ Benjamin Franklin

*In reading the lives of great men, I found that the
first victory they won was over themselves . . .
self-discipline with all of them came first.*

~ Harry S. Truman

*Leave all the afternoon for exercise and recreation,
which are as necessary as reading. I will rather say more
necessary because health is worth more than learning.*

~ Thomas Jefferson

*What counts, in the long run, is not what you read; it is what
you sift through your own mind; it is the ideas and impressions
that are aroused in you by your reading. It is the ideas stirred
in your own mind, the ideas which are a reflection of your
own thinking, which make you an interesting person.*

~ Eleanor Roosevelt

He that loves reading has everything within his reach.

~ William Godwin

*There are worse crimes than burning books.
One of them is not reading them.*

~ Ray Bradbury

*My alma mater was books, a good library . . . I could spend
the rest of my life reading, just satisfying my curiosity.*

~ Malcolm X

Books showed me there were possibilities in life, that there were actually people like me living in a world I could not only aspire to but attain. Reading gave me hope. For me, it was the open door.

~ OPRAH WINFREY

By reading the scriptures I am so renewed that all nature seems renewed around me and with me. The sky seems to be a pure, a cooler blue, the trees a deeper green. The whole world is charged with the glory of God and I feel fire and music under my feet.

~ THOMAS MERTON

We shouldn't teach great books; we should teach a love of reading.

~ B. F. SKINNER

The greatest luxury I know is sitting up reading in bed.

~ ELEANOR ROOSEVELT

I never feel lonely if I've got a book—they're like old friends. Even if you're not reading them over and over again, you know they are there. And they're part of your history. They sort of tell a story about your journey through life.

~ EMILIA FOX

Be careful about reading health books. You may die of a misprint.

~ MARK TWAIN

We all have a hungry heart, and one of the things we hunger for is happiness. So as much as I possibly could, I stayed where I was happy. I spent a great deal of time in my younger years just writing and reading, walking around the woods in Ohio, where I grew up.

~ MARY OLIVER

*A man only learns in two ways, one by reading, and
the other by association with smarter people.*

~ WILL ROGERS

*A capacity, and taste, for reading gives access to
whatever has already been discovered by others.*

~ ABRAHAM LINCOLN

*I love my friends and family, but I also love it when
they can't find me and I can spend all day reading or
walking all alone, in silence, eight thousand miles away
from everyone. All alone and unreachable in a foreign
country is one my most favorite possible things to be.*

~ ELIZABETH GILBERT

*A truly good book teaches me better than to read it. I
must soon lay it down, and commence living on its hint.
What I began by reading, I must finish by acting.*

~ HENRY DAVID THOREAU

*You can make positive deposits in your own economy every day by
reading and listening to powerful, positive, life-changing content
and by associating with encouraging and hope-building people.*

~ ZIG ZIGLAR

*During my days of deepest grief, in all of my shock,
sorrow, and struggle, I sat at the feet of God. I literally
spent hours each day reading God's word, meditating
on scripture and praying. I intentionally spent a
significant amount of time being still before God.*

~ RICK WARREN

All the people who fought for freedom were my heroes. I mean, that was the sort of story I liked reading . . . freedom struggles and so on.

~ Indira Gandhi

The best students come from homes where education is revered: where there are books, and children see their parents reading them.

~ Leo Buscaglia

Any book that helps a child to form a habit of reading, to make reading one of his deep and continuing needs, is good for him.

~ Maya Angelou

If one cannot enjoy reading a book over and over again, there is no use in reading it at all.

~ Oscar Wilde

The cool thing about reading is that when you read a short story or you read something that takes your mind and expands where your thoughts can go, that's powerful.

~ Taylor Swift

Some women have a weakness for shoes . . . I can go barefoot if necessary. I have a weakness for books.

~ Oprah Winfrey

I declare after all there is no enjoyment like reading! How much sooner one tires of anything than of a book! When I have a house of my own, I shall be miserable if I have not an excellent library.

~ Jane Austen

Consider starting a library in your home using a spare bedroom or even a corner area in your basement or attic. Create a lovely reading and relaxing space with organized bookshelves, good lighting, and, if room permits, add in a cozy chair where you can be by yourself, or with other family members, and read, read, read books. This new library and regular, positive reading experiences will color your life bright, cheerful, and uplifted.

Happy, Uplifting Reading!

The doctor of the future will no longer treat
the human frame with drugs, but rather will
cure and prevent disease with nutrition.

~ Thomas Edison

When we focus on what we love, we fashion our life around
our inner knowledge. We live the life we choose, surrounding
ourselves with people we love and objects that hold great meaning.
Home is a good place to begin our concentration because it is
our emotional center. Then we can branch out in all directions,
spreading the light of our true essence and heart's desire.

~ Alexandra Stoddard

Chapter 21

Uplift Your Life with
Wired for High-Level Wellness
and *A Hug in a Mug*

Bring out the best of what is in you.

~ ALEXANDRA STODDARD

Better to remain silent and be thought a fool
that to speak out and remove all doubt.

~ ABRAHAM LINCOLN

We are now on the last chapter and I am so delighted that you took this special, sacred journey with me to enrich your body and life physically, mentally, emotionally, and spiritually. Thank you for reading *Uplifted*. It feels like you are now part of my extended family. If you enjoyed this book, you may also enjoy and discover many more facets of holistic health in two of my other health- and life-enhancing books *Wired for High Level Wellness* and *A Hug in a Mug*.

To introduce you to these books, here's some information that might interest you. For additional, personally autographed copies of this book *Uplifted*, or for either of these two other books, please visit my website, SusanSmithJones.com, and select NEW BOOK in the navigation bar and click on the titles. There you will find the particulars on how to get autographed copies for you or sent to any of your family and friends anywhere in the world. These special autographed copies include a personal notecard from me along with a bookmark.

WIRED FOR HIGH-LEVEL WELLNESS: Simple Ways to Rejuvenate, Meditate & Prosper

A Holistic Health & Lifestyle Book That Will Transform Your Life for the Better. . . No Matter Your Age

In this captivating compendium, you'll read never-before-told-stories on how Susan's obstacles and challenging lessons shaped her life and were actually life-enriching catalysts that supercharged her whole-body healing from health-destroying illnesses and enabled her to come out the other side feeling rich with gratitude for every experience and in charge of her own high-level wellness destiny.

With candid and thoughtful insight throughout the pages of *Wired for High-Level Wellness*, Susan provides an enthralling narrative and precise roadmap on how to be truly healthy—physically, mentally, emotionally, and spiritually. As the reader, you will feel like you are sitting across from Susan at her kitchen table, visiting over a cup of fresh juice or tea while she shares her most sacred and coveted secrets with you on how to transform your life and live your highest dreams for yourself.

Susan's heartfelt personal stories will have you on the edge of your seat; her humor will have you laughing so hard that you will receive a great abdominal workout; and her sound nutritional and holistic lifestyle guidance will have you feeling healthier, happier, and more hopeful before you've even finished Chapter 1.

Some of the topics covered in this gem of a book include:

🌀 Hydrating superfoods

🌀 Tips for brain vitality ~ ways to keep your brain sharp at any age

🌀 Ways to detoxify and reinvigorate

🌀 How to be a magnet for prosperity and blessings

- Health benefits of oil pulling

- How to bring about soaring self-esteem

- The ABCs of stressless, effortless meditation ~ it's history and how to do it

- Weight-loss made easy

- How Earthing/grounding revitalizes

- Longevity practices that really work quickly

- Ways to create more fulfilling relationships

- The joys of living a faith- and God-centered life

Foreword Excerpt
by David Craddock, MA (Oxon)

"I am confident you will also derive tremendous value from this eclectic compendium, **Wired for High-Level Wellness.** *Susan reminds us that we were created by God and have been blessed with a miraculous body. She shows us how to not only heal the body but also create robust health at any age. Her easy-to-follow program is an indispensable and refreshing change from most health and self-improvement books that only focus on one particular aspect of health. No matter your reason for turning to this book—whether it's to find more happiness in life, look and feel better, find balance, discover how to eat healthier and be more positive, reinvigorate your body, boost your self-esteem, and live a more peaceful, hopeful, prosperous life with a heart full of faith and a strengthened relationship with God—this book will lead you in the right direction. Get ready to feel wonderful in body, mind, and spirit and enjoy the extraordinary life you were designed to live."*

Here's what a few other people have written about *Wired for High-Level Wellness*:

"Only a few people have the courage, vision, and love for humanity to be pioneers. Susan Smith Jones is one of them. Fortunately, where pioneers like her are willing to go, many people can follow more confidently. If your goals are health, happiness, balanced living, and a meaningful life, then *Wired for High-Level Wellness is for you.*"

~ BRIAN BOXER WACHLER, MD,
BOXER WACHLER VISION INSTITUTE

"Regardless of where you have looked for better health and how much 'dis-ease' you are experiencing now, you can begin to put it behind you by reading this book and placing yourself on a path to enjoy the life you deserve. In *Wired for High-Level Wellness*, Susan provides practical, yet powerful, techniques, tips, and delicious recipes to help manage stress, support brain health, bolster immunity, increase self-esteem, restore well-being, and live a more peaceful, happy, and balanced life."

~ ANGIE DUNKLING AVERILL, DMD, AND
GORDON AVERILL, DMD, 26TH STREET DENTAL

"*Wired for High-Level Wellness* is an important book for two reasons. First, it tells you that wellness is a choice. Second, it gives excellent advice on how to attain superb wellness once you've made the choice. Reading it will enable you to add to the vitality of the world."

~ FINLEY W. BROWN, JR., MD

"I think everyone wants to be all they can be and live an inspired life. In her upbeat book *Wired for High-Level Wellness*, Susan Smith Jones gives us some valuable choices and easy-to-follow guidelines that can be used as building blocks in our lives that will allow us to be the best we can be. Creating a healthy, happy, peaceful, and balanced life is now well within our grasp, thanks to this empowering book."

~ NANCY S. SCHORT, DDS

"*Wired for High-Level Wellness* is a beautiful, clear, uplifting book. A guide to living healthfully, joyfully, and peacefully, it is also a fine example of the God- and faith-centeredness that bring grace to life. As Susan writes about in her preface, the Bible is her favorite book that she consults every day, and she features many of her favorite Bible quotes throughout the pages of this life-enriching book. If you are ready to improve your diet, reduce stress in your life, exercise your way to vibrant health, increase your self-esteem, achieve your heartfelt goals, feel more hopeful and positive, and develop a closer relationship with God, *Wired for High-Level Wellness* is the book for you; it's loaded with secrets to improve the quality of your life."

~ Pastor Brittian Bowman

"Susan Smith Jones is the real thing. She's a walking, talking, living, breathing embodiment of what she gently preaches. For almost thirty years, Susan has been a regular guest on my many interview talk shows and has even filled in for me as host when I have been away. She always lights up the phone lines with her knowledge, enthusiasm, and humor, and I know that she will also light up your life with her healthy living books. All her beautifully designed books are filled with holistic health-enhancing information, and I've been captivated by all of them. But if I had to pick my favorite one, it would be *Wired for High-Level Wellness* because it has made such a profound difference in my life. As a result of her wisdom and guidance in this book, I lost all of my extra weight, upgraded my exercise program, healed my body, prospered in my life, feel more joyful, and am healthier and more energetic than ever. She has a unique ability to inspire and motivate in a way that makes you feel empowered and lets you know that your wellness destiny is under your control. My advice: get a copy of this book for yourself and then get several more copies to give as gifts to all your family and friends. Everyone will love it! And what better gift can you give than the gift of health?"

~ Nick Lawrence, Radio & TV Talk Show Host/Producer

"Susan Smith Jones has been a favorite guest of mine on my health radio shows for over fifteen years. Her enthusiasm, wealth of knowledge, and sense of humor shine through brightly in all of our radio discussions and my audiences always request her back soon. Even my production and recording team are delighted when she presents her healthy living topics. I first worked with Susan because of her wonderful books and work at UCLA as an expert in fitness and wellness. Susan is highly knowledgeable in holistic health and her books educate the public on how to achieve optimum health. In *Wired for High-Level Wellness*, she offers a beautiful and inspiring guide to living a life that is rooted in hope, faith, vitality, joy, and God's love. Reading about her Christian lifestyle and how her relationship with God is always at the center of her day-to-day activities will inspire and uplift you. When you read this book, you will feel like Susan is your friend, taking you by the hand and guiding you on your personal path to high-level wellness."

~ Karla Calumet, PhD, Health Psychologist

Susan's faith-filled guidance in the pages of this highly esteemed book will help you successfully overcome any health issues and other challenges you may be experiencing, and put you on your desired and deserving path of being physically, mentally, and spiritually balanced—calm, focused, energized, and joyful—something she has been practicing and teaching worldwide for over forty years.

"Getting back to the basics" is the foundation of this comprehensive book, *Wired for High-Level Wellness*. Her easy-to-follow program is an indispensable and refreshing change from most health and self-improvement books that only focus on one particular aspect of health. Susan believes in health by choice, not chance. Choose to read this book and you will see how easily and effortlessly your body, your health, and your life all change for the better. The transformation will astound you!

SUSAN SMITH JONES, PhD

A HUG IN A MUG
Using Herbal Teas, Culinary Spices
& Fresh Juices as Medicine

A HUG IN A MUG: Using Herbal Teas, Culinary Spices & Fresh Juices as Medicine

*Tea to the English is really
a picnic indoors.*

~ Alice Walker

*There are few hours in life more
agreeable than the hour dedicated to
the ceremony known as afternoon tea.*

~ Henry James

Herbal teas, culinary spices, and fresh juices are fashionable these days worldwide and for good reason. In most larger cities, you can find countless juicing and tea shops, and in most grocery stores, you can find all kinds of fresh and dried culinary herbs and spices. But did you know that many teas, spices, and juices are imbued with nature's healing components to keep your body vibrantly healthy? When I was a teenager, my grandmother started teaching me about the health benefits of nature's foods, including the health benefits of fresh juices, culinary spices, and herbal teas.

In *A Hug in a Mug*, I share my decades of knowledge and research on the best teas and juices to drink, along with the most salubrious spices to add to your diet on a regular basis such as turmeric, basil, oregano, cinnamon, cayenne pepper, ginger, and garlic. I offer fascinating stories about the history of these "naturefoods" and my secret tips to get the most out of the beverages or spices. As well, I have even included some of my favorite fresh juicing recipes and tea blend recipes (such as Blue Butterfly Pea tea combined with golden chamomile and bright hibiscus teas) that you can make in your home, along with the easiest and best ways to make and drink tea that you may have never considered.

There's a British tradition for afternoon tea using a variety of different teas and you'll learn about the history of this most enjoyable habit. I also cover in detail the history of tea-drinking around the world. You'll want to cozy up with a warm cup of herbal tea or freshly made juice while reading this enchanting and enriching book, learning countless, simple ways to upgrade your physical and mental health.

Culinary Spices

Here are a few of the things you will learn about culinary spices in this book:

- Cinnamon lowers blood sugar levels and has a powerful antidiabetic effect.

- Sage can improve function and memory.

- Peppermint relieves IBS pain and may reduce nausea.

- Turmeric contains curcumin, a substance with powerful anti-inflammatory effects.

- Holy basil helps fight infections and boosts immunity.

- Cayenne pepper contains capsaicin, which helps reduce appetite and may have anticancer properties.

- Ginger can treat nausea and has anti-inflammatory properties.

- Fenugreek improves blood sugar control.

- Rosemary can help prevent allergies and nasal congestion.

- Garlic can combat sickness and improve heart health.

Fresh Juices

Drinking juice with various fruits and vegetables has the ability to increase your nutrient intake, which will introduce vitamins and minerals into your body. These are helpful in the protection against diseases such as heart disease, high blood sugar, issues with the digestive system, immune disorders, high blood pressure, and more.

Here are only a few of the many benefits of juicing you'll learn about in the book:

- Juicing helps you to consume more fruits and veggies.

- Juicing can give you more energy.

- Juicing can help you sleep better.

🍋 Juicing can help you focus better.

🍋 Juicing can help you live longer.

🍋 Juicing can help you detox.

🍋 Juicing can help combat dehydration.

🍋 Juicing can help you to lose weight.

🍋 Juicing can help your digestive system.

🍋 Juicing can help bring your family together.

Herbal Teas

Here are just a few of the benefits of some herbal teas included in this book:

🍋 Chamomile tea is known for its calming effects and is frequently used as a sleep aid.

🍋 Peppermint tea is one of the most commonly used herbal teas in the world for digestive health.

🍋 Ginger tea is a spicy and flavorful drink to help fight inflammation and boost immunity.

🍋 Hibiscus tea may help lower high blood pressure and fight oxidative stress.

🍋 Echinacea tea is commonly used to prevent or shorten the duration of the common cold.

🍋 Rooibos tea may help improve bone health and reduce heart disease risk.

🍋 Sage tea improves cognitive function and memory.

🍋 Lemon balm tea increases antioxidant levels, improves heart and skin health, and relieves anxiety.

🍋 Rose hip tea is high in vitamin C and other antioxidants and has anti-inflammatory properties.

🍋 Passionflower tea helps improve sleep and reduce anxiety.

*Some people will tell you there is a great deal of
poetry and fine sentiment in a chest of tea.*

~ Ralph Waldo Emerson

*Once you get a spice in your home, you have it forever.
Women never throw out spices. The Egyptians were buried
with their spices. I know which one I'm taking with me when I go.*

~ Erma Bombeck

This **Uplifted** book you are reading now, combined with **Wired for High-Level Wellness** and **A Hug in a Mug,** make the perfect trio of healthy living books for you, your family, and your friends to help fast-track you to optimum health and a life brimming over with youthful vitality, happiness, faith, success, peace, and balance!

Where to purchase **Wired for High-Level Wellness**
and **A Hug in a Mug:**

These books are available in paperback and Kindle via Amazon. For personally autographed copies by Susan, which include a notecard and bookmark from her, please visit: **SusanSmithJones.com** and visit the book pages on the site. These books, as well as her other books—*Invest in Yourself with Exercise, Kitchen Gardening, Choose to Thrive,* and *Be the Change*—are also available in bookstores. If they are out of copies, ask the store's manager to order more.

Worry ends when faith begins.

~ 2 Corinthians 5:7

The earth laughs in flowers.
Adopt the pace of nature: her secret is patience.
Make the most of yourself for that is all there is of you.

~ Ralph Waldo Emerson

Whatsoever things are true,
Whatsoever things are honest,
Whatsoever things are just,
Whatsoever things are pure,
Whatsoever things are lovely,
Whatsoever things are of good report:
If there be any virtue,
and if there be any praise,
Think on these things.

~ Philippians 4:8

Afterword

If you can learn to love yourself and all the flaws, you can love
other people so much better. And that makes you so happy.

~ KRISTIN CHENOWETH

Love each other with genuine affection,
and take delight in honoring each other.

~ ROMANS 12:10

*N*ever forget that one of the greatest miracles on Earth, and a gift from God, is the human body. From head to toe, it was perfectly designed to function optimally well into your "goldenite" years, and it is stronger and wiser than you may realize. Your body was created to be self-healing, self-renewing, and self-rejuvenating. But to spark this natural restorative power of the mind and spirit to heal the physical body, you must first believe in your innate ability to self-heal.

Next, you must provide your body with the right nutriments, a positive attitude, and other self-repairing mental and physical tools and practices, and, at the same time, remove negative obstacles and interferences . . . and then your body will begin to heal and thrive physically, mentally, and spiritually. It may be a tall order, but it is so worth it. What's more, I know you can do it! You have the key to unlock your healing powers today so you can conquer illness, extend life, and be *uplifted* day in, day out.

Always remember that every day you have a choice to revitalize your body with positive energy and emotional success—and experience true vitality . . . or not. You can be filled with happiness, optimism, and hope. Demonstrate love by giving it to yourself daily. Falling in love with yourself first doesn't make you selfish or vain; it makes you indestructible. Remember: as you follow the guidance in this book and use my daily 12-Minute Action Steps and Affirmations, honor the gratitude and kindness practices, complete the Workbook, and more, you will be loving yourself completely and bringing an irresistible power of real joy and upliftment into your daily living experiences. *When you commit to living in joy, faith, peace, kindness, and vitality, then light and positivity will ripple out from you in every direction and make you a magnet for blessings and miracles.*

If you will now choose to take care of your miraculous body every day in the practical and surefire ways I have described in this book, it will reward you a thousand times over—improving your odds against disease, supporting mental health, giving you the courage of a lion, and putting wings under your self-esteem and confidence. You have the power to be and stay healthy, physically and mentally, because healing truly comes from within. Don't you think it's time to unlock your self-healing powers today?

Blessings and Godspeed,

Susan

Each day you must speak only lovingly and positively to yourself.
When you love yourself internally, you will glow externally.

~ Susan Smith Jones

Know your own happiness. You want nothing but patience—
or give it a more fascinating name, call it hope.

~ Jane Austen

Grownups never understand anything for themselves,
and it is tiresome for children to be always and
forever explaining things to them.

~ Antoine de Saint-Exupéry

About the Author

*The more you love, and the more you're love,
the lovelier you are.*

~ JUNE B. SMITH (SUSAN'S MOM)

*A cheerful heart is good medicine, but a
broken spirit saps a person's strength.*

~ PROVERBS 17:22

For a woman with three of America's and the UK's most ordinary names, **Susan Smith Jones, PhD,** has certainly made extraordinary contributions in the fields of holistic health, longevity, optimum nutrition, high-level fitness, and balanced, peaceful living. For starters, she taught students, staff, and faculty at UCLA how to be healthy and fit for thirty years!

Susan is the founder and president of Health Unlimited, a Los Angeles–based consulting firm dedicated to optimal wellness and holistic health education. As a renowned motivational speaker, Susan travels internationally as a frequent radio and TV talk show guest and motivational speaker (seminars, workshops, lectures, and keynote address); she's also the author of more than 2,500 magazine articles and over 33 books, including *Invest in Yourself with Exercise; A Hug in a Mug; Choose to Thrive; Be the Change; Kitchen Gardening;* and *Wired for High-Level Wellness: Simple Ways to Rejuvenate, Meditate & Prosper.*

Susan is in a unique position to testify on the efficacy of her basic message that health is the result of choice. When her back was fractured in an automobile accident, her physician told her that she would never be able to carry "anything heavier than a small purse." Susan chose not to accept this verdict; within six months, there was no longer any pain or evidence of the fracture. Soon, she fully regained her health and active lifestyle.

Susan attributes her healing to her natural-foods diet, a daily well-rounded fitness program, a strong God- and faith-centered life, along with the power of determination, balanced living, and a deep commitment to expressing her highest potential. Since that time, she has been constantly active in spreading the message that anyone can choose radiant health and rejuvenation. Her inspiring message and innovative techniques for achieving total health in body, mind, and spirit have won her a grateful and enthusiastic following and have put her in constant demand internationally as a health and fitness consultant and educator.

A gifted teacher, Susan brings together modern research and ageless wisdom in all her work. When she's not traveling the world, she resides in both West Los Angeles and England.

If you enjoyed this book, please visit: **SusanSmithJones.com, ChristianLifestyleMatters.com,** and **BooksToUplift.com** for more details on Susan and her work. Her books and websites are like having a "holistic health app" for anything related to holistic health and living a faith- and God-centered life.

If you'd like to receive Susan's free monthly *Healthy Living*
Newsletters filled with uplifting, empowering, and motivating
information, please go to **SusanSmithJones.com** and sign up
on the page Subscribe & Win! It takes only 10 seconds,
and you will also receive several gifts from Susan.

We make a living by what we get.
We make a life by what we give.

~ WINSTON CHURCHILL

Imagination is more important than knowledge. For
knowledge is limited to all we now know and understand,
while imagination embraces the entire world, and
all there ever will be to know and understand.

~ ALBERT EINSTEIN

Notes

Notes

Made in the USA
Middletown, DE
25 May 2022